Big Book of Chiptunes
Music for the Video Game Generations

Contents

0.1 Chiptune

A musician's chiptune setup involving Game Boys

A **chiptune**, also known as **chip music** or **8-bit music**, is synthesized electronic music which is 1) made for PSG sound chips (real or emulated) used in vintage computers, consoles, and arcade machines or 2) tracker format music which intentionally sounds similar to old PSG chip music or 3) music that combines PSG sounds and modern electronica/EDM music styles.[1][2]

In the early 1980s, personal computers became less expensive and more accessible than they had previously been. This led to a proliferation of outdated personal computers and game consoles that had been abandoned by consumers as they upgraded to newer machines. They were in low demand by consumers as a whole, and not difficult to find, making them a highly accessible and affordable method of creating sound or art. While it has been a mostly underground genre, chiptune has had periods of moderate popularity in the 1980s and 21st century, and has influenced the development of electronic dance music.

0.1.1 Overview

The terms "chip music" and "chiptune" refer to music made by the sound chips found within early gaming systems and microcomputers.[3][4][5]

A waveform generator is a fundamental module in a sound synthesis system. A waveform generator usually produces a basic geometrical waveform with a fixed or variable timbre and variable pitch. Common waveform generator configurations usually included two or three simple waveforms and often a single pseudo-random-noise generator (PRNG). Available waveforms often included pulse wave (whose timbre can be varied by modifying the duty cycle), square wave (a symmetrical pulse wave producing only odd overtones), triangle wave (which has a fixed timbre containing only odd harmonics, but is softer than a square wave), and

sawtooth wave (which has a bright raspy timbre and contains odd and even harmonics). Two notable examples of systems employing this technology comprise the Game Boy and the Commodore 64. The Game Boy uses two pulse channels (switchable between 12.5%, 25%, 50% and 75% wave duty cycle), a channel for 4-bit PCM playback, and a pseudo-random-noise generator. The Commodore 64, however, used the MOS Technology SID chip which offered 3 channels, each switchable between pulse, saw-tooth, triangle, and noise. Unlike the Game Boy, the pulse channels on the Commodore 64 allowed full control over wave duty cycles. The SID was a very technically advanced chip, offering many other features including ring modulation and adjustable resonance filters.[6]

0.1.2 History

The earliest precursors to chip music can be found in the early history of computer music. In 1951, the computers CSIRAC and Ferranti Mark 1 were used to perform real-time synthesized digital music in public.[7] One of the earliest commercial computer music albums came from the First Philadelphia Computer Music Festival, held August 25, 1978, as part of the Personal Computing '78 show. The First Philadelphia Computer Music Festival recordings were published by Creative Computing in 1979.[8]

Video game origins

See also: Video game music

Chiptune music began to appear with the video game music produced during the golden age of video arcade games. An early example was the opening tune in Tomohiro Nishikado's arcade game *Gun Fight* (1975). The first video game to use a continuous background soundtrack was Tomohiro Nishikado's 1978 release *Space Invaders*, which had four simple chromatic descending bass notes repeating in a loop, though it was dynamic and interacted with the player, increasing pace as the enemies descended on the player.[9] The first video game to feature continuous melodic background music was *Rally-X*, an arcade game released by Namco in 1980, featuring a simple tune that repeats continuously during gameplay.[10] It was also one of the earliest games to use a digital-to-analog converter to produce sampled sounds.[11] That same year, the first video game to feature speech synthesis was also released, Sunsoft's shoot 'em up arcade game *Stratovox*.[10]

In the late 1970s, the pioneering electronic dance/synthpop group Yellow Magic Orchestra (YMO) were using computers to produce synthesized music.[12] Some of their early music, including their 1978 self-titled debut album, were sampling sounds from popular arcade games such as *Space Invaders*[13] and *Gun Fight*. In addition to incorporating sounds from contemporary video games into their music, the band would later have a major influence on much of the video game and chiptune music produced during the 8-bit and 16-bit eras.[14][15] Sega's 1982 arcade game *Super Locomotive*, for example, featured a chiptune cover version of YMO's "Rydeen" (1979);[16] several later computer games also covered the song, such as *Trooper Truck* (1983) by Rabbit Software as well as *Daley Thompson's Decathlon* (1984) and *Stryker's Run* (1986) arranged by Martin Galway.[17]

By 1983, Konami's arcade game *Gyruss* utilized five sound chips along with a digital-to-analog converter, which were partly used to create an electronic rendition of J.S. Bach's *Toccata and Fugue in D minor*.[18] In 1984, former YMO member Haruomi Hosono released an album produced entirely from Namco arcade game samples entitled *Video Game Music*, an early example of a chiptune record[19] and the first video game music album.[20] The record featured the work of Namco's chiptune composers: Toshio Kai (*Pac-Man* in 1980), Nobuyuki Ohnogi (*Galaga*, *New Rally-X* and *Bosconian* in 1981, and *Pole Position* in 1982), and Yuriko Keino (*Dig Dug* and *Xevious* in 1982).[21]

FM synthesis

See also: Video game music

A major advance for chip music was the introduction of frequency modulation synthesis (FM synthesis), first commercially released by Yamaha for their digital synthesizers and FM sound chips, which began appearing in arcade machines from the early 1980s.[22][23] Arcade game composers utilizing FM synthesis at the time included Konami's Miki Higashino (*Gradius*, *Yie-Ar Kung Fu*, *Teenage Mutant Ninja Turtles*)[24] and Sega's Hiroshi Kawaguchi (*Space Harrier*, *Hang-On*, *Out Run*).[25]

By the early 1980s, significant improvements to personal computer game music were made possible with the introduction of digital FM synthesis sound. Yamaha began manufacturing FM synth boards for Japanese computers such as the NEC PC-8801 and PC-9801 in the early 1980s, and by the mid-1980s, the PC-8801 and FM-7 had built-in FM sound. This allowed computer game music to have greater complexity than the simplistic beeps from internal speakers. These FM synth boards produced a "warm and pleasant sound" that musicians such as Yuzo Koshiro and Takeshi Abo utilized to produce music that is still highly regarded within the chiptune community.[26] In the early 1980s, Japanese personal computers such as the NEC PC-88 and PC-98 featured audio programming languages

such as Music Macro Language (MML) and MIDI interfaces, which were most often used to produce video game music.[27] Fujitsu also released the *FM Sound Editor* software for the FM-7 in 1985, providing users with a user-friendly interface to create and edit synthesized music.[28]

The widespread adoption of FM synthesis by consoles would later be one of the major advances of the 16-bit era, by which time 16-bit arcade machines were using multiple FM synthesis chips.[22] A major chiptune composer during this period was Yuzo Koshiro.[29] Despite later advances in audio technology, he would continue to use older PC-8801 hardware to produce chiptune soundtracks for series such as *Streets of Rage* (1991–1994) and *Etrian Odyssey* (2007–present).[26] His soundtrack to *The Revenge of Shinobi* (1989) featured house[30][31] and progressive techno compositions[29] that fused electronic dance music with traditional Japanese music.[32] The soundtrack for *Streets of Rage 2* (1992) is considered "revolutionary" and "ahead of its time" for its "blend of swaggering house synths, dirty electro-funk and trancey electronic textures that would feel as comfortable in a nightclub as a video game."[33] For the soundtrack to *Streets of Rage 3* (1994), Koshiro created a new composition method called the "Automated Composing System" to produce "fast-beat techno like jungle,"[34] resulting in innovative and experimental sounds generated automatically.[35] Koshiro also composed chiptune soundtracks for series such as *Dragon Slayer*, *Ys*, *Shinobi*, and *ActRaiser*. Another important FM synth composer was the late Ryu Umemoto, who composed chiptune soundtracks for various visual novel and shoot 'em up games.[36]

SID music culture

See also: MOS Technology SID and Demoscene
Later on, several demo groups moved to using their own

MOS 6581 and 8580 Commodore 64 SID chips.

music instead of ripped game music. In 1986, Jeroen "Red" Kimmel studied Rob Hubbard's player routine and used it for original demo songs[37] before writing a routine of his own in 1987. Hobbyists were also writing their own dedicated music editor software, such as Chris Hülsbeck's

Soundmonitor which was released as a type-in listing in a 1986 issue of the German C-64 magazine 64'er.[38]

The practice of SID music composition has continued seamlessly until this day in conjunction with the Commodore 64 demoscene. The High Voltage SID Collection, a comprehensive archive of SID music, contains over 40,000 pieces of SID music.[39]

Tracker chiptunes

See also: Music tracker and Module file

Commodore Amiga (1985), with its wavetable and sample-based sound synthesis, distanced the concept of micro-computer music away from plain chip-synthesized sounds. Amiga tracker music software, beginning from Karsten Obarski's Ultimate Soundtracker (1987), inspired great numbers of computer enthusiasts to create computer music. As an offshoot of the burgeoning tracker music culture, a type of tracker music reminiscent of Commodore 64 SID music was born. This type of music came to be called "chiptunes".

Earliest examples of tracker chiptunes date back to 1989 and are attributed to the demoscene musicians 4mat, Baroque, TDK, Turtle and Duz. Tracker chiptunes are based on very short looped waveforms which are modulated by tracker effects such as arpeggio, vibrato, and portamento.

Musicians like Random Voice later included the technique of rapidly repeating series of offset waveforms in order to fully emulate one single SID instrument with trackers.

The small amount of sample data made tracker chiptunes far more space-efficient than most other types of tracker music, which made them appealing to size-limited demoscene demos and crack intros. Tracker chiptunes have also been commonly used in other warez scene executables such as keygens.

Nowadays, the term "chiptune" is also used to cover chip music using actual chip-based synthesis, but some sources, such as the Amiga Music Preservation project, still define a chiptune specifically as a small tracker module.[40]

Steps toward the mainstream music world

The heyday of chiptune music was the 1980s.[41] The earliest commercial chiptune records produced entirely from sampling arcade game sounds have existed since the mid-1980s, an early example being Haruomi Hosono's *Video Game Music* in 1984.[19] Though entirely chiptune records were uncommon at the time, many mainstream musicians

in the pop rock,[42] hip hop[43] and electronic music[44] genres were sampling arcade game sounds and bleeps during the golden age of video arcade games (late 1970s to mid-1980s), as early as Yellow Magic Orchestra's "Computer Game" in 1978.[13] Buckner & Garcia's "Pac-Man Fever" and the album of the same name were major hits in 1982.[42] Arcade game sounds were one of the foundational elements of the electro music genre, which in turn inspired many other electronic dance music genres such as techno and house music, which were sometimes referred to as "bleep music".[13] *Space Invaders* inspired Player One's "Space Invaders" (1979), which in turn provided the bassline for Jesse Saunders' "On and On" (1984),[45][46] the first Chicago house track.[47] Warp's record "Testone" (1990) by Sweet Exorcist sampled video game sounds from Yellow Magic Orchestra's "Computer Game" and defined Sheffield's bleep techno scene in the early 1990s.[48]

After the 1980s, however, chiptune music began declining in popularity.[41] Since then, up until the 2000s, chip music was rarely performed live and the songs were nearly exclusively spread as executable programs and other computer file formats. Some of the earliest examples of record label releases of pure chip music can be found in the late 1990s.[49] Chiptune music began gaining popularity again towards the end of the 1990s. The first electroclash record, I-F's "Space Invaders Are Smoking Grass" (1997), has been described as "burbling electro in a vocodered homage to Atari-era hi-jinks".[50]

By the mid-2000s, 8-bit chip music began making a comeback in mainstream pop music, when it was used by acts such as Beck (for example, the 2005 song "Girl"), The Killers (for example, the 2004 song "On Top"), No Doubt with the song "Running", and particularly The Postal Service in many of their songs. The low-quality digital MIDI styling of early game music composers such as Hiroshi Miyauchi also began gaining popularity.[51] In 2003, the J-pop girl group Perfume,[52][53] along with producer Yasutaka Nakata, began producing music combining chiptunes with synthpop and electro house;[53] their breakthrough came in 2007 with *Game*, which led to other Japanese female artists using a similar electronic style, including Aira Mitsuki, immi, Mizca, SAWA, Saori@destiny, and Sweet Vacation.[54] Electro house producer Deadmau5 in the late 1990s, with a chiptune and demoscene movements-influenced sound. Three self-released compilations Project 56, deadmau5 Circa 1998-2002 and A Little Oblique were finished in 2006.[55]

In 2007, the notable, entirely chiptune album *8-Bit Operators: The Music of Kraftwerk* was released on major mainstream label Astralwerks/EMI Records, which included several prominent and noted chipmusicians, including Nanoloop[56] creator Oliver Wittchow, and LittleSoundDJ[57] creator Johan Kotlinski who appears as the artist *Role Model*. Kraftwerk founding member Ralf Hütter personally selected the tracks.[58] A vinyl 12-inch single version was released on February 24, 2007 as a precursor to the full-length CD, and reached as high as number 17[59] on the Billboard magazine Hot Dance Singles Sales Chart. In March 2007, the CD release reached as high as number 1 on the *CMJ RPM* (North American college Electronic) charts.[60][61] Edinburgh born electronic musician Unicorn Kid has helped further popularize chiptune, especially with the song 'True Love Fantasy' and other songs from the EP 'Tidal Rave' being played on late night radio, including on BBC Radio 1, where he played live on the Festive Festival 2011. In Canada, Eightcubed and Crystal Castles helped the popularity further via the Toronto underground club scene and created a lasting impression with the music video "Heart Invaders" debuting on MuchMusic in 2008 [62] and the single "Alice Practice" hitting 29th on NME "150 Best Tracks of the Past 15 Years".[63]

A tracker loaded onto a Game Boy Advance

During the late 2000s, a new wave of chiptune culture took place, boosted by the release of software such as LittleSoundDJ for the Game Boy. This new culture has much more emphasis on live performances and record releases than the demoscene and tracker culture, of which the new artists are often only distantly aware.[64] In recent years, 8-bit chiptune sounds, or "video game beats", have been used by a number of mainstream pop artists. Examples include artists such as Kesha[65] (most notably in "Tik Tok",[52][66] the best-selling single of 2010),[67] 50 Cent with the hit single "Ayo Technology", Robyn, Snoop Dogg,[52][66] Eminem (for example, "Hellbound"), Nelly Furtado, and Timbaland (see Timbaland plagiarism controversy). The influence of video game sounds can also be heard in contemporary British electronica music by artists such as Dizzee Rascal and Kieran Hebden,[68] as well as in heavy metal bands such as DragonForce. Grime music in particular samples sawtooth wave sounds from video games which were popular in East London.[69] Dubstep producers have also been influenced by video game chiptunes, particularly the work of Yuzo Koshiro.[70][71][72] In 2010, a BBC article stated that the "sights and sounds of old-school games" (naming *Frogger* and *Donkey Kong* as examples) are "now becoming a part of mainstream music and culture."[41] Complextro pioneer Porter Robinson has also cited video game sounds, or chiptunes, as an influence on his style of music along with 1980s analog synth music.[73]

0.1.3 Today

The chip scene is far from dead with "compos" being held, groups releasing music disks and with the cracktro/demo scene. New tracker tools are making chip sounds available to less techy musicians. For example, Little Sound DJ for the Game Boy has an interface designed for use in a live environment and features MIDI synchronization. The NES platform has the MidiNES, a cartridge that turns the system into a full blown hardware MIDI controlled synthesizer. Recently, for the Commodore 64, the Mssiah has been released, which is very similar to the MidiNES, but with greater parameter controls, sequencing, analog drum emulation, and limited sample playback. The Commodore PET has the open-source PetSynth software, which uses the PET's 6522 chip for sound, allows the computer to be played like a piano keyboard, and features many effects. On the DOS platform, Fast Tracker is one of the most famous chiptune makers because of the ability to create hand-drawn samples with the mouse. Chiptune artist Pixelh8 has also designed music software such as Music Tech[74] for the Game Boy and the Pro Performer[75] for the Game Boy Advance and Nintendo DS which turn both machines into real time synthesizers.

In the last couple of years, chip music has returned to modern gaming, either in full chip music style or using chip samples in the music. Games that do this in their soundtrack include *Mega Man Battle Network*, *Reset Generation*, *Seiklus*, *Tetris DS*, *Sonic Rush*, *Scott Pilgrim vs. the World: The Game*, *Super Meat Boy*, *Bit.Trip Saga*, *VVVVVV*, *Super Hexagon*, and *Fez*. Furthermore, the Electronic Frontier Foundation in December 2010 used a faux 8-bit game with an 8-bit sound track by crashfaster to demonstrate its notable legal achievements for that year.[76]

On March 16, 2012 the Smithsonian American Art Museum's "The Art of Video Games" exhibit opened featuring a chipmusic soundtrack at the entrance by artists 8 Bit Weapon & ComputeHer. 8 Bit Weapon also created a track called "The art of Video Games Anthem" for the exhibit as well.[77]

0.1.4 Film

The NYC chiptune scene was the subject of a documentary called *Reformat the Planet* by 2 Player Productions. This film was an official selection at the 2008 South by Southwest.[78]

The documentary Europe in 8 Bits discusses the chiptune scene in Europe. Many of the persons involved in the European scene are interviewed, as well as a few chiptune artists from the United States, such as Bit Shifter.[79]

0.1.5 Television

There have been a number of television segments featuring chiptunes and chip music artists in the past few years. On April 11, 2005, 8 Bit Weapon played their songs "Bombs Away" and "Gameboy Rocker" on G4's *Attack of the Show* live broadcast Episode #5058.[80][81]

Another chipmusic feature include little-scale, Dot.AY, Ten Thousand Free Men & Their Families and Jim Cuomo on the ABC Australia television series Good Game.[82]

Br1ght Pr1mate, a Boston-based chiptune band, performed on Fox News on July 10, 2010.[83]

0.1.6 See also

- Atari Punk Console

- Circuit bending

- Chiptune Blaster   Online player for >400 different chiptune formats

- Elektron SidStation – Professional synthesizer with a built-in SID chip

- HardSID – A PCI card for modern computers that features from 1 to 4 actual SID chips

- SLAY Radio – Commodore 64 Remixes

- Pixelart

- Synthwave

- List of music software

0.1.7 Notes

[1] "Trackerien tarina - modit soivat yhä" (PDF). *Skrolli magazine*: 37. September 15, 2014. Retrieved 2015-08-30.

[2] Friedman, Ian. "Top 5 Chiptune Artists". DJZ.com. Retrieved March 13, 2012.

[3] Phelps, P. "A Modern Implementation of Chiptune Synthesis." (PDF). Retrieved 2009-09-21.

[4] Diaz & Driscoll. "Endless loop: A brief history of chiptunes". Transformative Works and Cultures. Retrieved 2009.

[5] Vice: Music Made On Game Boys Is a Much Bigger Deal Than You'd Think

[6] Waugh, I (1985) Commodore 64 Music: Making Music with Your Micro. Sunshine Books.

[7] Fildes, Jonathan (2008-06-17). "17 June 2008: 'Oldest' computer music unveiled". BBC News. Retrieved 2010-07-09.

[8] First Philadelphia Computer Music Festival

[9] Karen Collins (2008), *From Pac-Man to pop music: interactive audio in games and new media*, Ashgate, p. 2, ISBN 0-7546-6200-4

[10] Gaming's Most Important Evolutions, GamesRadar

[11] Collins, Karen (2008). *Game sound: an introduction to the history, theory, and practice of video game music and sound design*. MIT Press. p. 12. ISBN 0-262-03378-X. Retrieved June 12, 2011.

[12] "Computer rock music gaining fans". *Sarasota Journal*: 8. August 18, 1980. Retrieved 2011-05-25.

[13] David Toop (March 1996), "A-Z Of Electro", *The Wire* (145), retrieved 2011-05-29

[14] Daniel Robson (February 29, 2008). "YMCK takes 'chiptune' revolution major". *The Japan Times*. Retrieved 2011-06-11.

[15] Smith, David F. (June 2012). "Game Music Roots: Yellow Magic Orchestra". 1UP.com. Retrieved 6 August 2012.

[16] *Super Locomotive* at the Killer List of Videogames

[17] "Covers of Yellow Magic Orchestra songs". WhoSampled. Retrieved 21 July 2011.

[18] Collins, Karen (2008). *Game sound: an introduction to the history, theory, and practice of video game music and sound design*. MIT Press. p. 19. ISBN 0-262-03378-X. Retrieved June 12, 2011.

[19] *Haruomi Hosono – Video Game Music* at Discogs (list of releases)

[20] Carlo Savorelli. "Xevious". Hardcore Gaming 101. p. 2. Retrieved 2011-06-11.

[21] "Video Game Music". *VGMdb*. Retrieved September 6, 2011.

[22] Collins, Karen (2008). *Game sound: an introduction to the history, theory, and practice of video game music and sound design*. MIT Press. pp. 10–1. ISBN 0-262-03378-X. Retrieved June 12, 2011.

[23] Barnholt, Ray (June 2012). "The Magic of FM Synth". 1UP.com. Retrieved 6 August 2012.

[24] "Miki Higashino". *VGMdb*. Retrieved September 6, 2011.

[25] "Hiroshi Kawaguchi". *VGMdb*. Retrieved September 6, 2011.

[26] John Szczepaniak. "Retro Japanese Computers: Gaming's Final Frontier". Hardcore Gaming 101. Retrieved 2011-03-29. Reprinted from *Retro Gamer (67), 2009*

[27] Shimazu, Takehito (1994). "The History of Electronic and Computer Music in Japan: Significant Composers and Their Works". *Leonardo Music Journal* (MIT Press) **4**: 102–106 [104]. doi:10.2307/1513190. Retrieved 9 July 2012.

[28] "FM Sound Editor V1.0". *Oh!FM*. Archived from the original on 2 September 2012. Retrieved 2 September 2012.

[29] Santos, Wayne (December 2006). "Songs & Sounds In The 21st Century". *GameAxis Unwired* (SPH Magazines) (40): 39. ISSN 0219-872X. Retrieved 2011-08-05.

[30] Chris Greening & Don Kotowski (February 2011). "Interview with Yuzo Koshiro". Square Enix Music Online. Retrieved 2011-06-20.

[31] Yuzo Koshiro at Allgame

[32] RocketBaby (October 1999). "Interview with Yuzo Koshiro". Square Enix Music Online. Retrieved 8 August 2011.

[33] McNeilly, Joe (April 19, 2010). "Game music of the day: Streets of Rage 2". GamesRadar. Retrieved 28 July 2012.

[34] Davis, Jeff. "Interview with Yuzo Koshiro". *Gaming Intelligence Agency*. Retrieved 6 August 2011.

[35] Horowitz, Ken (February 5, 2008). "Interview: Yuzo Koshiro". *Sega-16*. Archived from the original on 21 September 2008. Retrieved 6 August 2011.

[36] Audi. "A Dragon's Journey: Ryu Umemoto in Europe". Hardcore Gaming 101. Retrieved 2011-08-23.

[37] "Kimmel, Jeroen "Red": Red Hubbard (C-64 demo)". Noname.c64.org. Retrieved 2010-07-09.

[38] "Hülsbeck, Chris: Soundmonitor 1.0 (C-64 program)". Noname.c64.org. Retrieved 2010-07-09.

[39] High Voltage SID Collection FAQ

[40] "Amiga Music Preservation FAQ". Amp.dascene.net. 2006-06-17. Retrieved 2010-07-09.

[41] Knowles, Jamillah (June 9, 2010). "How computer games are creating new art and music". BBC. Retrieved August 27, 2011.

[42] "Pac-Man Fever". Time Magazine. April 5, 1982. Retrieved October 15, 2009. Columbia/CBS Records' Pac-Man Fever...was No. 9 on the Billboard Hot 100 last week.

[43] David Toop (2000). *Rap attack 3: African rap to global hip hop, Issue 3* (3rd ed.). Serpent's Tail. p. 129. ISBN 1-85242-627-6. Retrieved 2011-06-06.

[44] "Electro". AllMusic. Retrieved 2011-05-25.

[45] "Jesse Saunders – On And On". Discogs. Retrieved 23 May 2012.

[46] Church, Terry (Feb 9, 2010). "Black History Month: Jesse Saunders and house music". beat portal. Retrieved 16 October 2011.

[47] Bracelin, Jason (May 22, 2007). "House music finds a home". *Las Vegas Review-Journal*. p. 1E. Retrieved 23 May 2012. A native of Chicago, where house was first popularized, Saunders is credited for producing and releasing the first house single, "On and On," on his own Jes Say Records label.

[48] Dan Sicko & Bill Brewster (2010), *Techno Rebels* (2nd ed.), Wayne State University Press, p. 76, ISBN 0-8143-3438-5, retrieved 2011-05-28

[49] "Carlsson, Anders "Goto80": Chip music timeline". Chipflip.wordpress.com. Retrieved 2010-07-09.

[50] D. Lynskey (22 March 2002), "Out with the old, in with the older", *Guardian.co.uk*, archived from the original on 16 February 2011

[51] Shaw, Jeff (May 25, 2006). "Music of the 8-bit variety makes a comeback". *Niagara Gazette*. Retrieved 7 May 2012.

[52] Daniel Robson (March 6, 2012). "Japan's chiptune heroes". *Nintendo Gamer*. Retrieved June 20, 2012.

[53] "Perfume Interview" (in Japanese). bounce.com. 2008-02-07. Archived from the original on 2008-12-09. Retrieved 2009-06-02. (English translation)

[54] "Perfume~🔲🔲🔲🔲🔲🔲!!" (in Japanese). All About 🔲🔲🔲🔲🔲.

[55] SectionZ (August 20, 2007). "SectionZ Electronic Music Community". Archived from the original on December 20, 2007. Retrieved May 9, 2012.

[56] (nanoloop.com) (retrieved November 21, 2011)

[57] LittleSoundDJ littlesounddj.com (retrieved November 20, 2011)

[58] http://8bitoperators.com/8BitFtWorthStar.pdf

[59] Hot Dance Singles Sales *Pocket Calculator* Allmusic.com (charts-awards/billboard-singles) retrieved September 20, 2011

[60] www.hypnote.com pdf of RPM issue #1008 chart(8-Bit Operators at #21 – high position #1)Retrieved September 20, 2011

[61] google.com search:north "american college electronic rpm charts 2007 8 bit 8bit operators" Retrieved September 20, 2011

[62] Dan Swan (Director) (6 January 2008). *Heart Invaders* (Television). London.

[63] 150 Best Tracks Of The Past 15 Years | NME.COM

[64] Yabsley, Alex. (2007) *The Sound of Playing: A Study into the Music and Culture of Chiptunes* [Bachelor of Music Technology thesis]. South Brisbane: Queensland Conservatorium, Griffith University.

[65] Miklewski, Michael (October 20, 2011). *"Music in Video Games: From 8-bit to Symphonies"*. *The Bottom Line*. Frostburg State University. Retrieved 18 June 2012.

[66] "Robyn: Body Talk, Pt. 2". Puls Music. 2010-09-10. Retrieved 2015-08-23. (Translation)

[67] "IFPI publishes Digital Music Report 2011".

[68] Lewis, John (July 4, 2008). "Back to the future: Yellow Magic Orchestra helped usher in electronica – and they may just have invented hip-hop, too". *The Guardian*. Retrieved May 25, 2011.

[69] Alex de Jong, Marc Schuilenburg (2006). *Mediapolis: popular culture and the city*. 010 Publishers. p. 106. ISBN 90-6450-628-0. Retrieved July 30, 2011.

[70] Lawrence, Eddy (11 January 2011). "Ikonika interview: Producer and DJ, Ikonika had an incredible 2010". *Time Out*. Retrieved 5 August 2011.

[71] "Recording Under the Influence: Ikonika". *Self-Titled Magazine*. April 21, 2010. Retrieved 5 August 2011.

[72] Lawrence, Eddy (18 January 2011). "Ikonika interview: Dubstep has taken the world by storm over the past 12 months". *Time Out*. Retrieved 6 August 2011.

[73] Hurt, Edd (June 28, 2012). "Electro wunderkind and self-described 'complextro' Porter Robinson recognizes no technological constraints". *Nashville Scene*. Retrieved 28 July 2012.

[74] Album on NES Cartridge, Synth on GameBoy, Create Digital Music Published July 4, 2007.

[75] Pixelh8 Music Tech Pro Performer Brings Live Performance to Game Boy, *Create Digital Music*. Published March 24, 2008.

[76] EFF 2010: Year in 8bit | Please Donate

[77] http://americanart.si.edu/pr/library/2012/taovg/taovg_release.pdf

[78] Archived December 7, 2009 at the Wayback Machine

[79] "Europe in 8 Bits". *http://europein8bits.com/*.

[80] "G4 – Attack of the Show – Episode History". G4tv.com. Retrieved 2011-06-21.

[81] "Intellivision® Music: 8 Bit Weapon". YouTube. 2007-01-15. Retrieved 2011-06-21.

[82] "Chiptunes". *Good Game Stories*. ABC Australia. April 6, 2009. Retrieved 2010-12-16.

[83] "Mesmerizing Electro-pop – Br1ght Pr1mate". *FOX & Friends*. FOX News. July 10, 2010. Retrieved 2010-12-16.

0.1.8 References

- Kevin, Driscoll; Diaz, Joshua (2009). "Endless loop: A brief history of chiptunes". *Transformative Works and Cultures* **2**. doi:10.3983/twc.2009.0096.

0.1.9 External links

- Chiptune Synthesis – modern and historical chiptune synthesis techniques

- "Bleep Bloop: The Charms of Chiptune" in The New Yorker

- Diggin' In The Carts: A Documentary Series About Japanese Video Game Music, Red Bull Music Academy

- Pulseboy – chiptune generator site

Chapter 1

Further Reading (Alphabetical Order)

1.1 Atari Punk Console

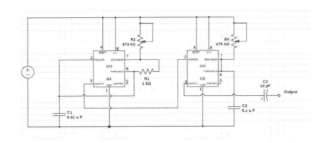

Circuit diagram of an implementation of Atari Punk Console

The **Atari Punk Console** (commonly shortened to APC) is a popular circuit that utilizes two 555 timer ICs or a single 556 dual timer IC. The original circuit, called a "Sound Synthesizer", was published in a Radio Shack booklet: "Engineer's Notebook: Integrated Circuit Applications" in 1980[1] and later called "Stepped Tone Generator" in "Engineer's Mini-Notebook - 555 Circuits" by its designer, Forrest M. Mims III (Siliconcepts, 1984).[2] It was named "Atari Punk Console" (APC) by Kaustic Machines crew because its "low-fi" sounds resemble classic Atari console games from the 1980s, with a square wave output similar to the Atari 2600. Kaustic Machines added a −4db line level output to the circuit which was originally designed to drive a small 8 ohm speaker.

Atari Punk console is an astable square wave oscillator driving a monostable oscillator that creates a single (square) pulse. There are two controls, one for the frequency of the oscillator and one to control the width of the pulse. The controls are usually potentiometers but the circuit can also be controlled by light, temperature, pressure etc. by replacing a potentiometer with a suitable sensor (e.g., photo resistor for light sensitivity). Most of the time there is also a power switch (often a toggle switch) and a volume knob.

The circuit is a simple DIY noisemaker circuit that is relatively inexpensive and easy to build, easily adaptable and is configurable in many ways. It has been built into a wide variety of cases, from metal IKEA bowls to light bulbs, an old Atari mouse or joystick. Its flexibility has led to wide scale popularity among electronics enthusiasts. It is often suggested as a good circuit to build for beginners.

1.1.1 See also

- Circuit bending
- Chiptune
- Drum Buddy

1.1.2 External links

- Original schematics
- Kaustic Machines added a line out to the APC
- Forrest M. Mims III web page
- PCB layout for dual 555 version
- Page describing the circuit + schematic + video sample
- Forrest M. Mims III Atari Punk Console Project description
- Atari Punk Console fan page

1.1.3 References

[1] "Engineer's Notebook: Integrated Circuit Applications". Jameco. Retrieved 13 September 2014.

[2] "Engineer's Mini-Notebook" (PDF). Radio Shack. Archived from the original (PDF) on 22 August 2013. Retrieved 13 September 2014.

1.2 Bitpop

Not to be confused with Britpop.

Bitpop is a type of electronic music and subgenre of chiptune music, where at least part of the music is made using the sound chips of old 8-bit (or 16-bit) computers and video game consoles.

1.2.1 Characteristics

Among systems used include the Atari 8-bit computer, NEC PC-8801, Commodore 64, Nintendo Entertainment System, Amiga, Game Boy, and Mega Drive / Genesis. The sounds produced from these systems can be combined to any degree with traditional instruments, such as guitar and drums, modern synthesizers and drum machines, or vocals and sound effects. Some artists use software-based emulators or virtual synthesizers to recreate the sounds of 8-bit systems, while some use hardware synths, which use the actual sound chips from those systems, such as the Sidstation, Midibox, and trackers.

1.2.2 History

The term bitpop was coined by artists who separated themselves from pure chiptune, as they used more modern production styles and equipment. The name has connotations of a pun on britpop, using the word bit.

Bitpop uses a mixture of old and new equipment often resulting a sound which is unlike Chiptune although containing 8-bit sourced sounds. For example, a bitpop production may be composed almost entirely of 8-bit sounds but with a live vocal, or overlaid live guitars. Conversely, a bitpop production may be composed almost entirely of live vocals and instruments, but feature a bassline or lead melody provided by an 8-bit device.[1][2][3]

One of the pioneers of bitpop music were Welle:Erdball, with their heavy use of Commodore 64 for their first album in 1992. Being a German-speaking group not using the term bitpop and who don't travel by plane, they remained popular among people listening to industrial music or electroclash.

Bitpop music began gaining popularity towards the end of the 1990s. The first electroclash record, I-F's "Space Invaders Are Smoking Grass" (1997), has been described as "burbling electro in a vocodered homage to Atari-era hijinks,"[4] particularly *Space Invaders*.[5] The Beastie Boys outer-space sci-fi themed album Hello Nasty (1998), included, among other potentially influencing tracks, the distinctively video game sound themed original composition track UNITE; garnering mainstream recognition years

ahead of the popular video game tune genre and movement. The trance song "Kernkraft 400" (1999), often played at sports events worldwide, was a remix of a chiptune song written by David Whittaker called "Stardust" for the 1984 Commodore 64 computer game *Lazy Jones*.

In 2003, Malcolm McLaren wrote an article on bitpop and chip music. It also noted a planned release in that style by McLaren.[6]

By the mid-2000s, 8-bit chip music began being incorporated in mainstream pop music, used by acts such as Beck (for example, the 2005 song "Girl"), The Killers (for example, the 2004 song "On Top"), and particularly The Postal Service in many of their songs. The low-quality digital MIDI styling of early game music composers such as Hiroshi Miyauchi also began gaining popularity.[7] In 2003, the J-pop girl group Perfume,[8][9] along with producer Yasutaka Nakata, began producing music combining chiptunes with synthpop and electro house;[9] their breakthrough came in 2007 with *Game*, which led to other Japanese female artists using a similar electronic style, including Aira Mitsuki, immi, Mizca, SAWA, Saori@destiny, and Sweet Vacation.[10]

In recent years, 8-bit chiptune sounds, or "video game beats", have been used by a number of mainstream pop artists. Examples in the Western world include artists such as Kesha[11] (most notably in "Tik Tok",[8][12] the best-selling single of 2010),[13] Robyn, Snoop Dogg,[8][12] Eminem (for example, "Hellbound"), Nelly Furtado, and Timbaland (see Timbaland plagiarism controversy). The influence of video game sounds can also be heard in contemporary British electronica music by artists such as Dizzee Rascal and Kieran Hebden.[14] Grime music in particular samples sawtooth wave sounds from video games which were popular in East London.[15] Dubstep producers have also been influenced by video game chiptunes, particularly the work of Yuzo Koshiro.[16][17][18] In 2010, a BBC article stated that the "sights and sounds of old-school games" (naming *Frogger* and *Donkey Kong* as examples) are "now becoming a part of mainstream music and culture."[19]

1.2.3 Notable artists

- 8 Bit Mayhem
- 8 Bit Weapon
- Adventure Kid
- Anamanaguchi
- Crystal Castles
- FantomenK

- Firebrand Boy

- Freezepop

- Machinae Supremacy

- Mr. Pacman

- Nullsleep

- Perfume

- Pluxus

- Puss

- she

- Slagsmålsklubben

- Solemn Camel Crew

- Superpowerless

- Thermostatic

- trash80

- Welle: Erdball

- Yasutaka Nakata

- YMCK

- You Love Her Coz She's Dead

1.2.4   See also

- SIDstation

- Circuit bending

- List of electronic music genres

- 8-bit (music)

- Game Boy music

1.2.5   External links

- Last.FM Bitpop Tag

- Bleepstreet Records

- 8 Bit Peoples

- 8 Bit Collective

- Bitpop

1.2.6   References

[1] What is Bitpop

[2] The Rise of Bitpop

[3] Listen to Bitpop

[4] D. Lynskey (March 22, 2002), "Out with the old, in with the older", *Guardian.co.uk*, archived from the original on February 16, 2011

[5] "I-f – Space Invaders Are Smoking Grass". Discogs. Retrieved May 25, 2012.

[6] Wired: 8-Bit Punk

[7] Shaw, Jeff (May 25, 2006). "Music of the 8-bit variety makes a comeback". *Niagara Gazette*. Retrieved May 7, 2012.

[8] Daniel Robson (March 6, 2012). "Japan's chiptune heroes". *Nintendo Gamer*. Retrieved June 20, 2012.

[9] "Perfume Interview" (in Japanese). bounce.com. February 7, 2008. Archived from the original on December 9, 2008. Retrieved June 2, 2009. (English translation)

[10] "Perfume~󠀪󠀪󠀪󠀪󠀪󠀪!!" (in Japanese). All About 󠀪󠀪󠀪󠀪󠀪.

[11] Miklewski, Michael (October 20, 2011). "Music in Video Games: From 8-bit to Symphonies". *The Bottom Line*. Frostburg State University. Retrieved June 18, 2012.

[12] "Robyn: Body Talk, Pt. 2". Puls Music. September 10, 2010. Retrieved July 21, 2012. (Translation)

[13] "IFPI publishes Digital Music Report 2011".

[14] Lewis, John (July 4, 2008). "Back to the future: Yellow Magic Orchestra helped usher in electronica – and they may just have invented hip-hop, too". *The Guardian*. Retrieved May 25, 2011.

[15] Alex de Jong, Marc Schuilenburg (2006). *Mediapolis: popular culture and the city*. 010 Publishers. p. 106. ISBN 90-6450-628-0. Retrieved July 30, 2011.

[16] Lawrence, Eddy (January 11, 2011). "Ikonika interview: Producer and DJ, Ikonika had an incredible 2010". *Time Out*. Retrieved August 5, 2011.

[17] "Recording Under the Influence: Ikonika". *Self-Titled Magazine*. April 21, 2010. Retrieved August 5, 2011.

[18] Lawrence, Eddy (January 18, 2011). "Ikonika interview: Dubstep has taken the world by storm over the past 12 months". *Time Out*. Retrieved August 6, 2011.

[19] Knowles, Jamillah (June 9, 2010). "How computer games are creating new art and music". BBC. Retrieved August 27, 2011.

Probing for "bend" using a jeweler's screwdriver and alligator clips

1.3 Circuit bending

Circuit bending is the creative, chance-based customization of the circuits within electronic devices such as low voltage, battery-powered guitar effects, children's toys and digital synthesizers to create new musical or visual instruments and sound generators.

Emphasizing spontaneity and randomness, the techniques of circuit bending have been commonly associated with noise music, though many more conventional contemporary musicians and musical groups have been known to experiment with "bent" instruments. Circuit bending usually involves dismantling the machine and adding components such as switches and potentiometers that alter the circuit.

1.3.1 Experimental process

A 1989 Kawasaki toy guitar used in a circuit bending project

Circuit bending is often practiced by those with no formal training in circuit theory or design, experimenting with second-hand electronics in a DIY fashion. Inexpensive key-boards, drum machines, and electronic children's toys (not necessarily designed for music production) are commonly used. Haphazard modifications can result in short circuits, resulting in the risk of fire, burning, or electrocution.

Aesthetic value, immediate usability and highly randomized results are often factors in the process of successfully bending electronics. Although the history of electronic music is often associated with unconventional sonic results, such innovators as Robert Moog[1] and Léon Theremin[2] were electrical engineers, and more concerned with the consistency and sound design of their instruments. Circuit bending is typified by inconsistencies in instruments built in an unscientific manner. While many pre-fitted circuit bent machines are on offer for sale at auction sites such as eBay, this somewhat contravenes the intention of most practitioners. Machines bent to a repeated configuration are more analogous to the well known practice of "mods", such as the Devilfish mod for the Roland TB-303, the famous Speak and Spell toys or various Analogman or Pedaldoc guitar pedal circuit modifications.

Circuit bending an audio device typically involves removing the rear panel of the device and connecting any two circuit locations with a "jumper" wire, sending current from one part of the circuit into another. Results are monitored through either the device's internal speaker or by connecting an amplifier to the speaker output. If an interesting effect is achieved, this connection would be marked for future reference or kept active by either soldering a new connection or bridging it with crocodile clips. Often other components are inserted at these points such as pushbuttons or switches, to turn the effect on or off; or components such as resistors or capacitors, to change the quality of the audio output. This is repeated on a trial and error basis. Other components added into the circuit can give the performer more expressiveness, such as potentiometers, photoresistors (for reaction to light) and pressure sensors.

A Yamaha PSR-6 used in a circuit bending project.

The simplest input, and the one most identified with circuit bending, is the body contact,[3] where the performer's touch causes the circuit to change the sound. Often metal knobs, plates, screws or studs are wired to these circuit points to give easier access to these points from the outside the case of the device.

Since creative experimentation[4] is a key element to the practice of circuit bending, there is always a possibility that short circuiting may yield undesirable results, including component failure. In particular, connecting the power supply or a capacitor directly to a computer chip lead can destroy the chip and make the device inoperable. Before beginning to do circuit bending, a person should learn the basic risk factors about working with electrical and electronic products, including how to identify capacitors (which can give a person a serious shock due to the electrical charge that they store), and how to avoid risks with AC power. For safety reasons, a circuit bender should have a few basic electronics tools, such as a multimeter (an electronic testing device which measures voltage, resistance and other factors). It is advised that beginner circuit benders should *never* "bend" any device that gets its power from mains electricity (household AC power), as this would carry a serious risk of electrocution.

1.3.2   Innovators

Although similar methods were previously used by other musicians and engineers, this method of music creation is believed to have been pioneered by Reed Ghazala in the 1960s. Ghazala's experience with circuit-bending began in 1966 when a toy transistor amplifier, by chance, shorted-out against a metal object in his desk drawer, resulting in a stream of unusual sounds.[5] While Ghazala says that he was not the first circuit bender, he coined the term Circuit Bending [6] and whole-heartedly promoted the proliferation of the concept and practice through his writings and internet site, earning him the title "Father of Circuit Bending".

Serge Tcherepnin, designer of the Serge modular synthesizers, discussed[7] his early experiments in the 1950s with the transistor radio, in which he found sensitive circuit points in those simple electronic devices and brought them out to "body contacts" on the plastic chassis. Prior to Mark's and Reed's experiments other pioneers also explored the body-contact idea, one of the earliest being Thaddeus Cahill (1897) whose telharmonium, it is reported, was also touch-sensitive.

Since 1984, Swiss duo Voice Crack created music by manipulating common electronic devices in a practice they termed "cracked everyday electronics." [8]

1.3.3   See also

Kraakdoos.

- Atari Punk Console
- Axesynth (Known as the "Atari", as used by the rock band MuteMath, and Velva (Chicago)
- Bent Festival
- Casper Electronics
- Chiptunes
- Electronic art music
- Glitch (music)
- Kraakdoos (CrackleBox)
- MIDIbox
- MOS Technology SID
- Music Tech Fest
- NIME
- No-Fi
- Noise music
- List of music software

1.3.4   References

Alexandre Marino Fernandez, Fernando Iazzetta, Circuit-Bending and DIY Culture

[1] "Robert Moog: Music Pioneer". *NPR.org*. 23 August 2005. Retrieved 3 June 2015.

[2] "No. 1818: Leon Theremin". Retrieved 3 June 2015.

[3] Reed Ghazala: http://www.anti-theory.com/soundart/circuitbend/cb14.html

[4] "circuit-bending". Retrieved 3 June 2015.

[5] Reed Ghazala: *Circuit-Bending, Build Your Own Alien Instruments*, Extreme Tech, 2006

[6] Reed Ghazala: "Circuit-Bending and Living Instruments," EMI Volume VIII #1, 1992

[7] Vail, Mark: *Vintage Synthesizers: Pioneering Designers, Groundbreaking Instruments, Collecting Tips, Mutants of Technology*, Backbeat Books; 2.00 edition (March 15, 2000)

[8] "YULE 2008". Retrieved 3 June 2015.

1.3.5 External links

- oddmusic.com's circuit bending section - Gallery of some of Reed Ghazala's work, facts, history, tutorial, benders guide, tools of the trade and more

- Q.R. Ghazala's How-To Ghazala's official website tutorial

- GetLoFi a circuit bending blog with a lot of circuit bending tips and resources

1.4 Computer music

"Computer Music" redirects here. For the magazine, see Computer Music (magazine).

Computer music is the applications of computing technology in music composition. It includes the theory and application of new and existing technologies and basic aspects of music, such as sound synthesis, digital signal processing, sound design, sonic diffusion, acoustics, and psychoacoustics. The field of computer music can trace its roots back to the origins of electronic music, and the very first experiments and innovations with electronic instruments at the turn of the 20th century.

More recently, with the advent of personal computing, and the growth of home recording, the term computer music is sometimes used to describe music that has been created using computing technology.

1.4.1 History

See also: Computer music programming languages

Much of the work on computer music has drawn on the relationship between music theory and mathematics. The world's first computer to play music was CSIRAC which was designed and built by Trevor Pearcey and Maston Beard. Mathematician Geoff Hill programmed the CSIRAC to play popular musical melodies from the very early 1950s. In 1951 it publicly played the "Colonel Bogey March"[1] of which no known recordings exist. However, CSIRAC played standard repertoire and was not used to extend musical thinking or composition practice which is current computer-music practice.

The oldest known recordings of computer generated music were played by the Ferranti Mark 1 computer, a commercial version of the Baby Machine from the University of Manchester in the autumn of 1951. The music program was written by Christopher Strachey. During a session recorded by the BBC, the machine managed to work its way through "Baa Baa Black Sheep", "God Save the King" and part of "In the Mood".[2]

Two further major 1950s developments were the origins of digital sound synthesis by computer, and of algorithmic composition programs beyond rote playback. Max Mathews at Bell Laboratories developed the influential MUSIC I program and its descendents, further popularising computer music through a 1963 article in *Science*.[3] Amongst other pioneers, the musical chemists Lejaren Hiller and Leonard Isaacson worked on a series of algorithmic composition experiments from 1956-9, manifested in the 1957 premiere of the *Illiac Suite* for string quartet.[4]

In Japan, experiments in computer music date back to 1962, when Keio University professor Sekine and Toshiba engineer Hayashi experimented with the TOSBAC computer. This resulted in a piece entitled *TOSBAC Suite*, influenced by the *Illiac Suite*. Later Japanese computer music compositions include a piece by Kenjiro Ezaki presented during Osaka Expo '70 and "Panoramic Sonore" (1974) by music critic Akimichi Takeda. Ezaki also published an article called "Contemporary Music and Computers" in 1970. Since then, Japanese research in computer music has largely been carried out for commercial purposes in popular music, though some of the more serious Japanese musicians used large computer systems such as the *Fairlight* in the 1970s.[5]

Early computer-music programs typically did not run in real time. Programs would run for hours or days, on multi-million-dollar computers, to generate a few minutes of music.[6][7] One way around this was to use a 'hybrid system', most notably the Roland MC-8 Microcomposer, where a microprocessor-based system controls an analog synthesizer, released in 1978.[5] John Chowning's work on FM synthesis from the 1960s to the 1970s allowed much more efficient digital synthesis,[8] eventually leading to the development of the affordable FM synthesis-based Yamaha

DX7 digital synthesizer, released in 1983.[9] In addition to the Yamaha DX7, the advent of inexpensive digital chips and microcomputers opened the door to real-time generation of computer music.[9] In the 1980s, Japanese personal computers such as the NEC PC-88 came installed with FM synthesis sound chips and featured audio programming languages such as Music Macro Language (MML) and MIDI interfaces, which were most often used to produce video game music, or chiptunes.[5] By the early 1990s, the performance of microprocessor-based computers reached the point that real-time generation of computer music using more general programs and algorithms became possible.[10]

> Interesting sounds must have a fluidity and changeability that allows them to remain fresh to the ear. In computer music this subtle ingredient is bought at a high computational cost, both in terms of the number of items requiring detail in a score and in the amount of interpretive work the instruments must produce to realize this detail in sound.[11]

1.4.2 Advances

Advances in computing power and software for manipulation of digital media have dramatically affected the way computer music is generated and performed. Current-generation micro-computers are powerful enough to perform very sophisticated audio synthesis using a wide variety of algorithms and approaches. Computer music systems and approaches are now ubiquitous, and so firmly embedded in the process of creating music that we hardly give them a second thought: computer-based synthesizers, digital mixers, and effects units have become so commonplace that use of digital rather than analog technology to create and record music is the norm, rather than the exception.

1.4.3 Research

Despite the ubiquity of computer music in contemporary culture, there is considerable activity in the field of computer music, as researchers continue to pursue new and interesting computer-based synthesis, composition, and performance approaches. Throughout the world there are many organizations and institutions dedicated to the area of computer and electronic music study and research, including the ICMA (International Computer Music Association), IRCAM, GRAME, SEAMUS (Society for Electro Acoustic Music in the United States), CEC (Canadian Electroacoustic Community), and a great number of institutions of higher learning around the world.

1.4.4 Computer-generated music

Computer-generated music is music composed by, or with the extensive aid of, a computer. Although any music which uses computers in its composition or realisation is computer-generated to some extent, the use of computers is now so widespread (in the editing of pop songs, for instance) that the phrase computer-generated music is generally used to mean a kind of music which could not have been created *without* the use of computers.

We can distinguish two groups of computer-generated music: music in which a computer generated the score, which could be performed by humans, and music which is both composed and performed by computers. There is a large genre of music that is organized, synthesized, and created on computers.

Music composed and performed by computers

Main article: Algorithmic composition
See also: Generative music, Evolutionary music and Genetic algorithm

Later, composers such as Gottfried Michael Koenig had computers generate the sounds of the composition as well as the score. Koenig produced algorithmic composition programs which were a generalisation of his own serial composition practice. This is not exactly similar to Xenakis' work as he used mathematical abstractions and examined how far he could explore these musically. Koenig's software translated the calculation of mathematical equations into codes which represented musical notation. This could be converted into musical notation by hand and then performed by human players. His programs Project 1 and Project 2 are examples of this kind of software. Later, he extended the same kind of principles into the realm of synthesis, enabling the computer to produce the sound directly. SSP is an example of a program which performs this kind of function. All of these programs were produced by Koenig at the Institute of Sonology in Utrecht in the 1970s.

Procedures such as those used by Koenig and Xenakis are still in use today. Since the invention of the MIDI system in the early 1980s, for example, some people have worked on programs which map MIDI notes to an algorithm and then can either output sounds or music through the computer's sound card or write an audio file for other programs to play.

Some of these simple programs are based on fractal geometry, and can map midi notes to specific fractals, or fractal equations. Although such programs are widely available and are sometimes seen as clever toys for the non-musician, some professional musicians have given them attention also. The resulting 'music' can be more like noise, or can sound quite familiar and pleasant. As with much algorithmic music, and algorithmic art in general, more depends on the way in which the parameters are mapped to aspects of these equations than on the equations themselves. Thus, for example, the same equation can be made to produce both a lyrical and melodic piece of music in the style of the mid-nineteenth century, and a fantastically dissonant cacophony more reminiscent of the avant-garde music of the 1950s and 1960s.

Other programs can map mathematical formulae and constants to produce sequences of notes. In this manner, an irrational number can give an infinite sequence of notes where each note is a digit in the decimal expression of that number. This sequence can in turn be a composition in itself, or simply the basis for further elaboration.

Operations such as these, and even more elaborate operations can also be performed in computer music programming languages such as Max/MSP, SuperCollider, Csound, Pure Data (Pd), Keykit, and ChucK. These programs now easily run on most personal computers, and are often capable of more complex functions than those which would have necessitated the most powerful mainframe computers several decades ago.

There exist programs that generate "human-sounding" melodies by using a vast database of phrases. One example is Band-in-a-Box, which is capable of creating jazz, blues and rock instrumental solos with almost no user interaction. Another is Impro-Visor, which uses a stochastic context-free grammar to generate phrases and complete solos.

Another 'cybernetic' approach to computer composition uses specialized hardware to detect external stimuli which are then mapped by the computer to realize the performance. Examples of this style of computer music can be found in the middle-80's work of David Rokeby (Very Nervous System) where audience/performer motions are 'translated' to MIDI segments. Computer controlled music is also found in the performance pieces by the Canadian composer Udo Kasemets such as the Marce(ntennia)l Circus C(ag)elebrating Duchamp (1987), a realization of the Marcel Duchamp process piece *Erratum Musical* using an electric model train to collect a hopper-car of stones to be deposited on a drum wired to an Analog:Digital converter, mapping the stone impacts to a score display (performed in Toronto by pianist Gordon Monahan during the 1987 Duchamp Centennial), or his installations and performance works (e.g. Spectrascapes) based on his Geo(sono)scope (1986) 15x4-channel computer-controlled audio mixer. In these latter works, the computer generates sound-scapes from tape-loop sound samples, live shortwave or sine-wave generators.

Computer-generated scores for performance by human players

Many systems for generating musical scores actually existed well before the time of computers. One of these was Musikalisches Würfelspiel *(Musical dice game*; 18th century), a system which used throws of the dice to randomly select measures from a large collection of small phrases. When patched together, these phrases combined to create musical pieces which could be performed by human players. Although these works were not actually composed with a computer in the modern sense, it uses a rudimentary form of the random combinatorial techniques sometimes used in computer-generated composition.

The world's first digital computer music was generated in Australia by programmer Geoff Hill on the CSIRAC computer which was designed and built by Trevor Pearcey and Maston Beard, although it was only used to play standard tunes of the day. Subsequently, one of the first composers to write music with a computer was Iannis Xenakis. He wrote programs in the FORTRAN language that generated numeric data that he transcribed into scores to be played by traditional musical instruments. An example is *ST/48* of 1962. Although Xenakis could well have composed this music by hand, the intensity of the calculations needed to transform probabilistic mathematics into musical notation was best left to the number-crunching power of the computer.

Computers have also been used in an attempt to imitate the music of great composers of the past, such as Mozart. A present exponent of this technique is David Cope. He wrote computer programs that analyse works of other composers to produce new works in a similar style. He has used this program to great effect with composers such as Bach and Mozart (his program *Experiments in Musical Intelligence* is famous for creating "Mozart's 42nd Symphony"), and also within his own pieces, combining his own creations with that of the computer.

Melomics, a research project from the University of Málaga, Spain, developed a computer composition cluster named Iamus, which composes complex, multi-instrument pieces for editing and performance. Since its inception, Iamus has composed a full album in 2012, appropriately named Iamus, which New Scientist described as "The first major work composed by a computer and performed by a full orchestra."[12] The group has also developed an API for developers to utilize the technology, and makes its music available on its website.

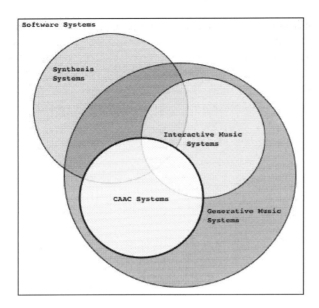

Diagram illustrating the position of CAAC in relation to other Generative music Systems

Computer-aided algorithmic composition

Computer-aided algorithmic composition (CAAC, pronounced "sea-ack") is the implementation and use of algorithmic composition techniques in software. This label is derived from the combination of two labels, each too vague for continued use. The label *computer-aided composition* lacks the specificity of using generative algorithms. Music produced with notation or sequencing software could easily be considered computer-aided composition. The label *algorithmic composition* is likewise too broad, particularly in that it does not specify the use of a computer. The term computer-aided, rather than computer-assisted, is used in the same manner as computer-aided design.

1.4.5   Machine improvisation

See also: Machine learning, Machine listening, Artificial intelligence and Neural networks

Machine improvisation uses computer algorithms to create improvisation on existing music materials. This is usually done by sophisticated recombination of musical phrases extracted from existing music, either live or pre-recorded. In order to achieve credible improvisation in particular style, machine improvisation uses machine learning and pattern matching algorithms to analyze existing musical examples. The resulting patterns are then used to create new variations "in the style" of the original music, developing a notion of stylistic reinjection. This is different from other improvisa-

tion methods with computers that use algorithmic composition to generate new music without performing analysis of existing music examples.

Statistical style modeling

Style modeling implies building a computational representation of the musical surface that captures important stylistic features from data. Statistical approaches are used to capture the redundancies in terms of pattern dictionaries or repetitions, which are later recombined to generate new musical data. Style mixing can be realized by analysis of a database containing multiple musical examples in different styles. Machine Improvisation builds upon a long musical tradition of statistical modeling that began with Hiller and Isaacson's *Illiac Suite for String Quartet* (1957) and Xenakis' uses of Markov chains and stochastic processes. Modern methods include the use of lossless data compression for incremental parsing, prediction suffix tree and string searching by factor oracle algorithm (basically a *factor oracle* is a finite state automaton constructed in linear time and space in an incremental fashion[13]).

Uses of machine improvisation

Machine improvisation encourages musical creativity by providing automatic modeling and transformation structures for existing music. This creates a natural interface with the musician without need for coding musical algorithms. In live performance, the system re-injects the musician's material in several different ways, allowing a semantics-level representation of the session and a smart recombination and transformation of this material in real-time. In offline version, machine improvisation can be used to achieve style mixing, an approach inspired by Vannevar Bush's memex imaginary machine.

Implementations

The first system implementing interactive machine improvisation by means of Markov models and style modeling techniques is the Continuator, , developed by François Pachet at Sony CSL Paris in 2002[14][15] based on work on non-real time style modeling.[16][17] Matlab implementation of the Factor Oracle machine improvisation can be found as part of Computer Audition toolbox.

OMax is a software environment developed in IRCAM. OMax uses OpenMusic and Max. It is based on researches on stylistic modeling carried out by Gerard Assayag and Shlomo Dubnov and on researches on improvisation with the computer by G. Assayag, M. Chemillier and G. Bloch (a.k.a. the *OMax Brothers*) in the Ircam Music Representations group.

Musicians working with machine improvisation

Gerard Assayag (IRCAM, France), Jeremy Baguyos (University of Nebraska at Omaha, USA) Tim Blackwell (Goldsmiths College, Great Britain), George Bloch (Composer, France), Marc Chemiller (IRCAM/CNRS, France), Nick Collins (University of Sussex, UK), Shlomo Dubnov (Composer, Israel / USA), Mari Kimura (Juilliard, New York City), George Lewis (Columbia University, New York City), Bernard Lubat (Pianist, France), François Pachet (Sony CSL, France), Joel Ryan (Institute of Sonology, Netherlands), Michel Waisvisz (STEIM, Netherlands), David Wessel (CNMAT, California), Michael Young (Goldsmiths College, Great Britain), Pietro Grossi (CNUCE, Institute of the National Research Council, Pisa, Italy), Toby Gifford and Andrew Brown (Griffith University, Brisbane, Australia), Davis Salks (jazz composer, Hamburg, PA, USA), Doug Van Nort (electroacoustic improviser, Montreal/New York)

1.4.6 Live coding

Main article: Live coding

Live coding[18] (sometimes known as 'interactive programming', 'on-the-fly programming',[19] 'just in time programming') is the name given to the process of writing software in realtime as part of a performance. Recently it has been explored as a more rigorous alternative to laptop musicians who, live coders often feel, lack the charisma and pizzazz of musicians performing live.[20]

Generally, this practice stages a more general approach: one of interactive programming, of writing (parts of) programs while they are interpreted. Traditionally most computer music programs have tended toward the old write/compile/run model which evolved when computers were much less powerful. This approach has locked out code-level innovation by people whose programming skills are more modest. Some programs have gradually integrated real-time controllers and gesturing (for example, MIDI-driven software synthesis and parameter control). Until recently, however, the musician/composer rarely had the capability of real-time modification of program code itself. This legacy distinction is somewhat erased by languages such as ChucK, SuperCollider, and Impromptu.

TOPLAP, an ad-hoc conglomerate of artists interested in live coding was formed in 2004, and promotes the use, proliferation and exploration of a range of software, languages and techniques to implement live coding. This is a parallel and collaborative effort e.g. with research at the Princeton Sound Lab, the University of Cologne, and the Computational Arts Research Group at Queensland University of Technology.

1.4.7 See also

1.4.8 References

[1] Doornbusch, Paul. "The Music of CSIRAC". *Melbourne School of Engineering, Department of Computer Science and Software Engineering.*

[2] Fildes, Jonathan (June 17, 2008). "'Oldest' computer music unveiled". *BBC News.* Retrieved 4 December 2013.

[3] Bogdanov, Vladimir (2001). *All Music Guide to Electronica: The Definitive Guide to Electronic Music.* Backbeat Books. p. 320. Retrieved 4 December 2013.

[4] Lejaren Hiller and Leonard Isaacson, *Experimental Music: Composition with an Electronic Computer* (New York: McGraw-Hill, 1959; reprinted Westport, Conn.: Greenwood Press, 1979). ISBN 0-313-22158-8.

[5] Shimazu, Takehito (1994). "The History of Electronic and Computer Music in Japan: Significant Composers and Their Works". *Leonardo Music Journal* (MIT Press) **4**: 102–106 [104]. doi:10.2307/1513190. Retrieved 9 July 2012.

[6] Cattermole, Tannith (May 9, 2011). "Farseeing inventor pioneered computer music". Gizmag. Retrieved 28 October 2011.
"In 1957 the MUSIC program allowed an IBM 704 mainframe computer to play a 17-second composition by Mathews. Back then computers were ponderous, so synthesis would take an hour."

[7] Mathews, Max (1 November 1963). "The Digital Computer as a Musical Instrument". *Science* **142** (3592): 553–557. doi:10.1126/science.142.3592.553. Retrieved 28 October 2011.
"The generation of sound signals requires very high sampling rates.... A high speed machine such as the I.B.M. 7090 ... can compute only about 5000 numbers per second ... when generating a reasonably complex sound."

[8] Dean, R. T. (2009). *The Oxford handbook of computer music.* Oxford University Press. p. 20. ISBN 0-19-533161-3.

[9] Dean, R. T. (2009). *The Oxford handbook of computer music.* Oxford University Press. p. 1. ISBN 0-19-533161-3.

[10] Dean, R. T. (2009). *The Oxford handbook of computer music.* Oxford University Press. pp. 4–5. ISBN 0-19-533161-3.
"... by the 90s ... digital sound manipulation (using MSP or many other platforms) became widespread, fluent and stable."

[11] Loy, D. Gareth (1992). Roads, Curtis, ed. *The Music Machine: Selected Readings from Computer Music Journal*. MIT Press. p. 344. ISBN 0-262-68078-5.

[12] "Computer composer honours Turing's centenary". *News Scientist.* 5 July 2012.

[13] Jan Pavelka; Gerard Tel; Miroslav Bartosek, eds. (1999). *Factor oracle: a new structure for pattern matching; Proceedings of SOFSEM'99; Theory and Practice of Informatics.* Springer-Verlag, Berlin. pp. 291–306. ISBN 3-540-66694-X. Retrieved 4 December 2013. Lecture Notes in Computer Science 1725

[14] Pachet, F., The Continuator: Musical Interaction with Style. In ICMA, editor,Proceedings of ICMC, pages 211-218, Göteborg, Sweden, September 2002. ICMA. Best paper award.

[15] Pachet, F. Playing with Virtual Musicians: the Continuator in practice. IEEE Multimedia,9(3):77-82 2002.

[16] G. Assayag, S. Dubnov, O. Delerue, "Guessing the Composer's Mind : Applying Universal Prediction to Musical Style", In Proceedings of International Computer Music Conference, Beijing, 1999.

[17] S. Dubnov, G. Assayag, O. Lartillot, G. Bejerano, "Using Machine-Learning Methods for Musical Style Modeling", IEEE Computers, 36 (10), pp. 73-80, Oct. 2003.

[18] Collins, N.; McLean, A.; Rohrhuber, J.; Ward, A. (2004). "Live coding in laptop performance". *Organised Sound* **8** (03). doi:10.1017/S135577180300030X.

[19] Wang G. & Cook P. (2004) "On-the-fly Programming: Using Code as an Expressive Musical Instrument", In *Proceedings of the 2004 International Conference on New Interfaces for Musical Expression (NIME)* (New York: NIME, 2004).

[20] Collins, N. (2003). "Generative Music and Laptop Performance". *Contemporary Music Review* **22** (4): 67–79. doi:10.1080/0749446032000156919.

1.4.9   Further reading

- Ariza, C. 2005. "Navigating the Landscape of Computer-Aided Algorithmic Composition Systems: A Definition, Seven Descriptors, and a Lexicon of Systems and Research." In *Proceedings of the International Computer Music Conference*. San Francisco: International Computer Music Association. 765-772. Internet: http://www.flexatone.net/docs/nlcaacs.pdf

- Ariza, C. 2005. *An Open Design for Computer-Aided Algorithmic Music Composition: athenaCL.* Ph.D. Dissertation, New York University. Internet: http://www.flexatone.net/docs/odcaamca.pdf

- Berg, P. 1996. "Abstracting the future: The Search for Musical Constructs" *Computer Music Journal* 20(3): 24-27.

- Boulanger, Richard, ed. (March 6, 2000). *The Csound Book: Perspectives in Software Synthesis, Sound Design, Signal Processing, and Programming.* The MIT Press. p. 740. ISBN 0-262-52261-6. Retrieved 3 October 2009.

- Chadabe, Joel. 1997. *Electric Sound: The Past and Promise of Electronic Music.* Upper Saddle River, New Jersey: Prentice Hall.

- Chowning, John. 1973. "The Synthesis of Complex Audio Spectra by Means of Frequency Modulation". *Journal of the Audio Engineering Society* 21, no. 7:526–34.

- Collins, Nick (2009). *Introduction to Computer Music.* Chichester: Wiley. ISBN 978-0-470-71455-3.

- Dodge, Charles; Jerse (1997). *Computer Music: Synthesis, Composition and Performance.* Thomas A. (2nd ed.). New York: Schirmer Books. p. 453. ISBN 0-02-864682-7.

- Doornbusch, P. 2009. "A Chronology / History of Electronic and Computer Music and Related Events 1906 - 2011" http://www.doornbusch.net/chronology/

- Heifetz, Robin (1989). *On the Wires of Our Nerves.* Lewisburg Pa.: Bucknell University Press. ISBN 0-8387-5155-5.

- Manning, Peter (2004). *Electronic and Computer Music* (revised and expanded ed.). Oxford Oxfordshire: Oxford University Press. ISBN 0-19-517085-7.

- Perry, Mark, and Thomas Margoni. 2010. "From Music Tracks to Google Maps: Who Owns Computer-Generated Works?". *Computer Law and Security Review* 26: 621–29.

- Roads, Curtis (1994). *The Computer Music Tutorial.* Cambridge: MIT Press. ISBN 0-262-68082-3.

- Supper, M. 2001. "A Few Remarks on Algorithmic Composition." *Computer Music Journal* 25(1): 48-53.

- Xenakis, Iannis (2001). *Formalized Music: Thought and Mathematics in Composition.* Harmonologia Series No. 6. Hillsdale, NY: Pendragon Pr. ISBN 1-57647-079-2.

1.4.10 External links

1.5 Demoscene

The **demoscene** is an international computer art subculture that specializes in producing demos: small, self-contained computer programs that produce audio-visual presentations. The main goal of a demo is to show off programming, artistic, and musical skills.

The demoscene's roots are in the home computer revolution of the late 1970s, and the subsequent advent of software cracking. Crackers illegally distributed video games, adding introductions of their own making ("cracktros"), and soon started competing for the best presentation.[1] The making of intros and standalone demos eventually evolved into a new subculture, independent of the gaming[2]:29–30 and software piracy scenes.

1.5.1 Concept

Screen shot from Second Reality, a famous[3] demo by Future Crew.

Prior to the popularity of IBM PC compatibles, most home computers of a given line had relatively little variance in their basic hardware, which made their capabilities practically identical. Therefore, the variations among demos created for one computer line were attributed to programming alone, rather than one computer having better hardware. This created a competitive environment in which demoscene groups would try to outperform each other in creating outstanding effects, and often to demonstrate why they felt one machine was better than another (for example Commodore 64 or Amiga versus Atari 800 or ST).

Demo writers went to great lengths to get every last bit of performance out of their target machine. Where games and application writers were concerned with the stability and functionality of their software, the demo writer was typically interested in how many CPU cycles a routine would consume and, more generally, how best to squeeze great

activity onto the screen. Writers went so far as to exploit known hardware errors to produce effects that the manufacturer of the computer had not intended. The perception that the demo scene was going to extremes and charting new territory added to its draw.

Recent computer hardware advancements include faster processors, more memory, faster video graphics processors, and hardware 3D acceleration. With many of the past's challenges removed, the focus in making demos has moved from squeezing as much out of the computer as possible to making stylish, beautiful, well-designed real time artwork – a directional shift that many "old school demosceners" seem to disapprove of. This can be explained by the break introduced by the PC world, where the platform varies and most of the programming work that used to be hand-programmed is now done by the graphics card. This gives demo-groups a lot more artistic freedom, but can frustrate some of the old-schoolers for lack of a programming challenge. The old tradition still lives on, though. Demo parties have competitions with varying limitations in program size or platform (different series are called compos). On a modern computer the executable size may be limited to 64 kB or 4 kB. Programs of limited size are usually called intros. In other compos the choice of platform is restricted; only old computers, like the 8-bit Atari 800 or Commodore 64, or the 16-bit Amiga or Atari ST, or mobile devices like handheld phones or PDAs are allowed. Such restrictions provide a challenge for coders, musicians and graphics artists and bring back the old motive of making a device do more than was intended in its original design.

1.5.2 History

The earliest computer programs that have some resemblance to demos and demo effects can be found among the so-called display hacks. Display hacks predate the demoscene by several decades, with the earliest examples dating back to the early 1950s.

Demos in the demoscene sense began as software crackers' "signatures", that is, crack screens and crack intros attached to software whose copy protection was removed. The first crack screens appeared on the Apple II computers in the late 1970s and early 1980s, and they were often nothing but plain text screens crediting the cracker or his group. Gradually, these static screens evolved into increasingly impressive-looking introductions containing animated effects and music. Eventually, many cracker groups started to release intro-like programs separately, without being attached to pirated software. These programs were initially known by various names, such as *letters* or *messages*, but they later came to be known as *demos*.[4]

Simple demo-like music collections were put together on

the C64 in 1985 by Charles Deenen, inspired by crack intros, using music taken from games and adding some homemade color graphics. In the following year the movement now known as the demoscene was born. The Dutch groups 1001 Crew and The Judges, both Commodore 64-based, are often mentioned as the earliest demo groups. Whilst competing with each other in 1986, they both produced pure demos with original graphics and music involving more than just casual work, and used extensive hardware trickery. At the same time demos from others, such as Antony Crowther (Ratt), had started circulating on Compunet in the United Kingdom. On the ZX Spectrum, Castor Cracking Group released their first demo called *Castor Intro* in 1986. The ZX Spectrum demo scene was slow to start, but it started to rise in the late 1980s, most noticeably in Eastern Europe.

1.5.3   Demoscene culture

The demoscene is mainly a European phenomenon, and is traditionally male-dominated.[5] It is a competition-oriented subculture, with groups and individual artists competing against each other in technical and artistic excellence. Those who achieve excellence are dubbed "elite", while those who do not follow the demoscene's implicit rules are called "lamers"; such rules emphasize creativity over "ripping" (or buying) the works of others, having good contacts within the scene, and showing effort rather than asking for help.[5] Both this competitiveness and the sense of cooperation among demosceners have led to comparisons with the earlier hacker culture in academic computing.[5][6]:159 The demoscene is a closed subculture, which seeks and receives little mainstream public interest.[2]:4 As of 2010, the size of the scene was estimated at some 10.000.[7]

In the early days, competition came in the form of setting records, like the number of "bobs" (blitter objects) on the screen per frame, or the number of DYCP (different Y Character position) scrollers on a C64. These days, there are organized competitions, or compos, held at demoparties, although there have been some online competitions as well. It has also been common for diskmags to have voting-based *charts* which provide ranking lists for the best coders, graphicians, musicians, demos and other things. However, the respect for charts has diminished since the 1990s.

Party-based competitions usually require the artist or a group member to be present at the event. The winners are selected by a public voting amongst the visitors and awarded at a prizegiving ceremony at the end of the party. Competitions at a typical demo event include a *demo compo*, an *intro compo* (usually 4kB and 64kB), a *graphics compo* and

a *music compo*. Most parties also split some categories by platform, format or style.

There are no criteria or rules the voters should be bound by, and a visitor typically just votes for those entries that made the biggest impression on them. In the old demos, the impression was often attempted with programming techniques introducing new effects and breaking performance records in old effects. Over the years, the emphasis has moved from technical excellence to more artistic values such as overall design, audiovisual impact and mood.

In recent years, an initiative to award demos in an alternative way arose by the name of the Scene.org Awards. The essential concept of the awards was to avoid the subjectivity of mass-voting at parties, and select a well-renowned jury to handle the task of selecting the given year's best productions on several aspects, such as Best Graphics or Best 64k Intro. This award was canceled in 2012.

Groups

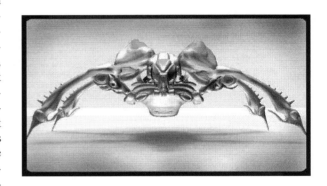

PC-Demo: Interceptor by Black Maiden.

Main article: Demogroup

Demosceners typically organize in small, tightly-knit groups, centered around a *coder* (programmer), a *musician* and a *graphician* (graphics designer). Various other supporting roles exist and groups can grow to dozens of people, but most demos are actually created by a small number of people.[2]:32–33

Groups always have names, and similarly the individual members pick a handle by which they will be addressed in the large community. While the practice of using handles rather than real names is a borrowing from the cracker/warez culture, where it serves to hide the identity of the cracker from law enforcement, in the demoscene (oriented toward legal activities) it mostly serves as a manner of self-expression. Group members tend to self-identify with the group, often extending their handle with their group's name, following the patterns "*Handle* of *Group*" or "*Han*-

dle/Group".[2]:31–32

Parties

Assembly 2004 – a combination of a demoparty and a LAN party

Main article: Demoparty

A demoparty is an event which gathers demomakers and provides them competitions to compete in. A typical demoparty is a non-stop event lasting over a weekend, providing the visitors a lot of time for socializing. The competing works, at least those in the most important competitions, are usually shown at night, using a video projector and big loudspeakers.[8]

Demoparties started to appear in the 1980s in the form of copyparties where software pirates and demomakers gathered to meet each other and share their software. Competitions did not become a major aspect of the events until the beginning of the 1990s.

Demoscene events are most frequent in Europe, with around fifty parties every year. North America has the second highest number of demoparties historically, currently with two parties per year.[9] Most events are local, gathering demomakers mostly from a single country, while the largest international parties (such as Revision and Assembly) attract visitors from all over the globe.

1.5.4   Demo types

Main article: Demo (computer programming)

The demoscene still exists on many platforms, including the PC, C64, MSX, ZX Spectrum, Amstrad CPC, Amiga, Atari, Dreamcast and Game Boy Advance. The large variety of platforms makes their respective demos hard to com-

pare. Some 3D benchmark programs also have a demo or showcase mode, which derives its roots from the days of the 16-bit platforms.

There are several categories demos are informally classified into, the most important being the division between the "full-size" **demos** and the size-restricted **intros**, a difference visible in the competitions of nearly any demo party. The most typical competition categories for intros are the **64K intro** and the **4K intro**, where the size of the executable file is restricted to 65536 and 4096 bytes, respectively.

1.5.5   Influence

Although demos are still a more or less obscure form of art even in the traditionally active demoscene countries, the scene has had an impact on areas such as computer games industry and new media art.

A great deal of European game programmers, artists and musicians have come from the demoscene, often cultivating the learned techniques, practices and philosophies in their work. For example, the Finnish company Remedy Entertainment, known for the Max Payne series of games, was founded by the PC group Future Crew, and most of its employees are former or active Finnish demosceners.[10][11] Sometimes demos even provide direct influence even to game developers that have no demoscene affiliation: for instance, Will Wright names demoscene as a major influence on the Maxis game Spore, which is largely based on procedural content generation.[12] Similarly, at QuakeCon in 2011, John Carmack noted that he "thinks highly" of people who do 64k intros, as an example of artificial limitations encouraging creative programming.[13] Jerry Holkins from Penny Arcade claimed to have an "abiding love" for the demoscene, and noted that it is "stuff worth knowing".[14]

Certain forms of computer art have a strong affiliation with the demoscene. Tracker music, for example, originated in the Amiga games industry but was soon heavily dominated by demoscene musicians; producer Adam Fielding[15] claims to have tracker/demoscene roots. Currently, there is a major tracking scene separate from the actual demoscene. A form of static computer graphics where demosceners have traditionally excelled is pixel art; see *artscene* for more information on the related subculture.

Over the years, desktop computer hardware capabilities have improved by orders of magnitude, and so for most programmers, tight hardware restrictions are no longer a common issue. Nevertheless, demosceners continue to study and experiment with creating impressive effects on limited hardware. Since handheld consoles and cellular phones have comparable processing power or capabilities to the desktop platforms of old (such as low resolution screens which require pixel-art, or very limited storage and memory for music replay), many demosceners have been able to apply their niche skills to develop games for these platforms, and earn a living doing so. One particular example is Angry Birds, whose lead designer Jaakko Iisalo was an active and well-known demoscener in the 90s.[16]

Some attempts have been made to increase the familiarity of demos as an art form. For example, there have been demo shows, demo galleries and demoscene-related books, sometimes even TV programs introducing the subculture and its works.[17]

The museum IT-ceum in Linköping, Sweden, have an exhibition about the demo scene.[18]

Sometimes a demoscene-based production may become very famous in technical contexts. For example, the 96-kilobyte FPS game *.kkrieger* by Farbrausch uses procedural content generation algorithms that are quite common on today's 64K intros but largely unknown to the computer games enthusiasts and the US-based game development community.

Video games industry

4players.de reported that "numerous" demo and intro programmers, artists, and musicians were employed in the games industry by 2007. Video game companies with demoscene members on staff include Digital Illusions, Starbreeze, Ascaron,[19] 49Games, Remedy Entertainment, Techland, Lionhead Studios,[20] Bugbear Entertainment, Digital Reality, and Akella.[21]

1.5.6   See also

1.5.7   References

[1] Reunanen, Markku (15 April 2014). "How Those Crackers Became Us Demosceners". WiderScreen. Retrieved 13 October 2014.

[2] Markku Reunanen (2010). *Computer Demos—What Makes Them Tick?* (Lic.). Aalto University.

[3] "Slashdot's "Top 10 Hacks of All Time"". slashdot.org. 13 December 1999. Retrieved 25 December 2010. *Second Reality by Future Crew – Awesome, Mindblowing, Unbelievable, Impossible. Some of the words used to describe what this piece of code from demoscene gods Future Crew did on 1993-era PC hardware. Even by today's standards, what this program can do without relying on any kind of 3D graphics acceleration is impressive. As if the graphics weren't impressive enough, it can even playback in Dolby Surround Sound.*

[4] http://janeway.exotica.org.uk/author.php?id= 3596[Database search for just one of many groups producing intros for cracks early, and later producing demos.]

[5] Reunanen, Markku; Silvast, Antti (2009). *Demoscene Platforms: A Case Study on the Adoption of Home Computers*. History of Nordic Computing. pp. 289–301. doi:10.1007/978-3-642-03757-3_30.

[6] Turner-Rahman, Gregory (2013). "the demoscene". In Chris, Cynthia; Gerstner, David A. *Media Authorship*. Routledge.

[7] Hartmann, Doreen (2010). *Computer Demos and the Demoscene: Artistic Subcultural Innovation in Real-Time."* (PDF). 16th International Symposium of Electronic Art.

[8] Williams, Jeremy (2002). "Demographics: Behind the Scene". archive.org. Retrieved 17 February 2011.

[9] http://demoscene.us/parties/

[10] Bobic (18 January 2007). "Sceners in the Games Industry". 4players.de. Retrieved 17 February 2011.

[11] "Jaakko Lehtinen appointed as a Professor in the School of Science". 2012-09-28. The so-called demoscene has laid a foundation for the active and internationally astonishingly successful Finnish games industry.

[12] Dave 'Fargo' Kosak (2005-03-14). "Will Wright Presents Spore... and a New Way to Think About Games". *GameSpy*.

[13] "QuakeCon 2011 - John Carmack Keynote". *YouTube*. 2011-08-05.

[14] "Lickr". 2012-04-13.

[15] Artist Feature: Adam Fielding on YouTube

[16] http://www.edge-online.com/features/ meet-man-behind-angry-birds/

[17] scene.org – file browser

[18] "Linköping - Do & See - Datamuseet It-ceum". and visitors can also learn more about today's demo scene

[19] Bobic (January 18, 2007). "Spielkultur | Special | 4Sceners". *4players.de*. p. 1. Archived from the original on September 21, 2014. Retrieved September 21, 2014.

[20] Bobic (January 18, 2007). "Spielkultur | Special | 4Sceners". *4players.de*. p. 2. Archived from the original on September 21, 2014. Retrieved September 21, 2014.

[21] Bobic (January 18, 2007). "Spielkultur | Special | 4Sceners". *4players.de*. p. 3. Archived from the original on September 21, 2014. Retrieved September 21, 2014.

1.5.8 Further reading

- Polgár, Tamás ("Tomcat") (2005). *FREAX: Volume 1.* CSW-Verlag. ISBN 3-9810494-0-3.

- Vigh, David and Polgár, Tamás ("Tomcat"): *FREAX Art Album.* CSW-Verlag 2006

- Tasajärvi, Lassi (2004). *DEMOSCENE: the Art of Real-Time.* Evenlake Studios. ISBN 952-91-7022-X.

- Tasajärvi, Lassi (2009). *DEMOSCENE: the Art of Real-Time eBook (pdf).* Evenlake Studios. ISBN 978-952-92-6129-1.

- *DEMOing: Art or Craft? 1984–2002* (PDF), *Write-up* by Shirley Shor *about the demoscene*

- Green, Dave (July 1995). "Demo or Die!". Wired magazine. Retrieved 31 December 2007.

- Demoscene Research – bibliography of scientific publications about the demoscene.

- *The Demoscene* (PDF), *Flyer by* Digitale Kultur e. V. *about the demoscene*

- Vigh, David: *Pixelstorm* (PDF), – *selected artworks of demoscene graphicians 2003, bugfixed 2007*

- Demoscene & Paris art scene – Special issue of mustekala.info webzine focused on demoscene with several articles, some only on Finnish though.

- Reunanen, Markku (2010). *Computer Demos – What Makes Them Tick?* (PDF). Aalto University School of Science and Technology.

1.5.9 External links

- demoscene.info, *A webportal providing information on the demoscene*

- demozoo.org, *An extensive database of demos, demoscene music, graphics, demosceners and demoparties*

- slengpung.com, *Pictures from parties and demoscene related events*

- demoparty.net, *Database of past and future demoparties, location and travel info*

- bitfellas.org, *Demoscene community and information portal*

- , *What Is Demoscene?* an introductory movie by demoscene.tv.

- Pouet.net Database of demos, with download links

- SceneSat *Demoscene radio station with music from the demoscene and live shows from demoparties*

- CGM UKScene Radio, *Demoscene radio station featuring demoscene music created on; Amiga, Atari, C64, Spectrum and PC.*

1.6 Drum machine

For the early "drum machine" computers that used a rotating cylinder as their main memory, see drum memory.

A **drum machine** is an electronic musical instrument

A Yamaha RY30 Drum Machine

designed to imitate the sound of drums, cymbals or other percussion instruments. Drum machines are most commonly associated with electronic music genres such as house music, but are also used in many other genres. They are also used when session drummers are not available or if the production cannot afford the cost of a professional drummer.

In the 2010s, most modern drum machines are sequencers with a sample playback (rompler) or synthesizer component that specializes in the reproduction of drum timbres. Though features vary from model to model, many modern drum machines can also produce unique sounds, and allow the user to compose unique drum beats and patterns.

1.6.1 History

Early drum machines

Rhythmicon (1930–1932)

In 1930–32, the spectacularly innovative and hard to use *Rhythmicon* was realized by Leon Theremin at the request

Chamberlin Rhythmate (1957)

In 1957 Californian Harry Chamberlin constructed a tape loop-based drum machine called the *Chamberlin Rhythmate*. It had 14 tape loops with a sliding head that allowed playback of different tracks on each piece of tape, or a blending between them. It contained a volume and a pitch/speed control and also had a separate amplifier with bass, treble, and volume controls, and an input jack for a guitar, microphone or other instrument. The tape loops were of real acoustic jazz drum kits playing different style beats, with some additions to tracks such as bongos, clave, castanets, etc.

First commercial product – Wurlitzer Sideman (1959)

Rhythmicon (1932) and Joseph Schillinger, a music educator

Wurlitzer Sideman *(1959, inner view)*

of Henry Cowell, who wanted an instrument which could play compositions with multiple rhythmic patterns, based on the overtone series, were far too hard to perform on existing keyboard instruments. The invention could produce sixteen different rhythms, each associated with a particular pitch, either individually or in any combination, including en masse, if desired. Received with considerable interest when it was publicly introduced in 1932, the Rhythmicon was soon set aside by Cowell and was virtually forgotten for decades. The next generation of rhythm machines played only pre-programmed rhythms such as mambo, tango, or bossa nova.

In 1959 Wurlitzer released an electro-mechanical drum machine called the *Sideman*, which was the first-ever commercially produced drum machine. The Sideman was intended as a percussive accompaniment for the Wurlitzer organ range. The Sideman offered a choice of 12 electronically generated, predefined rhythm patterns with variable tempos. The sound source was a series of vacuum tubes which created 10 preset electronic drum sounds. The drum sounds were 'sequenced' by a rotating wiper arm with contact brushes on it that swept around a phenolic panel with corresponding contacts arranged in a pattern of concentric circles across its face; these were spaced in certain patterns to generate parts of a particular rhythm. Combinations of these different sets of rhythms and drum sounds created popular rhythmic patterns of the day, e.g. waltzes, fox trots etc. These combinations were selected by a rotary knob on the top of the Sideman box. The tempo of the patterns was controlled by a slider that increased the speed of rotation of the wiper arm. The Sideman had a panel of 10 buttons for manually triggering drum sounds, and a remote player to control the machine while playing from an organ keyboard. The Sideman was housed in a mahogany cabinet that contained the sound-generating circuitry, amplifier and speaker.[1]

Raymond Scott (1960–1963)

In 1960, Raymond Scott constructed the *Rhythm Synthesizer* and, in 1963, a drum machine called *Bandito the Bongo Artist*. Scott's machines were used for recording his album "Soothing Sounds for Baby" series (1964).

First fully transistorized drum machines – Seeburg/Gulbransen (1964)

Seeburg/Gulbransen *Rhythm Prince* using mechanical wheel, as seen on bailed out left panel

Seeburg/Gulbransen *Select-A-Rhythm*, an earliest fully transistorized rhythm machine

During the 1960s, implementation of rhythm machines were evolved into fully solid-state (transistorized) from early electro-mechanical with vacuum tubes, and also size were reduced to desktop size from earlier floor type. In the early 1960s, a home organ manufacturer, Gulbransen (later acquired by Fender) cooperated with an automatic musical equipment manufacturer Seeburg Corporation, and released early compact rhythm machines *Rhythm Prince* (PRP),[2] although, at that time, these size were still as large as small guitar amp head, due to the use of bulky electro-mechanical pattern generators. Then in 1964, Seeburg invented a compact electronic rhythm pattern generator using "diode matrix" (U.S. Patent 3,358,068 in 1967),[3] and

fully transistorized electronic rhythm machine with pre-programmed patterns, *Select-A-Rhythm* (SAR1),[4][5] was released. As the result of its robustness and enough compact size, these rhythm machines were gradually installed on the electronic organ as accompaniment of organists, and finally spread widely.

Keio-Giken (Korg), Nippon Columbia, and Ace Tone (1963–1967)

Korg Donca-Matic DA-20 *(1963)*

In the early-1960s, a nightclub owner in Tokyo, Tsutomu Katoh was consulted from Tadashi Osanai, a notable accordion player, about the rhythm machine he used for accompaniment in club, Wurlitzer Sideman. Osanai, a graduate of the Department of Mechanical Engineering at University of Tokyo, convinced Katoh to finance his efforts to build better one.[6] In 1963, their new company Keio-Giken (later Korg) released their first rhythm machine, Donca-Matic DA-20 using vacuum tube circuit for sound and mechanical-wheel for rhythm patterns. It was a floor-type machine with built-in speaker and keyboard featuring the manual play, in addition to the multiple automatic rhythm patterns, and the price was comparable with the average annual income of Japanese at that time.[7]

Then, their effort was focused on the improvement of reliability and performance, along with the size reduction and the cost down. Unstable vacuum tube circuit was replaced with reliable transistor circuit on Donca-Matic DC-11 in mid-1960s, and in 1966, bulky mechanical-wheel was also replaced with compact transistor circuit on Donca-Matic DE-20 and DE-11. In 1967, Mini Pops MP-2 was developed as an option of Yamaha Electone (electric organ), and Mini Pops was established as a series of the compact desktop rhythm machine. In the United States, Mini Pops MP-3, MP-7, etc. were sold under Univox brand by the distributor at that time, Unicord Corporation.[7]

In 1965, Nippon Columbia filed a patent for an automatic rhythm instrument. It described it as an "automatic rhythm player which is simple but capable of electronically producing various rhythms in the characteristic tones of a drum, a piccolo and so on." It has some similarities to Seeburg's slightly earlier 1964 patent.[8]

In 1967, Ace Tone founder Ikutaro Kakehashi (later founder of Roland Corporation) developed the preset rhythm-pattern generator using *diode matrix* circuit, which has some similarities to the earlier Seeburg and Nippon Columbia patents. Kakehashi's patent describes his device as a "plurality of inverting circuits and/or clipper circuits" which "are connected to a counting circuit to synthesize the output signal of the counting circuit" where the "synthesized output signal becomes a desired rhythm."[9]

Ace Tone commercialized its preset rhythm machine, called the FR-1 Rhythm Ace, in 1967. It offered 16 preset patterns, and four buttons to manually play each instrument sound (cymbal, claves, cowbell and bass drum). The rhythm patterns could also be cascaded together by pushing multiple rhythm buttons simultaneously, and the possible combination of rhythm patterns were more than a hundred (on the later models of Rhythm Ace, the individual volumes of each instrument could be adjusted with the small knobs or faders). The FR-1 was adopted by the Hammond Organ Company for incorporation within their latest organ models. In the US, the units were also marketed under the Multivox brand by Peter Sorkin Music Company, and in the UK, marketed under the Bentley Rhythm Ace brand.[10]

Early preset drum machine users

A number of other preset drum machines were released in the 1970s, but early examples of the use can be found on The United States of America's eponymous album from 1967–8. The first major pop song to use a drum machine was "Saved by the Bell" by Robin Gibb, which reached #2 in Britain in 1969. Drum machine tracks were also heavily used on the Sly & the Family Stone album *There's a Riot Goin' On*, released in 1971. The German krautrock band Can also used a drum machine on their song "Peking O".

The 1972 Timmy Thomas single "Why Can't We Live Together"/"Funky Me" featured a distinctive use of a drum machine and keyboard arrangement on both tracks. Another early example of electronic drums used by a rock group, is Obscured by Clouds by Pink Floyd, from early in 1972. The first album on which a drum machine produced all the percussion was Kingdom Come's *Journey*, recorded in November 1972 using a Bentley Rhythm Ace. French singer-songwriter Léo Ferré mixed a drum machine with a symphonic orchestra in the song "Je t'aimais bien, tu sais..." in his album *L'Espoir*, released in 1974. Osamu Kitajima's progressive psychedelic rock album *Benzaiten* (1974) also utilized drum machines, and one of the album's contributors, Haruomi Hosono,[11] would later start the electronic music band Yellow Magic Orchestra (as "Yellow Magic Band") in 1977.[12]

Drum sound synthesis

A key difference between such early machines and more modern equipment is that they use sound synthesis rather than digital sampling in order to generate their sounds. For example, a snare drum or maraca sound would typically be created using a burst of white noise whereas a bass drum sound would be made using sine waves or other basic waveforms. This meant that while the resulting sound was not very close to that of the real instrument, each model tended to have a unique character. For this reason, many of these early machines have achieved a certain "cult status" and are now sought after by producers for use in production of modern electronic music, most notably the Roland TR-808.[13]

Programmable drum machines

Eko ComputeRhythm (1972),
One of the first programmable drum machines

In 1972, Eko released the ComputeRhythm (1972), which was the first programmable drum machine. It had a 6-row push-button matrix that allowed the user to enter a pattern manually. The user could also push punch cards with pre-programmed rhythms through a reader slot on the unit.[14] Another stand-alone drum machine, the PAiA Programmable Drum Set released in 1975, was also one of the first programmable drum machines,[15] and was sold as a kit with parts and instructions which the buyer would use to build the machine.

Also in 1975, Ace Tone released its successor to the Rhythm Ace series, the Rhythm Producer FR-15, which provided the feature to modify the pre-programmed rhythms.[16] In 1978, the Roland CR-78 drum machine was released.[17] It was a programmable rhythm machine, and had four memory locations which allowed users to store their own patterns. The following year, Roland offered a simpler version, the Boss DR-55. It had only four sounds.

Digital sampling

Linn LM-1 (1980)

The Linn LM-1 Drum Computer (released in 1980 at $4,995) was the first drum machine to use digital samples. Only about 500 were ever made, but its effect on the music industry was extensive. Its distinctive sound almost defines 1980s pop, and it can be heard on hundreds of hit records from the era, including The Human League's *Dare*, Gary Numan's *Dance*, Devo's "New Traditionalists", and Ric Ocasek's *Beatitude*. Prince bought one of the very first LM-1s and used it on nearly all of his most popular recordings, including *1999* and *Purple Rain*.

Many of the drum sounds on the LM-1 were composed of two chips that were triggered at the same time, and each voice was individually tunable with individual outputs. Due to memory limitations, a crash cymbal sound was not available except as an expensive third-party modification. A cheaper version of the LM-1 was released in 1982 called the LinnDrum. Priced at $2,995, not all of its voices were tunable, but crash cymbal was included as a standard sound.

Like its predecessor the LM-1, it featured swappable sound chips. The LinnDrum can be heard on records such as The Cars' *Heartbeat City* and Giorgio Moroder's soundtrack for the film *Scarface*.

It was feared the LM-1 would put every session drummer in Los Angeles out of work and it caused many of L.A's top session drummers (Jeff Porcaro is one example) to purchase their own drum machines and learn to program them themselves in order to stay employed. Linn even marketed the LinnDrum specifically to drummers.[18]

Oberheim DMX (1981)

SCI Drumtraks (1984)

Following the success of the LM-1, Oberheim introduced the DMX, which also featured digitally sampled sounds and a "swing" feature similar to the one found on the Linn machines. It became very popular in its own right, becoming a staple of the nascent hip-hop scene.

Other manufacturers soon began to produce machines, e.g. the Sequential Circuits Drum-Traks and Tom, the E-mu Drumulator and the Yamaha RX11.

In the 1986, SpecDrum by Cheetah Marketing, an inexpensive 8-bit sampling drum external module for ZX Spectrum,[19] was introduced. And its price was less than £30 when similar models cost around £250.[20]

Roland TR-808 and TR-909 machines

See also: Roland TR-808 and Roland TR-909

The famous Roland TR-808, a programmable drum machine, was also launched in 1980. At the time it was received with little fanfare, as it did not have digitally sampled sounds; drum machines using digital samples were much more popular. In time, though, the TR-808, along with its successor, the TR-909 (released in 1983), would become a fixture of the burgeoning underground dance, electro, house, techno, R&B and hip-hop genres, mainly because of its low cost (relative to that of the Linn machines) and the unique character of its analogue-generated sounds,

Roland TR-808 Rhythm Composer (1980)

which included five unique percussion sounds: "the hum kick, the ticky snare, the tishy hi-hats (open and closed) and the spacey cowbell." It was first utilized by Yellow Magic Orchestra in the year of its release, after which it would gain further popularity with Marvin Gaye's "Sexual Healing" and Afrikaa Bambaataa's "Planet Rock" in 1982.[13]

In a somewhat ironic twist it is the analogue-based Roland machines that have endured over time as the Linn sound became somewhat overused and dated by the end of the decade. The TR-808 and TR-909's beats have since been widely featured in pop music, and can be heard on countless recordings up to the present day.[13] Because of its bass and long decay, the kick drum from the TR-808 has also featured as a bass line in various genres such as hip hop and drum and bass. Since the mid-1980s, the TR-808 and TR-909 have been used on more hit records than any other drum machine,[21] and has thus attained an iconic status within the music industry.[13]

MIDI breakthrough

E-mu SP-1200

Because these early drum machines came out before the introduction of MIDI in 1983, they use a variety of methods of having their rhythms synchronized to other electronic devices. Some used a method of synchronization called DIN-sync, or Sync-24. Some of these machines also output analog CV/Gate voltages that could be used to synchronize or control analog synthesizers and other music equipment. The Oberheim DMX came with a feature allowing it to be synchronized to its proprietary Oberheim Parallel Buss interfacing system, developed prior to the introduction of MIDI.

Alesis SR-16 (1991)

By the year 2000, standalone drum machines became much less common, being partly supplanted by general-purpose hardware samplers controlled by sequencers (built-in or external), software-based sequencing and sampling and the use of loops, and music workstations with integrated sequencing and drum sounds. TR-808 and other digitized drum machine sounds can be found in archives on the Internet. However, traditional drum machines are still being made by companies such as Roland Corporation (under the name Boss), Zoom, Korg and Alesis, whose SR-16 drum machine has remained popular since it was introduced in 1991.

There are percussion-specific sound modules that can be triggered by pickups, trigger pads, or through MIDI. These are called drum modules; the Alesis D4 and Roland TD-8 are popular examples. Unless such a sound module also features a sequencer, it is, strictly speaking, not a drum machine.

1.6.2 Programming

See also: Music sequencer

Programming of drum machines are varied by the products. On most products, it can be done in **real time**: the user

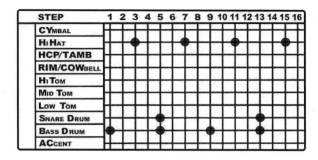

4-on-the-floor on Roland TR-707

creates drum patterns by pressing the trigger pads as though a drum kit were being played; or using **step-sequencing**: the pattern is built up over time by adding individual sounds at certain points by placing them, as with the TR-808 and TR-909, along a 16-step bar. For example, a generic 4-on-the-floor dance pattern could be made by placing a closed high hat on the 3rd, 7th, 11th, and 15th steps, then a kick drum on the 1st, 5th, 9th, and 13th steps, and a clap or snare on the 5th and 13th. This pattern could be varied in a multitude of ways to obtain fills, break-downs and other elements that the programmer sees fit, which in turn could be sequenced with **song-sequence** — essentially the drum machine plays back the programmed patterns from memory in an order the programmer has chosen. The machine will quantize entries that are slightly off-beat in order to make them exactly in time.

If the drum machine has MIDI connectivity, then one could program the drum machine with a computer or another MIDI device.

1.6.3   Comparison with live drumming

While recordings in the 2010s are increasingly using drum machines, "...scientific studies show there are certain aspects of human-created rhythm that machines cannot replicate, or can only replicate poorly" such as the "feel" of human drumming and the ability of a human drummer to respond to changes in a song as it is being played live onstage.[22] Human drummers also have the ability to make slight variations in their playing, such as playing "ahead of the beat" or "behind the beat" for sections of a song, in contrast to a drum machine which plays a pre-programmed rhythm. As well, human drummers play a "...tremendously wide variety of rhythmic variations" that drum machines cannot reproduce.[22]

1.6.4   Labor costs

Drum machines developed out of a need to create drum beats when a drum kit was not available. Increasingly, drum machines and drum programming are used by major record labels to undercut the costly expense of studio drummers.[23]

1.6.5   See also

- Electronic drum
- Music sequencer

1.6.6   References

[1] US patent 3207835, Howard E. Holman and Joseph H. Hearne (Wurlitzer Company), "Rhythm Device", issued 1965-09-21

[2] "Vintage Seeburg Rhythm Prince Drum Machine". MatrixSynth. February 02, 211. Check date values in: |date= (help)

[3] US patent 3358068, Richard H. Campbell, Jr., Gilford, N.H. (Seeburg Corporation), "Musical Instruments", issued 1967-12-12
— When this patent was filed in 1964-06-26, also Automatic Rhythm Device, Automatic Repetitive Rhythm Instrument Timing Circuitry, and its sound circuits Snare Drum Instrument and Cow Bell Instrument were filed at the same time.

[4] *Seeburg Portable Select-A-Rhythm Service Manual* (PDF). Seeburg Sales Corporation. Archived from the original (PDF) on 2012-04-25. — rhythm patterns were fully electronically generated by 48-step binary counter using 6-stage flip-flops

[5] "Seeburg Select-a-Rhythm Vintage Drum Machine". MatrixSynth. May 3, 2011.

[6] Colbeck, Julian (1996). *Keyfax Omnibus Edition*. MixBooks. p. 52. ISBN 978-0-918371-08-9.

[7] "Donca-Matic (1963)". *Korg Museum*. Korg.

[8] http://www.google.ms/patents/US3482027

[9] US patent 3651241, Ikutaro Kakehashi (Ace Electronics Industries, Inc.), "Automatic Rhythm Performance Device", issued 1972-03-21

[10] Reid, Gordon (2004), "The History Of Roland Part 1: 1930–1978", Sound on Sound *(November), retrieved 19 June 2011*

[11] *Osamu Kitajima – Benzaiten* at Discogs

[12] *Harry Hosono And The Yellow Magic Band – Paraiso* at Discogs

[13] Jason Anderson (November 28, 2008). "Slaves to the rhythm: Kanye West is the latest to pay tribute to a classic drum machine". CBC News. Retrieved 2011-05-29.

[14] "The EKO ComputeRhythm – Jean Michel Jarre's Drum Machine". synthtopia.com.

[15] "Programmable Drum Set". Synthmuseum.com. Retrieved 2007-06-16.

[16] "Ace Tone Rhythm Producer FR-15". *ESTECHO.com.* — Sakata Shokai/Ace Tone Rhythm Producer, a successor of Rhythm Ace after the reconstruction of Ace Tone brand in 1972, provided feature to modify the pre-programmed rhythms.

[17] The History of Roland

[18] "Why Drummers Prefer LinnDrum to Other Drum Machines". Modern Drummer Magazine. 1984.

[19] Ryan Block (2005-10-28). "Music Thing: The ZX Spectrum SpecDrum module". *engadget.com.*

[20] P Henning; A Pateman. "Specdrum". *Crash Magazine.*

[21] Peter Wells (2004), *A Beginner's Guide to Digital Video*, AVA Books, p. 18, ISBN 2-88479-037-3, retrieved 2011-05-20

[22] Barnes, Tom (23 March 2015). "Science shows why drum machines will never replace live drummers". *http://mic.com". Music.mic. Retrieved 20 September 2015.*

[23] D Arditi. "Digital Downsizing: The Effects of Digital Music Production on Labor". *Journal of Popular Music Studies.*

1.6.7   External links

- WikiRecording's How to Make Real Drums Sound like an 80s Drum Machine

- http://drum-machines-history.blogspot.co.uk/

1.7   Electro house

Electro house is a hard form of house music.[1] Electro house is characterized by a prominent bassline and/or kick drum and a tempo between 125 and 135 beats per minute.[2][3] Its origins were influenced by electro,[4] electroclash,[5] pop,[6] synthpop,[5][7] and tech house.[5][6][7] The term has been used to describe the music of many *DJ Mag* Top 100 DJs, including Dimitri Vegas & Like Mike, Hardwell, Skrillex,[8][9] and Steve Aoki.[10]

(From left to right) Porter Robinson, Zedd, and Skrillex perform at the 2012 South by Southwest music festival.

1.7.1   Characteristics

Electro-house is typified by its heavy bass.[3] This is often in the form of buzzing basslines,[3] such as those created with sawtooth waves and distortion.[11] It is also often in the form of large bass drum sounds[3] in a four-to-the-floor pattern.[11] The tempo of electro house is usually around 130 beats per minute.[2] Electro house sometimes resembles tech house,[4] but it can contain melodic elements[2] and electro-influenced samples and synths.[4]

1.7.2   History

The genre has been described as a fusion genre of house and electro,[12] either in its original form or as fused with synthpop and techno in its late-1990s revival, electroclash.[5] It has also been seen as a term created from using "electro" as an adjective (meaning "futuristic" or "hard") for "house".[1]

Early songs that have been labelled retroactively as electro-house include "Dark Invader" by Arrivers in 1996 and "Raw S*it" by Basement Jaxx in 1997.[13] Mr. Oizo's 1999 hit "Flat Beat" has also been considered an early example of the genre.[14]

Benny Benassi, with his track "Satisfaction" released in 2002, is seen as the forerunner of electro-house who brought it to the mainstream.[5][6] By the mid 2000s, electro-house saw an increase in popularity.[2][15] In November 2006, electro-house tracks "Put Your Hands Up For Detroit" by Fedde Le Grand and "Yeah Yeah" by Bodyrox and Luciana held the number one and number two spots, respectively, in the UK Top 40 singles charts.[16] Since then, electro-house producers such as Feed Me, Knife Party, The M Machine, Porter Robinson, Skrillex,[9] and Yasutaka Nakata[17] have emerged.

1.7.3 Subgenres

Big room

In the early 2010s, a type of electro-house known as "big room" began to develop, particularly gaining popularity through electronic dance music-oriented events and festivals such as Tomorrowland. Big room songs resemble Dutch house, often incorporating drops, minimalist percussion, regular beats, sub-bass layered kicks, simple melodies, and synth-driven breakdowns.[18][19] The layout of a big room track is very similar to the layout of a typical electro-house song. Big room is thought of as a subgenre of electro-house.

Big room has become controversial in the EDM scene, being criticized by some producers for becoming a stereotypical "EDM" sound lacking originality and creativity, and that the whole genre sounds homogenous. Mixmag described big room tracks as consisting of "titanic breakdowns and spotless, monotone production aesthetics (read: lowest common denominator 'beats')." In a Reddit AMA, Wolfgang Gartner described big room as a "joke", and considered it, along with conglomerates such as SFX Entertainment, the oversaturation of events in North America, and "major label A&R's shoving digestible cheap dance music down teenager's throats [*sic*]" as the biggest problems affecting the EDM industry. Notable producers such as Axwell and Steve Angello of now-defunct Swedish House Mafia (who had been credited with their influence to progressive house) have emphasized the need for more creative and experimental EDM tracks overall.[19][20]

In mid-2013, Swedish duo Daleri posted a mix on SoundCloud entitled "Epic mashleg", consisting purely of drops from 15 "big room" songs on Beatport's charts at the time (including artists such as Dimitri Vegas & Like Mike, Hardwell, and W&W) played in succession. The intent of the mashup was to serve as a commentary on the "big room" movement and the lack of differentiation between tracks; member Eric Kvarnström commented that "the scary thing is that there are new tracks like this every day. Every day, new tracks, all the same. It just keeps coming all the time." The duo defended their use of big room characteristics in their own music (particularly their releases on the Armada Music imprint Trice, which releases many big room tracks), by emphasizing their complextro influences.[18] In the midst of a feud between Deadmau5 and Afrojack over social media regarding originality in dance music culminating with Afrojack creating a style parody of Deadmau5's music entitled "something_", Deadmau5 posted a song on SoundCloud, "DROP DA BOMB", satirizing the style of "commercial" house music and big room.[21][22]

Complextro

Complextro is typified by glitchy, intricate basslines and textures created by sharply cutting between instruments in quick succession.[23][24] The term, a portmanteau of the words "complex" and "electro",[23][24][25] was coined by Porter Robinson to describe the sound of the music he was making in 2010.[25][26] He has cited video game sounds, or chiptunes, as an influence on his style of music along with 1980s analog synth music.[27] Other producers of the genre include Adventure Club, Kill The Noise, Knife Party, Lazy Rich,[28] The M Machine, Madeon, Skrillex,[23] Wolfgang Gartner, and Zedd.

Dutch house

Dutch house, sometimes referred to as 'Dirty Dutch', is a style of electro-house that originated in the Netherlands and found prominence by 2009,[29] mainly pioneered by Vato Gonzalez and DJ Chuckie. It is primarily defined by complex rhythms made from Latin-influenced drum kits, a lower emphasis on basslines, and squeaky, high-pitched lead synths. Influences on the subgenre include Detroit techno, hip hop and other urban styles of music.[30] Related artists include Afrojack, Chuckie, Fedde Le Grand, R3hab, Sidney Samson, Switch, Hardwell, W&W, and Blasterjaxx.

Fidget house

Fidget house, or fidget, is "defined by snatched vocal snippets, pitch-bent dirty basslines and rave-style synth stabs over glitchy 4/4 beats."[31] It contains influences from Chicago house, Baltimore club, Kuduro, bassline, bouncy techno, rave, dubstep, hip hop and world music.[31] Purveyors of the genre include The Bloody Beetroots, Crookers, Danger, Naeleck, Hervé, Sinden, and Switch. The term fidget house was coined by DJs/producers Jesse Rose and Switch, "as a joke, which has now gone a little too far."[31][32]

Moombahton

Main article: Moombahton

Moombahton is a mixture of Dutch house and reggaeton.[33] Its identifying characteristics include "a thick, spread-out bass line; some dramatic builds; and a two-step pulse, with quick drum fills",[34] but it has "no real rules beyond working within a 108 bpm range."[35] A portmanteau of "moombah" and "reggaeton", moombahton was created by DJ Dave Nada when he slowed down the tempo of the Afrojack remix of the Silvio Ecomo &

Chuckie song "Moombah" to please party-goers with tastes in reggaeton.[34] Other producers of the genre include Dillon Francis, Diplo, and Munchi.[35]

Moombahcore is a style of moombahton with elements of breakcore, dubstep, gabber, and techstep.[36][37] Characteristics of the genre include chopped vocals, dubstep-influenced bass sounds, and extensive build-ups.[37] Artists who have produced moombahcore include Delta Heavy, Dillon Francis, Feed Me, Knife Party, and Noisia.

1.7.4   See also

- List of electro house artists

- List of electronic music genres

1.7.5   Notes

[1] Lopez, Korina (13 December 2011). "Electronic dance music glossary". USA Today. Retrieved 17 May 2012. Electro: 'It's meant so many things in the last 30 years. Originally, it meant futuristic electronic music and was used to describe Kraftwerk and Afrika Bambaataa. Now, it means hard electronic dance music.' Electro can be used as an adjective, such as electro-house and electro-pop.

[2] "Electro House". *Beat Explorers' Dance Music Guide*. Electro House rose to prominence in the early to mid 00's as a heavier alternative to other house subgenres that were prevalent at the time. [...] Electro House usually sits somewhere between 125-135bpm and tracks are arranged in a way that gives a large focus on the climax or drop. This usually contains a heavy bassline, and frequently includes melodic elements to help establish cohesion within the track.

[3] "Electro House". *DI Radio*. Digitally Imported. Buzzing basslines, huge kicks, party rocking drops. House music packed full of gigantic bass and massive synths.

[4] "Music Definitions - House music : styles". *DJ Cyclopedia*. 3345. Electro house : Sometimes resembles tech house, but often influenced by the 'electro' sound of the early 1980's, aka breakdancing music, via samples or just synthesizer usage.

[5] "Electro House". Tumblr. Retrieved 12 June 2012. It was in the early 2000s when a big movement of electroclash being mixed with synthpop. Meanwhile, tech house was also becoming more known and gaining some serious buzz. When the two were combined that is when Electro House came to be the way it is now. ... 'Satisfaction' was one of those songs that people would have stuck in their head for days. This song still continues to receive a lot of attention even now. It won world wide rewards as well as make Benny Benassi the father of Electro House.

[6] music2electro. "Electro House of Style Music". HubPages. Many people want to find out exactly where did this style of music emerge from. There isn't any factual evidence to prove anything. As with most music history, it isn't certain. ... It is noted that about ten years ago there was a large revolutionary time in electro music being mixed with pop. At the same time tech house was gaining popularity. When the two were mixed that is when Electro House came to be the way it is now.

[7] Electro Man. "Quick Introduction to Electro House Genre". *Electronic Music Blog!*. Blogger. Retrieved 12 June 2012. It was in the early 2000s when a big movement of electroclash being mixed with synthpop. At the same time tech house was gaining popularity. With the right events happening at the right times, the two came together [to form electro house].

[8] Edwards, Owen. "Skrillex". *DJ Mag*.

[9] Lester, Paul (1 September 2011). "Skrillex (No 1,096)". *New band of the day* (London: The Guardian). Retrieved 25 August 2012. ... Skrillex, a 23-year-old electro-house/dubstep producer ...

[10] Roullier, Ian. "Steve Aoki". *DJ Mag*. Steve Aoki's stock has risen once again over the past 12 months as he continues to perform the biggest, most audacious EDM sets across the globe and pump out his stomping, strutting electro house productions.

[11] Suhonen, Petri (2011-10-11). "How To Create Electro House Style Bass". *How to Make Electronic Music*. Retrieved 2012-08-17.

[12] "Electro House" (in Russian). oXidant. Retrieved 5 June 2012. Electro House - это смесь двух стилей Electro и House.

[13] "Electro House". Beatport. Retrieved 15 December 2012.

[14] "Flat Beat". Beatport. Retrieved 10 June 2012.

[15] Peterson, Angus. "Eric Prydz - Eric Prydz presents Pryda". inthemix. Retrieved 5 June 2012. But even more defining was the '80s aesthetic, one of the key inspirations behind the explosion of electro house in 2005.

[16] "UK Top 40 Hit Database". everyHit.com. Retrieved 25 August 2012.

[17] "Perfume Interview" (in Japanese). bounce.com. 2008-02-07. Archived from the original on 2008-12-09. Retrieved 2009-06-02. (English translation)

[18] "Swedish DJs Daleri Mock EDM Cliche With Hilarious Viral Mini-Mix 'Epic Mashleg'". *Spin*. Retrieved 20 January 2014.

[19] "EDM Will Eat Itself: Big Room stars are getting bored". *Mixmag*. Retrieved 20 January 2014.

[20] "Wolfgang Gartner's Reddit AMA RECAP, States His Distaste For The Big Room Movement & Claims There Is An "Over saturation" of Festivals". *YourEDM*. YourEDM, LLC. Retrieved 20 January 2014.

[21] "Deadmau5 has a dig at commercial house with "DROP DA BOMB" mix". *Mixmag*. Retrieved 20 January 2014.

[22] "Afrojack and Deadmau5 argue over what's "good music"". *Mixmag*. Retrieved 20 January 2014.

[23] Barboza, Trenton. "What is Complextro? An Emerging Genre Explained". *Voices*. Yahoo!. Retrieved 25 June 2012. The genre's name is a combination of the words 'Complex' and 'Electro' creating 'Complextro.' Producing this form of music is incredibly intricate and often requires a large amount of instruments that are layered close to each other within a piece of music sequencing software. This often results in a glitch, giving the genre its unique feel. ... Complextro is slowly gaining worldwide popularity due to high profile electronic producers such as Skrillex, Porter Robinson, and Crookers.

[24] Nutting, P.J. (April 21, 2011). "Electronic Music... through 18-year-old eyes". Boulder Weekly. Retrieved 25 June 2012. It is said to have elements of dubstep and fidget house.Like conducting for a punchy electro orchestra, each 'instrument' gets a moment of focus before leaping to another, uniting them all in a compelling way. YouTube generation musicologists have dubbed this sound 'complextro' (a mash-up of 'complex' and 'electro') ...

[25] "Tweet by Porter Robinson". when i made [the word 'complextro'], i wanted a portmanteu to describe my sound. complex+electro=complextro. it has since became the name of the style:)

[26] "Porter Robinson: Skrillex's Best Advice - Lollapalooza 2012 - YouTube". YouTube. 2012-08-06. Retrieved 2012-12-05.

[27] Hurt, Edd (June 28, 2012). "Electro wunderkind and self-described 'complextro' Porter Robinson recognizes no technological constraints". *Nashville Scene*. Retrieved 28 July 2012.

[28] "Salacious Sound Exclusive Interview: Porter Robinson". *Salacious Sound*. Feb 4, 2011. Retrieved 8 October 2013. He really is one of the founding fathers of this "complextro" thing that we're bearing witness to now.

[29] "Dutch House Music". Retrieved 2012-08-19.

[30] Dirty Dutch (17 Jul 2012). "Dirty Dutch moves from RAI to Ziggo Dome". Retrieved 2012-08-03. Known for their fusion of musical genres such as house, hip-hop, electro, urban and techno showcasing both Dutch and internationally acclaimed artists alike, the Dirty Dutch events have escalated to accommodate the huge demand, consistently selling out to tens of thousands of partygoers.

[31] McDonnell, John (September 8, 2008). "Welcome to the fidget house". *Music Blog* (London: The Guardian). Retrieved 26 June 2012. ... fidget house - a joke term made up a few years ago by Switch and Jesse Rose. ... Fidget producers like to think of themselves as global music connoisseurs, hand-picking bits from genres such as Chicago house, rave, UK garage, US hip-hop, Baltimore club, Kuduro and other 'authentic' world music genres.

[32] "Jesse Rose Interview". DJMag.com. Retrieved 26 June 2012. We came up with 'fidget house' as a joke, which has now gone a little too far.

[33] Yenigun, Sami (18 March 2011). "Moombahton: Born In D.C., Bred Worldwide". *The Record*. NPR Music. Retrieved 25 August 2012. ... Moombahton is a cross between Dutch house music and reggaeton.

[34] Fischer, Jonathan L. (December 24, 2010). "Our Year in Moombahton: How a local DJ created a genre, and why D.C.'s ascendant dance scene couldn't contain it". Washington City Paper. Retrieved November 17, 2011. The sound has a few basic identifying characteristics: A thick, spread-out bass line; some dramatic builds; and a two-step pulse, with quick drum fills.

[35] Patel, Puja. "Hot New Sound: Moombahton Goes Boom!". *Spin*. Retrieved 16 February 2012. Nada says Moombahton has 'no real rules beyond working within a 108 bpm range.' ... Munchi, a 21-year-old Dutchman who released heavily club-influenced Moombahton tracks ...

[36] "MTV Artist To Watch: Dillon Francis". *Mr.M*. Mr.M. Retrieved 5 January 2014. Yep, Dillon remixes ultra-DJs, generates unique function, helped found two little movements called "moombahton" (a fusion of house and reggaeton) and "moombahcore" (a variation of moombahton only infusing other weird phrases like gabber, breakcore, techstep, and dubstep), and he was our unique correspondent at last spring's Hangout Fest!

[37] "Moombahcore". *Freaky Loops*. Loopmasters. Retrieved 25 August 2012. The sound proved irresistible on the dance floor – slow and sexy like reggaeton, but hard-edged like electro house even dubstep at the same time. ... Characteristics of the Moombahcore; chopped vocals, monster dubstep basses, extended and enhanced build-ups and the introduction of fat kicks and percussion elements.

1.8 Electroclash

Not to be confused with Electropunk or Electronicore.

Electroclash, also known as **retro electro**, **tech pop**, **nouveau disco**, the **new new wave**, and **Neo-Electro**,[3][6] is a genre of music that fuses 1980s electro, new wave and synthpop with 1990s techno, retro-style electropop and electronic dance music.[4][7][8] It emerged in New York and Detroit in the later 1990s, pioneered by acts including Collider, I-F and those associated with Gerald Donald, and is associated with acts including Peaches, Adult,[9] Legowelt,[9] and Fischerspooner.[9]

1.8.1 Terminology and characteristics

The term electroclash was coined by New York DJ and promoter Larry Tee[7][8] to describe music that combined synthpop, techno, punk and performance art. The genre was in reaction to the rigid formulations of techno music, putting an emphasis on song writing, showmanship and a sense of humour,[4] described by *The Guardian* as one of "the two most significant upheavals in recent dance music history".[10] The visual aesthetic of electroclash has been associated with the 1982 cult film *Liquid Sky*.[11]

1.8.2 History

Electroclash emerged in New York at the end of the 1990s. It was pioneered by I-F with his 1997 track "Space Invaders Are Smoking Grass"[4][12] (which, "introducing old-fashioned verse-chorus dynamics to burbling electro in a vocodered homage to Atari-era hi-jinks," is the "record widely credited with catalysing" the electroclash movement),[4] as well as Collider with their 1998 album *Blowing Shit Up* (though Collider called its own style "electropunk" as the genre had not yet been named).[13] The style was pursued by artists including Felix da Housecat,[14] Peaches and Chicks on Speed.[15] During the early years, Ladytron were sometimes labeled as electroclash, but they rejected this tag.[16] Goldfrapp's albums *Black Cherry* (2003) and *Supernature* (2005) incorporated electroclash influences.[17][18]

It came to media attention in 2001, when the Electroclash Festival was held in New York.[19] The Electroclash Festival was held again in 2002 with subsequent live tours across the US and Europe in 2003 and then 2004. Other notable artists who performed at the festivals and subsequent tours include: Scissor Sisters, ADULT., Fischerspooner, Erol Alkan, Princess Superstar, Mignon, Miss Kittin & The Hacker, Mount Sims, Tiga and Spalding Rockwell. The style spread to scenes in London and Berlin, but rapidly faded as a recognisable genre as acts began to experiment with a variety of forms of music.[20][21]

1.8.3 Popularity chart

Successful records from the electroclash movement include:

1.8.4 References

[1] David Madden (2012). "Crossdressing to Backbeats: The Status of the Electroclash Producer and the Politics of Electronic Music". Retrieved January 3, 2015. Electroclash combines the extended pulsing sections of techno, house and other dance musics with the trashier energy of rock and new wave.

[2] Ishkur (2005). "Ishkur's guide to Electronic Music". Retrieved January 3, 2015.

[3] Carpenter, Susan (August 6, 2002). "Electro-clash builds on '80s techno beat". The Spectator. Retrieved 25 July 2012.

[4] D. Lynskey (22 March 2002). "Out with the old, in with the older". *Guardian.co.uk*. Archived from the original on 16 February 2011

[5] Reynolds, Simon (2013). *Energy Flash: A Journey Through Rave Music and Dance Culture*. Soft Skull Press. Go to Berliniamsburg, the Brooklyn club at the epicentre of New York's eighties-inspired 'electroclash' scene, and you feel a peculiar sensation: it's not exactly like time travel, more like you've stepped into a parallel universe, an alternative history scenario where rave never happened.

[6] "Neo-Electro | Significant Albums, Artists and Songs | AllMusic". *AllMusic*. Retrieved 2015-06-12.

[7] "The Electroclash Mix by Larry Tee". *Entertainment Weekly*. Retrieved 18 April 2015.

[8] Larry Tee Biography on Yahoo! Music

[9] Ishkur (2005). "Ishkur's guide to Electronic Music". Retrieved January 3, 2015.

[10] "The female techno takeover", *The Guardian*, May 24, 2008

[11] "The Great Electroclash Swindle". Retrieved August 10, 2008.

[12] "I-f – Space Invaders Are Smoking Grass". Discogs. Retrieved 25 July 2012.

[13] Potter, Josh (3 November 2011). "Walking Mix Tape". *Metroland*. Retrieved 21 April 2012.

[14] M. Goldstein (22 March 2002). "This cat is housebroken". *Boston Globe*. Archived from the original on 16 February 2011.

[15] J. Walker (5 October 2002). "Popmatters concert review: ELECTROCLASH 2002 Artists: Peaches, Chicks on Speed, W.I.T., and Tracy and the Plastics". *Boston Globe*. Archived from the original on 16 February 2011.

[16] "3/29 - Ladytron - 'Best Of: 00 - 10'". *nettskinny.com*. Retrieved 18 April 2015.

[17] Phares, Heather. "Black Cherry – Goldfrapp". AllMusic. Rovi Corporation. Retrieved 11 October 2011.

[18] Oculicz, Edward (23 August 2005). "Goldfrapp – Supernature". *Stylus Magazine*. Retrieved 11 October 2011.

[19] Quinnon, Michael: "Electroclash". World Wide Words, 2002

[20] Harris, John (2009). *Hail! Hail! Rock'n'Roll: The Ultimate Guide to the Music, the Myths and the Madness*. Sphere. p. 78. ISBN 978-1-84744-293-2.

[21] "So-cool U.K. quartet Ladytron brings electro-pop to Gothic.

[22] Search song on EveryHit.com database

1.8.5 External links

- Profile of Electroclash movement in FACT Magazine

1.8.6 See also

- List of electroclash bands and artists

1.9 Electronic dance music

Electronic dance music (also known as **EDM, electronic dance, dance music**,[1] **club music**, or simply **dance**) is a broad range of percussive electronic music genres produced largely for nightclubs, raves, and festivals. Produced for playback by disc jockeys (DJs), EDM is generally used in the context of a live mix, where a DJ creates a seamless selection of tracks by segueing from one recording to the next.[2]

The term "electronic dance music" and the initialism "EDM" was adopted by the U.S. music industry and music press as a buzzword to describe the increasingly commercial American electronic music scene that developed in the early 2010s. In this context, EDM does not refer to a specific genre, but serves as an umbrella term for several commercially-popular genres, including techno, house, trance, hardstyle, drum and bass, dubstep, trap, Jersey club and their respective subgenres.[3][4][5][6]

1.9.1 History

See also: Electronic music, Euro Disco, Italo disco, Hi-NRG and Electronic body music

Notable early examples include the 1977 songs "I Feel Love" (by Donna Summer and Giorgio Moroder)[7] and "Was Dog a Doughnut" (by Cat Stevens), the work of Kraftwerk and Yellow Magic Orchestra during the late 1970s to early 1980s, and 1980s genres such as electro, early house (particularly Chicago House), and Detroit techno, influenced by the sounds of the Roland TR-808 and TR-909 drum machines and the Roland TB-303 bass synthesizer.

By late 2011, *Music Trades* was describing electronic dance music as the fastest-growing genre in the world.[8] Elements of electronic music also became increasingly prominent in pop music.[9] Radio and television also contributed to dance music's mainstream acceptance.[10]

Acid house and rave

See also: Acid house, Techno, Rave and Second Summer of Love

By 1988, house music exploded in the West with acid

Roland TB-303: The bass line synthesizer that was used prominently in acid house.

house becoming increasingly popular.[11] There was also a warehouse party subculture based around the sound system scene; the music at warehouse parties was predominantly house. In 1988 the Balearic party vibe associated with Ibiza-based DJ Alfredo Fiorito was transported to London, when Danny Rampling and Paul Oakenfold opened the clubs Shoom and Spectrum, respectively. Both places became synonymous with acid house, and it was during this period that MDMA gained prominence as a party drug. Other important UK clubs included Back to Basics in Leeds, Sheffield's Leadmill and Music Factory, and The Haçienda in Manchester, where Mike Pickering and Graeme Park's spot, Nude, was an important proving ground for American underground dance music.[Note 1] Acid house fever escalated in London and Manchester. MDMA-fueled clubgoers, faced with a 2 a.m. close, sought refuge at all-night underground warehouse parties. Within a year, however, up to 10,000 people at a time were attending commercially organized mass parties called raves.[1]

[12] The success of house and acid house paved the way for Detroit Techno, a style that was initially supported by a handful of house music clubs in Chicago, New York, and Northern England, with Detroit clubs catching up later.[13] According to British DJ Mark Moore, Derrick May's "Strings of Life" led London clubgoers to accept house: "because most people hated house music and it was all rare groove and hip hop...I'd play 'Strings of Life' at the Mudd Club and clear the floor".[14][Note 2]

EDM in the United States

Initially, electronic dance music achieved limited popular exposure in America when it was marketed as "electronica" during the mid-to-late 1990s.[16] At the time, a wave of electronic music bands from the UK, including The Prodigy, The Chemical Brothers, Fatboy Slim and Underworld, had been prematurely associated with an "American electronica revolution".[9][17] But rather than finding mainstream success, EDM was relegated to the margins of the industry.[9] Madonna's 1998 album, *Ray of Light*, is credited as bringing the genre into the mainstream and is considered an EDM release by contemporary critics.[18][19] However, despite media interest in electronica in the late 1990s, American house and techno producers continued to travel abroad to establish their careers as DJs and producers.[9]

A number of factors led to the increased prominence for dance acts in North America in the mid-2000s. In 2004, Tiësto opened the 2004 Summer Olympics in Athens, Greece.[20] According to *Spin*, Daft Punk's performance at Coachella in 2006 was the "tipping point" for EDM—it introduced the duo to a new generation of "rock kids".[9] In 2009, French house musician David Guetta began to gain prominence in mainstream pop music thanks to several crossover hits on Top 40 charts such as "When Love Takes Over", as well as his collaborations with U.S. pop and hip-hop acts such as Akon ("Sexy B*tch") and The Black Eyed Peas ("I Gotta Feeling").[21] YouTube and SoundCloud helped fuel interest in EDM, as well as electro house and dubstep. Skrillex popularized a harsher sound nicknamed "brostep".[22][23]

The increased popularity of EDM was also influenced by live events. Promoters and venues realized that DJs could generate larger profits than traditional musicians; Diplo explained that "a band plays [for] 45 minutes; DJs can play for four hours. Rock bands—there's a few headliner dudes that can play 3,000-4,000-capacity venues, but DJs play the same venues, they turn the crowd over two times, people buy drinks all night long at higher prices—it's a win-win."[9]

Electronic music festivals like the Electric Daisy Carnival (EDC) also grew in size, placing an increased emphasis on visual experiences (such as video and lighting), fashion (characterized by *The Guardian* as an evolution from the 1990s "kandi raver" into "[a] slick and sexified yet also kitschy-surreal image midway between Venice Beach and Cirque Du Soleil, Willy Wonka and a Gay Pride parade"), and the DJs themselves, who began to attain a celebrity status.[22][23] Other major acts that gained prominence like Avicii and Swedish House Mafia held concert tours at major music venues like arenas rather than nightclubs; in December 2011, Swedish House Mafia became the first electronic music act to sell out New York City's Madison Square Garden.[22]

In 2011 *Spin* declared a "new rave generation" led by acts like David Guetta, Deadmau5, and Skrillex.[9] In January 2013, *Billboard* introduced a new EDM-focused Dance/Electronic Songs chart, tracking the top 50 electronic songs based on sales, radio airplay, club play, and online streaming.[24] According to Eventbrite, EDM fans are more likely to use social media to discover and share events or gigs. They also discovered that 78% of fans say they are more likely to attend an event if their peers do, compared to 43% of fans in general. EDM has many young and social fans.[25][25]

Corporate investment

The mainstream success of EDM made it increasingly attractive to investors to the point where there were comparisons to the dot-com boom of the late-1990s. Corporate consolidation in the EDM industry began in 2012—especially in terms of live events. In June 2012, media executive Robert F. X. Sillerman—founder of what is now Live Nation—re-launched SFX Entertainment as an EDM conglomerate, and announced his plan to invest $1 billion to acquire EDM businesses. His acquisitions included regional promoters and festivals (including ID&T, which organizes Tomorrowland), two nightclub operators in Miami, and Beatport, an online music store for EDM.[26][27] Live Nation also acquired Cream Holdings and Hard Events, and announced a "creative partnership" with EDC organizers Insomniac Events in 2013 that would allow it to access its resources whilst remaining an independent company;[28] Live Nation CEO Michael Rapino described EDM as the "[new] rock 'n' roll".[16][29][30]

U.S. radio conglomerate iHeartMedia, Inc. (formerly Clear Channel Media and Entertainment) has also made efforts to align itself with EDM. It hired noted British DJ and BBC Radio 1 personality Pete Tong to produce programming for its "Evolution" dance radio brand,[31] and announced a partnership with SFX in January 2014 to co-produce live concerts and EDM-oriented original programming for its top 40 radio stations. iHeartMedia president John Sykes explained that he wanted his company's properties to be the "best destination [for EDM]".[32][33]

Major brands have also used the EDM phenomena as a means of targeting millennials [34][35] and EDM songs and artists have increasingly been featured in television commercials and programs.[36] Avicii's manager Ash Pournouri compared these practices to the commercialization of hip-hop in the early 2000s.[36] Heineken has a marketing relationship with the Ultra Music Festival, and has incorporated Dutch producers Armin van Buuren and Tiësto into its ad campaigns. Anheuser-Busch has a similar relationship as beer sponsor of SFX Entertainment events.[36] In 2014, 7 Up launched "7x7Up"—a multi-platform campaign centered around EDM that includes digital content, advertising featuring producers, and branded stages at both Ultra and Electric Daisy Carnival.[34][37][38] Wireless carrier T-Mobile US entered into an agreement with SFX to become the official wireless sponsor of its events, and partnered with Above & Beyond to sponsor its 2015 tour.[35]

1.9.2 Criticism

Despite the growing mainstream acceptance of EDM, a number of producers and DJs, including Carl Cox, Steve Lawler, and Markus Schulz, have raised concerns that the perceived over-commercialization of dance music has impacted the "art" of DJing. Cox saw the "press-play" approach of EDM DJs as unrepresentative of what he called "DJ ethos".[22] Writing in *Mixmag*, DJ Tim Sheridan argued that "push-button DJs" who use auto-sync and play pre-recorded sets of "obvious hits" has resulted in a situation overtaken by "the spectacle, money and the showbiz".[39]

Some house producers openly admitted that "commercial" EDM needed further differentiation and creativity. Avicii, whose 2013 album *True* featured songs incorporating elements of bluegrass, such as lead single "Wake Me Up", stated that most EDM lacked "longevity".[40] Deadmau5 has criticized the homogenization of EDM, stating that the music he hears "all sounds the same", underlining his diversification into other genres like techno. During the 2014 Ultra Music Festival, Deadmau5 made critical comments about up-and-coming EDM artist Martin Garrix and later played an edited version of Garrix's "Animals" remixed to the melody of "Old McDonald Had a Farm". Afterwards, Tiësto criticized Deadmau5 on Twitter for "sarcastically" mixing Avicii's "Levels" with his own "Ghosts 'n' Stuff".[41][42][43][44]

In May 2014, the NBC comedy series *Saturday Night Live* parodied the stereotypes of EDM culture and push-button DJs in a Digital Short entitled "When Will the Bass Drop?". It featured a DJ named "Davvincii" who goes about performing everyday activities—playing a computer game, frying eggs, collecting money—who then presses a giant "BASS" button, which explodes the heads of concertgoers.[45][46][47]

International expansion

China is a market where EDM has made relatively few inroads, and because it is hard for DJs to sell tickets, they hardly ever perform there. The country's first EDM festival, Storm, took place in Shanghai in November 2013; among the 25,000 fans that were attending, most were expatriates. The second Storm Festival, held in October 2014 at a large Shanghai park called Xu Hui Binjiang Green Space, was considered more of a success than the first one.[48] For example, there were more than 80 pre-parties and six larger warehouse parties in 20 Chinese cities in the leadup to the festival; in 2013 there were only five pre-parties.[49] Another example of the international expansion of EDM is when Deadmau5 became the first Canadian ever to headline Toronto's Rogers Centre in November, 2011, he turned the dome from an unwelcoming concrete hangar into the perfect rave venue.[50]

1.9.3 Terminology

The term "electronic dance music" was used in the United States as early as 1985, although the term "dance music" did not catch on as a blanket term until the late 1990s, when the U.S. music industry created music charts for "dance".[51] In July 1995, Nervous Records and *Project X Magazine* hosted the first awards ceremony, calling it the "Electronic Dance Music Awards".[Note 3][53]

In *The Guardian*, journalist Simon Reynolds noted that the music industry's adoption of EDM as a term of art was thanks to an intentional effort to re-brand U.S. "rave culture" and differentiate it from the 1990s rave scene.[23] In the UK, "dance music" or "dance" are more common terms for EDM.[54]

What is widely perceived to be "club music" has changed over time; it now includes different genres and may not always encompass EDM. Similarly, *electronic dance music* can mean different things to different people. Both "club music" and EDM seem vague, but the terms are sometimes used to refer to distinct and unrelated genres (club music is defined by what is popular, whereas EDM is distinguished by musical attributes).[55]

1.9.4 Genres

Main article: List of electronic music genres

Like other music genres, EDM has various subgenres that evolved over the past 30 years that are often defined by their varying tempo (BPM), rhythm, instrumentation, and time period. For example; hardstyle, dubstep, trance, electro, hardcore, trap, chillstep, chillout, drum and bass, house, and some other genres which came from combinations from the genre above.

1.9.5 Production

Typical tools for EDM production: computer, MIDI keyboard and mixer/sound recorder.

In a 2014 interview with Tony Andrew, the owner and founder of the Funktion-One sound system—considered a foremost model of audio technology and installed in famous venues including Berghain, Output, and Trouw—Andrew explained the critical importance of bass to dance music:

> Dance music would not be so successful without bass. If you think about it, we've really only had amplified bass for around 50 years. Big bass is only a couple of generations old. Before the invention of speakers that could project true bass frequencies, humans really only came across bass in hazardous situations—for example, when thunder struck, or an earthquake shook, or from explosions caused by dynamite or gunpowder. That is probably why it is by far the most adrenaline-inducing frequency that we have. Bass gets humans excited basically. Below 90 or 100 Hz, bass becomes more of a physical thing. It vibrates specific organs. It vibrates our bones. It causes minor molecular rearrangement,

and that is what makes it so potent as a force in dance music. The molecular vibration caused by bass is what gives dance music its power. It is what makes dance music so pleasurable to hear through a proper sound system.[56]

Andrew warned that too much bass—and too much sound in general—can be harmful, stating that a "good sound engineer will understand that there is a window between enough sound to give excitement and so much that it is damaging".[56]

1.9.6 Festivals

Main article: List of electronic music festivals
See also: List of trance festivals
Electronic dance music was often played at illegal under-

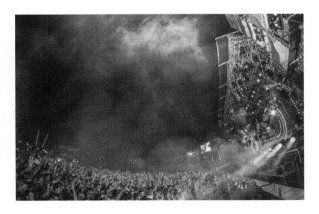

An EDM festival in 2013 with over 100,000 attendees,[57] exhibiting the large crowds and dramatic lighting common at such events since the early 2000s.[23]

ground rave parties. These were held in secret locations, for example, warehouses, abandoned bridges, fields and any other large, open areas. In the 1990s and 2000s, aspects of the underground rave culture of the 1980s and early 1990s began to evolve into legitimate EDM concerts and festivals. Major festivals often feature a large number of acts representing various EDM genres spread across multiple stages. Festivals have placed a larger emphasis on visual spectacles as part of their overall experiences, including elaborate stage designs with complex lighting systems, laser shows, and pyrotechnics, along with the attire of their attendees.[37] These events differed from underground raves by their organized nature, often taking place at major venues, and measures to ensure the health and safety of attendees.[58] MTV's Rawley Bornstein described electronic music as "the new rock and roll",[59] as has Lollapalooza organizer Perry Ferrell.[60]

Ray Waddell of *Billboard* noted that festival promoters

have done an excellent job at branding.[59] Larger festivals have been shown to have positive economic impacts on their host citiesl[58] the 2014 Ultra Music Festival brought 165,000 attendees—and over $223 million—to the Miami/South Florida region's economy.[38] The inaugural TomorrowWorld brought $85.1 million to the Atlanta area—as much revenue as its hosting of the NCAA Final Four earlier in the year.[61] The increasing mainstream prominence of electronic music has also led major U.S. multi-genre festivals, such as Lollapalooza and Coachella, to add more electronic and dance acts to their lineups, along with dedicated, EDM-oriented stages. Even with these accommodations, some major electronic acts, such as Deadmau5 and Calvin Harris respectively, have made appearances on main stages during the final nights of Lollapalooza and Coachella, respectively—spots traditionally reserved for prominent non-electronic genres, such as rock and alternative.[62][63]

Russell Smith of *The Globe and Mail* felt that the commercial festival industry was an antithesis to the original concepts of the rave subculture, citing "the expensive tickets, the giant corporate sponsors, the crass bro culture— shirtless muscle boys who cruise the stadiums, tiny popular girls in bikinis who ride on their shoulders – not to mention the sappy music itself."[64] Drug-related incidents, as well as other complaints surrounding the behaviour of their attendees, have contributed to negative perceptions and opposition to electronic music events by local authorities;[64][65] After Ultra Music Festival 2014, where a crowd of gatecrashers trampled a security guard on its first day, Miami's city commissioners considered banning the festival from being held in the city, citing the trampling incident, lewd behavior, and complaints by downtown residents of being harassed by attendees. The commissioners voted in favor of allowing UMF to be held in Miami due to its positive economic effects, under the condition that organizers address security, drug usage and lewd behavior by attendees[66][67][68]

Association with recreational drug use

See also: Club drug and Party pills

Dance music has a long association with recreational drug use.[69] Russell Smith noted that the association of drugs and music was by no means exclusive to electronic music, citing previous examples such as Psychedelic rock and LSD, disco music and cocaine, and punk music and heroin.[64]

Reports of alleged drug related deaths

A number of deaths related to alleged drug use have occurred at major festivals in recent years, involving such drugs as MDMA and meth. Electric Daisy Carnival was forced to move to Las Vegas in 2011, when the Los Angeles Memorial Coliseum refused to host any it or any other Insomniac-organized electronic music events after an underaged attendee died from an MDMA overdose at the 2010 edition.[58][70][71][72] Drug-related deaths during Electric Zoo 2013 in New York City, United States, and Future Music Festival Asia 2014 in Kuala Lumpur, Malaysia, prompted the final day of both events to be outright cancelled,[71][73] while Life in Color cancelled a planned event in Malaysia out of concern for the incident at Future Music Festival Asia, and ther drug-related deaths that occurred at the A State of Trance 650 concerts in Jakarta, Indonesia.[74][75][76]

1.9.7 Industry awards

1.9.8 See also

- Timeline of electronic music genres

- List of electronic dance music record labels

- List of electronic musicians

- List of electronic dance music venues

- Freetekno

- Rave music

- Remix

1.9.9 Notes

[1] Fikentscher (2000), p. 5, in discussing the definition of underground dance music as it relates to post-disco music in America, states that: "The prefix 'underground' does not merely serve to explain that the associated type of music - and its cultural context - are familiar only to a small number of informed persons. Underground also points to the sociological function of the music, framing it as one type of music that in order to have meaning and continuity is kept away, to large degree, from mainstream society, mass media, and those empowered to enforce prevalent moral and aesthetic codes and values."

[2] "Although it can now be heard in Detroit's leading clubs, the local area has shown a marked reluctance to get behind the music. It has been in clubs like the Powerplant (Chicago), The World (New York), The Hacienda (Manchester), Rock City (Nottingham) and Downbeat (Leeds) where the techno

sound has found most support. Ironically, the only Detroit club which really championed the sound was a peripatetic party night called Visage, which unromantically shared its name with one of Britain's oldest new romantic groups".[15]

[3] "Josh Wink, Moby, and the Future Sound Of London were among the fortunate folks honored at the first Electronic Dance Music Awards presented on July 27 in New York produced by Nervous Records and *Project X* magazine. Winners were tallied from ballots from *Project X* readers".[52]

1.9.10 References

[1] Koskoff (2004), p. 44

[2] Butler (2006), pp. 12–13, 94

[3] "Is EDM a Real Genre?". *Noisey*. Vice. Retrieved 25 February 2015.

[4] RA Roundtable: EDM in AmericaResident Advisor,. "RA Roundtable: EDM In America". N. p., 2012. Web. 18 May. 2014.

[5] "The FACT Dictionary: How 'Dubstep', 'Juke', 'Cloud Rap' And Many More Got Their Names'", *FACT Mag*, July 10, 2013.

[6] "Hardstyle music's growing influence" *Dailytrojan*, Web. Mar 3, 2014.

[7] [http://www.billboard.com/biz/search/charts?page=41&f{[}0{]}=ts_chart_artistname%3A*donna%20summer*&f{[}1{]}=ss_bb_type%3Achart_item&type=2&artist=donna%20summer "Chart Search - Billboard"]. *billboard.com*.

[8] "Just How Big is EDM?". *Music Trades Magazine*. Retrieved 14 June 2014.

[9] Sherburne, Philip. "Harder, Better, Faster, Stronger", *Spin Magazine*, pages 41-53, October 2011

[10] "The Year EDM Sold Out: Swedish House Mafia, Skrillex and Deadmau5 Hit the Mainstream". *Billboard*. Retrieved 27 January 2014.

[11] Rietveld (1998), pp. 40–50

[12] Rietveld (1998), pp. 54–59

[13] Brewster (2006), pp. 398–443

[14] Brewster (2006), p. 419

[15] Cosgrove 1988a

[16] Ben Sisario (April 4, 2012). "Electronic Dance Concerts Turn Up Volume, Tempting Investors". *New York Times*.

[17] Chaplin, Julia & Michel, Sia. "Fire Starters", *Spin Magazine*, page 40, March 1997, Spin Media LLC.

[18] The 30 Greatest EDM Albums of All Time, Rolling Stone, 2 August 2012

[19] Ray of Light - Madonna Allmusic

[20] "The EDM Bubble: What Caused It". EDM Exclusives.

[21] "DJ David Guetta leads the EDM charge into mainstream". *USA Today*. June 5, 2012.

[22] Jim Fusilli (June 6, 2012). "The Dumbing Down of Electronic Dance Music". *Wall Street Journal*.

[23] "How Rave Music Conquered America". *The Guardian*. August 2, 2012.

[24] "New Dance/Electronic Songs Chart Launches With Will.i.am & Britney at No. 1". *Billboard*. Retrieved 13 August 2014.

[25] Peoples, Glenn. "EDM's Social Dance." Billboard - The International Newsweekly of Music, Video and Home Entertainment Jul 06 2013: 8. ProQuest. Web. 20 July 2015.

[26] "Exclusive: SFX Acquires ID&T, Voodoo Experience". *Billboard*. Retrieved 18 April 2013.

[27] "SFX Purchases 75% Stake in ID&T, Announce U.S. Edition of Tomorrowland at Ultra". *Billboard*. Retrieved 16 April 2013.

[28] Zel McCarthy (June 20, 2013). "Live Nation Teams With Insomniac Events in 'Creative Partnership'". *Billboard*.

[29] "Live Nation Acquires L.A. EDM Promoter HARD: Will the Mainstream Get More Ravey?". *Spin*. Retrieved 25 April 2014.

[30] Dan Rys (May 9, 2012). "Live Nation Buys EDM Entertainment Company Cream Holdings Ltd, Owner of Creamfields Festivals". *Billboard*.

[31] Ben Sisario (December 20, 2012). "Boston Radio Station Switches to Electronic Dance Format". *New York Times*.

[32] Kerri Mason (January 6, 2014). "SFX and Clear Channel Partner for Digital, Terrestrial Radio Push". *Billboard*.

[33] Kerri Mason (January 6, 2014). "John Sykes, Robert Sillerman on New Clear Channel, SFX Partnership: 'We Want to Be the Best'". *Billboard*.

[34] "7Up Turns to Electronic Dance Music to Lift Spirits -- and Sales". *Advertising Age*. Retrieved 27 June 2015.

[35] "Exclusive: Bolstering Massive EDM Strategy, T-Mobile Debuts Above & Beyond Video Series". *Billboard*. Retrieved 27 June 2015.

[36] "Booming business: EDM goes mainstream". *Miami Herald*. March 26, 2014.

[37] Valerie Lee (June 27, 2014). "An Electric Desert Experience: The 2014 EDC Las Vegas Phenomenon". *Dancing Astronaut.*

[38] Roy Trakin (April 3, 2014). "Ultra Music Festival's 16th Anything but Sweet, Though Still Potent". *The Hollywood Reporter.*

[39] "Is EDM killing the art of DJing?". *Mixmag.* Retrieved 7 June 2014.

[40] "EDM Will Eat Itself: Big Room stars are getting bored". *Mixmag.* Retrieved 20 January 2014.

[41] "Deadmau5 Trolls Martin Garrix with 'Old MacDonald Had a Farm' Remix of 'Animals' at Ultra". *radio.com.* March 31, 2014.

[42] "Deadmau5 gives reason for techno track: "EDM sounds the same to me"". *Mixmag.* Retrieved 25 April 2014.

[43] "Deadmau5: The Man Who Trolled the World". *Mixmag.* Retrieved 25 April 2014.

[44] "Afrojack and Deadmau5 argue over what's "good music"". *Mixmag.* Retrieved 20 January 2014.

[45] "SNL Digital Shorts return with 'Davvincii' to skewer EDM and overpaid DJs". *The Verge.* May 18, 2014.

[46] "Watch Saturday Night Live Mock Big Room DJ Culture". *Mixmag.* Retrieved 7 June 2014.

[47] "SNL takes stab at EDM culture in new digital short featuring 'Davvincii'". *Dancing Astronaut.* May 2014.

[48] Ako (October 14, 2014). "Shanghai's Storm 2014 Raises The Ante For Music Festivals In China". *EDM Tunes.*

[49] Hannah Karp (October 5, 2014). "In China, Concert Promoter Wants EDM in the Mix". *Wall Street Journal.*

[50] Doherty, Mike (Spring 2012). "Electronic Dance Music Breaks Through". *Words & Music.*

[51] Jonathan Bogart (10 July 2014). "Buy the Hype: Why Electronic Dance Music Really Could Be the New Rock". *The Atlantic.*

[52] Larry Flick (August 12, 1995). = xAsEAAAAM-BAJ&lpg=PA24&pg=PA24#v=onepage&q&f=false "Gonzales Prepares More Batches of Bucketheads" Check |url= scheme (help). *Billboard*: 24.

[53] David Prince (1995). "Rhythm Nation". *Rolling Stone* (705): 33.

[54] "Definition".

[55] Kembrew McLeod (2001). "Genres, Subgenres, Sub-Subgenres and More: Musical and Social Difference Within Electronic/Dance Music Communities" (PDF). *Journal of Popular Music Studies* 13: 59–75. doi:10.1111/j.1533-1598.2001.tb00013.x.

[56] Terry Church (April 10, 2014). "Funktion-One's Tony Andrews on Setting Up Soundsystems – From Wembley Stadium to Your Bedroom". *DJTechTools.*

[57] http://www.technoton-magazin.com/veranstaltung26_technotonontour_electriclove2014.html

[58] "A fatal toll on concertgoers as raves boost cities' income". *Los Angeles Times.* February 3, 2013.

[59] Lisa Rose, "N.J. basks in the glow of the brave new rave: Electronic dance festivals go mainstream", *Newark Star Ledger*, May 16, 2012.

[60] Sarah Maloy (August 4, 2012). "Lollapalooza's Perry Farrell on EDM and Elevating the Aftershow: Video". *Billboard.*

[61] Melissa Ruggieri (April 8, 2014). "Study: TomorrowWorld had $85m impact". *Atlanta Journal-Constitution.*

[62] "House Music Comes Home: How Chicago's Summer of Music Festivals Has Reinvigorated the City's Dance Spirit". *Noisey* (Vice).

[63] "How Coachella's final day symbolizes the electronic music fever pitch". *Las Vegas Weekly.* April 14, 2014.

[64] "Russell Smith: Exposés on EDM festivals shift long overdue blame". *The Globe and Mail.* July 12, 2015. Retrieved 3 October 2015.

[65] "Music festival safety recommendations come too late for family". *CBC News.* Retrieved 3 October 2015.

[66] "Ultra Fest to Stay in Miami, City Commission Decides". *Rolling Stone.* Retrieved 25 April 2014.

[67] "Miami Commission: Ultra stays in downtown Miami". *Miami Herald.* Retrieved 25 April 2014.

[68] "Ultra Music Announces Review After Festival Security Draws Criticism". *Billboard.com.* Retrieved 7 April 2014.

[69] Electronic Dance Music's Love Affair with Ecstasy

[70] "Man dies at Electric Daisy Carnival in Las Vegas". *Chicago Tribune.* June 22, 2014.

[71] Jon Pareles (September 1, 2014). "A Bit of Caution Beneath the Thump". *New York Times.*

[72] "Electric Zoo to Clamp Down on Drugs This Year". *Wall Street Journal.* 28 August 2014.

[73] "Six dead from 'meth' at Future Music Festival Asia 2014: police". *Sydney Morning Herald* (Fairfax Media). Retrieved 3 October 2015.

[74] "Blanked out: Life In Color cancelled due to drug deaths". *Malaysia Star.* Retrieved 7 April 2014.

[75] "Police Probe 'A State of Trance' Festival Drug Deaths". *Jakarta Globe.* Retrieved 7 April 2014.

[76] "Three Dead After State of Trance Festival in Jakarta, Drugs Suspected". *Spin.com*. Retrieved 3 October 2015.

[77] "Hardwell Wins DJ Mag's Top 100 DJs Poll". *Billboard*. Retrieved 12 August 2014.

[78] Rodriguez, Krystal (23 September 2014). "Here are the winners of this year's Ibiza DJ Awards". *In the Mix Webzine Australia*.

[79] Zalokar, Gregor. "DJ Awards 2014 Winners". *EMF Magazine*. Retrieved 25 March 2015.

[80] "30th Annual International Dance Music Awards - Winter Music Conference 2015 - WMC 2015". *Winter Music Conference*.

[81] "American Music Awards 2012: A big night for Justin Bieber". *CBS News*. November 18, 2012.

[82] "Choose your Nomination Category". *worldmusicawards.com*. World Music Awards. Retrieved 7 June 2015.

[83] "Best Dance Music Artist". *worldmusicawards.com*. World Music Awards. Retrieved 7 June 2015.

Bibliography

- Butler, Mark Jonathan (2006). *Unlocking the Groove: Rhythm, Meter, and Musical Design in Electronic Dance Music*. Indiana University Press. ISBN 9780253346629.

- Fikentscher, Kai (2000). *'You Better Work'!: Underground Dance Music in New York*. Hanover, NH: Wesleyan University Press. ISBN 9780819564047.

- Koskoff, Ellen (2004). *Music Cultures in the United States: an Introduction*. Routledge. ISBN 9780415965897.

- Rietveld, Hillegonda C. (1998). *This is Our House: House Music, Cultural Spaces, and Technologies*. Popular Cultural Studies **13**. Ashgate. ISBN 9781857422429.

1.9.11 Further reading

- Hewitt, Michael. *Music Theory for Computer Musicians*. 1st Ed. U.S. Cengage Learning, 2008. ISBN 978-1-59863-503-4

- "Electronic dance music glossary" by Moby for *USA Today* (December 13, 2011)

1.10 Game Boy music

This article is about the use of the Nintendo Game Boy as a musical instrument. For music from Game Boy games, see Video game music.

Game Boy music is a type of chip music produced using a portable gaming device from the Game Boy line of consoles. To produce music of this genre, one needs a Game Boy and a cartridge containing appropriate tracking software, such as Little Sound DJ.

1.10.1 Software

There are several pieces of software available, but most Game Boy musicians use Nanoloop, Little Sound DJ, Pixelh8 Pro Performer or Pixelh8 Music Tech. Other software includes Carillon Editor, Music Box, Pocket Music, the Game Boy Camera among others.

Nanoloop was programmed by Oliver Wittchow, a German art student. The user interface is minimalistic and distinct from conventional musical user interfaces. Little Sound DJ was programmed by Johan Kotlinski, who lives in Stockholm. Little Sound DJ is a type of four-track tracker.

1.10.2 Timeline

- In 1997, Oliver Wittchow and Sebastian Burdach started to work on programming music applications for the Game Boy. During three nights, Sebastian Burdach wrote a very simple sequencer in Game Boy BASIC, probably the very first sequencer for the Game Boy, which allows the user to edit loops in real time.

- In 1998, the Game Boy Camera was released (in Japan under the name "Pocket Camera"). Besides incorporating the ability to take photos, the camera also incorporates gaming capabilities. One of these will lead the player to the DJ game, a sequencer known as "Trippy-H".

- In 1998, Oliver Wittchow switched to programming the Game Boy in C. He performed for the first time with his newly written program "Nanoloop" at the "Liquid Sky Club", Cologne, at a lo-fi contest, which he won. He recorded a 7" single, which was released 1999 on the xxc3 label.[1]

- In 1999, Alec Empire released under the project name "Nintendo Teenage Robots" an album titled "We Punk Einheit!". The music consisted solely of Game Boy sounds, made with the dj program of the Game Boy

Camera. Later Alec Empire also used Nanoloop live on stage.

- In 1999, "Nanoloop 0.8" was sold on flash cartridges, in Germany only.

- In 2000, "Nanoloop 1.0" was sold on ROM cartridges, made in Hong Kong. This version is marketed internationally. It was quite buggy, and was replaced later this year with the more stable version 1.1.

- In 2000, the German electronic music duo "Klangstabil", consisting of Maurizio Blanco and Boris May, released two albums, "Sprite Storage Format" (12" lp), and "Gioco Bambino" (cd), consisting mainly of Game Boy music made with the Game Boy Camera, with some external effects and filtering.[2]

- In 2000, Aleksi Eeben (a.k.a. "Heatbeat", from the Commodore Amiga demoscene) released his program "Carillon". Although it was not intended for live use, one could nonetheless program one's own music, and one could (and still can) download it for free.

- In 2000, Johan Kotlinski created the program Little Sound DJ. Before that, according to Johan Kotlinski, "it was just a hack 'instrumentor.gb' that I sent to my demo group friends." At this early stage, lsdj was nowhere near finished. The first versions, which were put on cartridges and sold, came out 2001.

- In 2001, Chris McCormick, from Chrism and Fenris, created the program Looper Advance. It is a looper/sequencer for the Game Boy Advance.

- In 2002, Jester Interactive created Pocket Music for the Game Boy Color and Game Boy Advance which was published by Rage. They are Sample based sequencers and the Game Boy Advance version has a mild dub of Eminem's single "My Name Is."

- In 2002, the now defunct label "Disco Bruit" released the various artists compilation "Nanoloop 1.0". Several in the electronic music scene established artists (like Dat politics, Merzbow, Felix Kubin, etc.) were given nanoloops.[3] Supposedly also Aphex Twin was to contribute, but somehow it didn't happen.[4]

- In 2003, the CD "Boy Playground" was released on the Relax Beat label.[5] Most of the tracks were created using the program Little Sound DJ and the record was gathering the best Game Boy musicians worldwide (Johan Kotlinski, Bit Shifter, Covox, Lo-Bat, Mark DeNardo, Tobiah, The Hardliner, Goto80, Nim, Handheld, Bud Melvin, Adlib Sinner Forks, Dilemma, Keichi Hirao, Puss, Teamtendo).

- In 2003, Malcolm McLaren (of Sex Pistols fame) was collaborating with Relax Beat producers Jacques Fantino and Thierry Criscione who initiated him to Chip music during the studio sessions. After listening to the first Game Boy track, Malcolm McLaren's comment was : "It sounds ugly... but this music is so beautiful !". Malcolm McLaren was so excited to discover this new genre that he proposed to write a promotional article in Wired for the release of the CD "Boy Playground". He wrote an article in Wired magazine, claiming Game Boy music (or 8-bit music, or chiptunes in general) to be the new punk rock.[6] This article was very controversial, and McLaren's effort to create a hype around the new "8-bit punk" was not welcome by very many chipmusicians, and resulted in an open letter by chipmusician gwEm (Gareth Morris).[7] McLaren did arrange a "Fashion Beast" party in Florence, Italy, in 2004. Chinese girl group "Wild Strawberries", and Game Boy musicians Covox and Lo-bat were playing.[8] Lately it has become a bit silent around McLaren's "8-bit punk". In 2005 he designed clothing for kids, seemingly inspired by 8-bit aesthetics.[9]

- In 2005 8 Bit Weapon played their songs "Bombs Away" & "Gameboy Rocker" off an old Game Boy using LSDJ on G4's Attack of the Show live broadcast Episode #5058. [6] [7]

- In 2006, the CD "Glitter & Bleep : Joystick Pop" was produced by the Relax Beat label.[10] It features original songs by the greatest talents of the European 8-bit scene. Besides Game Boys also various other 8-bit consoles were used.

- In 2007, the cd "8-Bit Operators: The Music of Kraftwerk" was released on the Astralwerks label. It features cover versions of Kraftwerk songs by several prominent chiptune artists. Besides Game Boys also various other 8-bit consoles were used.

- The Game Boy music scene is quite small and spread around the world, with musicians creating music in a wide range of styles. Several major signed artists have also been known to use LSDJ and Nanoloop.

- In late 2007 Pixelh8 designed music software such as Music Tech[11] for the Nintendo Game Boy which turns the Game Boy into real time synthesizer, whereby the user can design the sound and play notes by using the keys.

- In 2008 the Pixelh8 designed Pro Performer[12] for the Nintendo Game Boy Advance and Nintendo DS which was an upgraded version of the Music Tech for Game Boy.

- April 15, 2009 Pixelh8 released Pixelh8 Music Tech V2.0, Pro Performer, Drum Tech and Death Ray software free for download[13] from his official website.[14]

- In April 2009, Sony Creative Software released "8 Bit Weapon: A Chiptune Odyssey" loop and sample Library. The library contains music loops and samples made by the band using various vintage computers and video game consoles, including the original Nintendo Game Boy.

1.10.3 Artists

- 8 Bit Weapon
- Anamanaguchi
- Autechre [15]
- Bubblyfish
- Cinematronic
- Chipzel
- Danimal Cannon
- Derpancakes
- Doctor Octoroc
- Dead Choir Anthology
- GyroMan Band
- Horse the Band
- Huoratron
- I Fight Dragons
- Lukhash
- Manhattan-DIY
- Melted Moon
- Nullsleep
- Noedell
- PDF Format (the band)
- Bit Shifter
- Pixelh8
- Electric Children
- Pulselooper
- Droid-on

- SSB
- Rainbowdragoneyes
- Knife city
- Glomag
- Trash80
- Console killer
- Unicorn Kid
- Starpulse
- fantomenk
- Zef
- l-tron
- Starscream
- Covox
- RainbowCrash88
- YMCK
- PixelPanic

1.10.4 References

[1] "Nanoloop - 01 (7")". Discogs. Retrieved 2009-01-02.

[2] http://www.klangstabil.com/

[3] "Various - Nanoloop 1.0 (CD)". Discogs. Retrieved 2009-01-02.

[4] "Aphex Twin creates Game Boy music?". The Aphex Twin Community. Retrieved 2009-01-02.

[5] "Boy Playground - An introduction to Game Boy Chip music". Relaxbeat.net. Retrieved 2009-01-02.

[6] McLaren, Malcolm (November 2003). "8-Bit Punk" (11.11). Wired. Retrieved 2009-01-02.

[7] gwEm. "Open Letter to Malcolm McLaren". micromusic.net. Retrieved 2009-01-02.

[8] McLaren, Malcolm (8 January 2004). "hustler of culture: malcolm mclaren's fashion beast". Hustlerofculture.typepad.com. Retrieved 2009-01-02.

[9] "Futuristicky: December 2005". Futuristicky.com. 2005-12-23. Retrieved 2009-01-02.

[10] "GLITTER & BLEEP - Joystick Pop". Relaxbeat.net. Retrieved 2009-01-02.

[11] Album on NES Cartridge, Synth on GameBoy, Create Digital Music Published July 4, 2007.

[12] Pixelh8 Music Tech Pro Performer Brings Live Performance to Game Boy, *Create Digital Music*. Published March 24, 2008.

[13] www.pixelh8.co.uk, *Pixelh8*. Published April 15, 2009.

[14] www.pixelh8.co.uk, *Pixelh8*. Published April 15, 2009.

[15] "Autechre Gear List". Mike Baas. Retrieved 2012-03-29.

1.11 Glitch (music)

Glitch is a genre of electronic music that emerged in the late 1990s. It has been described as a genre that adheres to an "aesthetic of failure," where the deliberate use of glitch-based audio media, and other sonic artifacts, is a central concern.[1]

Sources of glitch sound material are usually malfunctioning or abused audio recording devices or digital electronics, such as CD skipping, electric hum, digital or analog distortion, bit rate reduction, hardware noise, software bugs, crashes, vinyl record hiss or scratches and system errors.[2] In a *Computer Music Journal* article published in 2000, composer and writer Kim Cascone classifies glitch as a subgenre of electronica, and used the term *post-digital* to describe the glitch aesthetic.[1]

1.11.1 History

The origins of the glitch aesthetic can be traced to the early 20th century, with Luigi Russolo's Futurist manifesto *The Art of Noises*, the basis of noise music. He also constructed noise generators, which he named *intonarumori*. Later musicians and composers made use of malfunctioning technology, such as Michael Pinder of The Moody Blues in 1968's "The Best Way to Travel," and Christian Marclay, who used mutilated vinyl records to create sound collages beginning in 1979. The title track of OMD's popular 1981 album *Architecture & Morality* makes use of invasive computer- and industrial noise snippets, and has been cited as an early incarnation of glitch.[3] Yasunao Tone used damaged CDs in his *Techno Eden* performance in 1985, while Nicolas Collins's 1992 album *It Was a Dark and Stormy Night* included a composition that featured a string quartet playing alongside the stuttering sound of skipping CDs.[4] Yuzo Koshiro's electronic soundtrack for 1994 video game *Streets of Rage 3* used automatically randomized sequences to generate "unexpected and odd" experimental sounds.[5]

Glitch originated as a distinct movement in Germany with the musical work and labels (especially Mille Plateaux) of Achim Szepanski.[6][7] While the movement initially slowly gained members (including bands like Oval),[8] the techniques of Glitch later quickly spread around the world as many artists followed suit. Trumpeter Jon Hassell's 1994 album *Dressing for Pleasure*—a dense mesh of funky trip hop and jazz—features several songs with the sound of skipping CDs layered into the mix.

Oval's *Wohnton*, produced in 1993, helped define the genre by adding ambient aesthetics to it.[9]

The mid-nineties work of Warp Records artists Aphex Twin (*Richard D. James Album, Windowlicker, Come to Daddy* EP) *chan-EL*, and Autechre (Tri Repetae, Chiastic Slide) were also influential in the development of the digital audio manipulation technique and aesthetic.

1.11.2 Production techniques

Glitch is often produced on computers using modern digital production software to splice together small "cuts" (samples) of music from previously recorded works. These cuts are then integrated with the signature of glitch music: beats made up of glitches, clicks, scratches, and otherwise "erroneously" produced or sounding noise. These glitches are often very short, and are typically used in place of traditional percussion or instrumentation. Skipping CDs, scratched vinyl records, circuit bending, and other noise-like distortions figure prominently into the creation of rhythm and feeling in glitch; it is from the use of these digital artifacts that the genre derives its name. However, not all artists of the genre are working with erroneously produced sounds or are even using digital sounds. Some artists also use digital synthesizer such as the Clavia Nord Modular G2 and Elektron Machinedrum and Monomachine.

Popular software for creating glitch includes trackers like Jeskola Buzz and Renoise, as well as modular software like Reaktor, Ableton Live, Reason, AudioMulch, Bidule, SuperCollider, FLStudio, Max/MSP, Pure Data, and ChucK. Circuit bending, the intentional modification of low power electronic devices to create new musical devices, also plays a significant role on the hardware end of glitch music and its creation.

1.11.3 Notable artists

- Alva Noto (Carsten Nicolai)
- Farmers Manual
- Frank Bretschneider
- Kid606
- Kim Cascone

- Mokira (Andreas Tilliander)

- OMFG

- Oval

- Pan Sonic

- Pole

- Prefuse 73

- Ryoji Ikeda

- The Glitch Mob

- Tipper

- Death Grips

1.11.4   Glitch hop

Glitch hop is a subgenre of glitch and fuses it with hip hop elements. While it does not necessarily include rap it fuses funky hip hop beats with glitchy effects and techniques[10] such as beat repeaters, sweeps cutting, skipping, repeating, chopping and bit crush reduction.[11] The genre took shape at about the year 2001 with the early works of Prefuse 73 on Warp Records and became popular at about the year 2004.[11][12] While it was once based on heavily twisted, sliced and distorted glitchy hip hop beats modern glitch hop has become a more defined standalone genre, quite detached from its hip hop origins and also takes increased influence of dubstep and the drum and bass subgenre neurofunk with whose neurohop variant it shares many similarities.[13][14] Popular artists of the genre include edIT, Bassnectar, KOAN Sound, Pretty Lights, GRiZ, Opiuo, Mr. Bill, Skope, Shurk, and The Glitch Mob.

1.11.5   See also

- Circuit bending

- Clicks & Cuts Series

- Generative music

- Microsound

- Noise music

- Raster-Noton

1.11.6   References

[1] "The glitch genre arrived on the back of the electronica movement, an umbrella term for alternative, largely dance-based electronic music (including house, techno, electro, drum'n'bass, ambient) that has come into vogue in the past five years. Most of the work in this area is released on labels peripherally associated with the dance music market, and is therefore removed from the contexts of academic consideration and acceptability that it might otherwise earn. Still, in spite of this odd pairing of fashion and art music, the composers of glitch often draw their inspiration from the masters of 20th century music who they feel best describe its lineage." *THE AESTHETICS OF FAILURE: 'Post-Digital' Tendencies in Contemporary Computer Music*, Kim Cascone, Computer Music Journal 24:4 Winter 2000 (MIT Press)

[2] Cox, Christoph and Warner, Daniel, eds. (2004). *Audio Culture: Readings in Modern Music*. Continuum Books. p. 393.

[3] *The Pioneers of Electropop*. 23 September 2001. 17 minutes in. Channel 4. Channel Four Television Corporation. Paul Gambaccini: There's even a track on there [*Architecture & Morality*]—the title cut, in fact—that, when you listen to [it], is really like an early incarnation of glitch techno."

[4] 1995 Interview with Nicolas Collins, by Brian Duguid

[5] Horowitz, Ken (February 5, 2008). "Interview: Yuzo Koshiro". *Sega-16*. Archived from the original on 21 September 2008. Retrieved 6 August 2011.

[6] "First championed by the ideological German techno figure Achim Szepanski and his stable of record labels—Force Inc, Mille Plateaux, Force Tracks, Ritornell—this tight-knit scene of experimental artists creating cerebral hybrids of experimental techno, minimalism, digital collage, and noise glitches soon found themselves being assembled into a community."Allmusic

[7] "Random Inc.", "Allmusic"

[8] "Glitch", "Allmusic"

[9] "Although Oval are perhaps more well-known for how they make their music than for the music they actually make, the German experimental electronic trio have provided an intriguing update of some elements of avant-garde composition in combination with techniques of digital sound design.[...]" Allmusic

[10] *FutureMusic - Issues 178-182*. Future Pub. 2006. Even when it's beautiful, Glitch Hop is disturbing. It's the wrinkle in the bedsheet, the sand in the vaseline. Artists like Prefuse 73, Telefon Tel Aviv, Matmos, Kid606, and others fuse hip hop beats with clicky, digital tones that are as gorgeous as they are defective. Glitch Hop producers are not content to make mathematical abstractions. Instead they combine this with funky, head-nodding beats to make a music that is both challenging and instinctively booty-shakin'. And now Big Fish Audio and producer Brian Saitzyk have distilled the essence of this sound into Glitch Hop.

[11] Michael, John (1 July 2010). "What is Glitch Hop?". Retrieved 5 July 2015.

[12] Duthel, C. *Pitbull - Mr. Worldwide*. p. 155. ISBN 9781471090356. Retrieved 5 July 2015.

[13] "Glitch Hop Guide". TheDanceMusicGuide. Retrieved 5 July 2015.

[14] "What Is Neurohop? Its Beginnings, Pioneers and Future". BassGorilla. Retrieved 26 August 2015.

1.11.7 Further reading

- Andrews, Ian, *Post-digital Aesthetics and the return to Modernism*, MAP-uts lecture, 2000, available at author's website.

- Bijsterveld, Karin and Trevor J. Pinch. "'Should One Applaud?': Breaches and Boundaries in the Reception of New Technology in Music." *Technology and Culture*. Ed. 44.3, pp. 536–559. 2003.

- Byrne, David. "What is Blip Hop?" *Lukabop*, 2002. Available here.

- Collins, Adam, "Sounds of the system: the emancipation of noise in the music of Carsten Nicolai", *Organised Sound*, 13(1): 31–39. 2008. Cambridge University Press.

- Collins, Nicolas. Editor. "Composers inside Electronics: Music after David Tudor." *Leonardo Music Journal*. Vol. 14, pp. 1–3. 2004.

- Krapp, Peter, Noise Channels: Glitch and Error in Digital Culture. Minneapolis: University of Minnesota Press 2011.

- Prior, Nick, "Putting a Glitch in the Field: Bourdieu, Actor Network Theory and Contemporary Music", *Cultural Sociology*, 2: 3, 2008: pp. 301–319.

- Thomson, Phil, "Atoms and errors: towards a history and aesthetics of microsound", *Organised Sound*, 9(2): 207–218. 2004. Cambridge University Press.

- Sangild, Torben: "Glitch—The Beauty of Malfunction" in *Bad Music*. Routledge (2004, ISBN 0-415-94365-5)

- Young, Rob: "Worship the Glitch", *The Wire* 190/191 (2000)

- Noah Zimmerman, "Dusted Reviews, 2002"

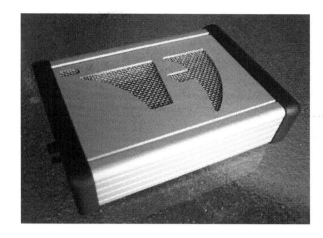

HardSID UPlay

1.12 HardSID

The **HardSID** is a family of sound cards, produced by a Hungarian company Hard Software and originally conceived by Téli Sándor.

The HardSID cards are based on the MOS Technology SID (Sound Interface Device) chip which was popularised and immortalized by the Commodore 64 home computer. It was the third non-Commodore SID-based device to enter market (the first was the SID Symphony from Creative Micro Designs and the second was the SidStation MIDI synthesiser, by Elektron). HardSID's major advantage over SidStation (apart from the fact that the SidStation has been sold out long since, with only few used pieces surfacing now and then) is that it is a simple hardware interface to a SID chip, making it far more suitable for emulator use, SID music players and even direct programming - SidStation only responds to MIDI information and requires music events to be converted to MIDI and back.

The original **HardSID** (1999) was a card for the ISA bus (instantaneously anachronizing the item), containing a slot for one SID chip. From the beginning, HardSID has supported both the 6581 and the 8580 models of SID, including all revisions.

The ISA model was subsequently replaced with a version for the PCI bus. As well as a standard 1-SID version, they launched the **HardSID Quattro**, which includes slots for four SID chips and a cooling fan.

An USB line of HardSID products was introduced with two new models: the **HardSID 4U**, a USB device with sockets for four SID chips and the **HardSID 4U Studio Edition** with improved electrical isolation and screening to reduce noise in the signal.

As of May 2010, there are three USB HardSID devices

available: the **HardSID Uno** with one SID chip, the **HardSID UPlay** with two SID chips and the already known **HardSID 4U Studio Edition** with four SID chips.

HardSID cards are supported by most modern SID music playing applications, including sidplay and ACID64 Player and some trackers such as GoatTracker. The ISA cards have official device drivers for Microsoft Windows, and the PCI ones for Mac OS X as well as Windows. The PCI Windows drivers support up to 32-bit Windows XP, and there are no 64-bit drivers or Windows Vista/7 support at all. Unofficial drivers are available for Linux.

The HardSID USB devices are shipped with Windows drivers for XP/Vista/7 only. Mac OS X support was already worked on but dropped in May 2009, officially "due to the lack of/minimal interest" (source: official, now closed Yahoo group) before any (beta) drivers were released. There are also no Linux drivers available.

Separate MIDI drivers, which allowed any MIDI-capable instrument or sequencer program to drive the card, were available for both the ISA and PCI versions of the HardSID.

The HardSID 4U unit has dedicated on-board CPU power, as opposed to the earlier HardSID units. This makes the 4U able to play SID-files with digi-contents at full speed and quality, without eating up the host computer's CPU power. The older revisions depended on the player software's emulation to accomplish this, due to the lack of an on-board CPU or memory buffer. The result was virtually always a very high CPU load when playing digi-tunes.

1.12.1   External links

- The Official HardSID Facebook page

- HardSID Linux driver

- HardSID support for sidplay 2.x

- Simon White's SID Player Music Library V2 - includes sidgroups a SID voice selection program

- sidplay2/w - Cycle exact emulation by Simon White with support for HardSID; user interface by Adam Lorentzon

- ACID64 Player - A cycle exact SID player with support for all HardSID devices by Wilfred Bos

1.13   List of audio programming languages

This is a **list of audio programming languages** including languages optimized for sound production, algorithmic composition, and sound synthesis.

- abc, a language for notating music using the ASCII character set

- Alda, a music programming language for musicians

- ChucK, strongly timed, concurrent, and on-the-fly audio programming language

- Cmix, Real-time Cmix, a MUSIC-N synthesis language somewhat similar to Csound

- CMusic

- Common Lisp Music (CLM), a music synthesis and signal processing package in the Music V family

- Csound, a MUSIC-N synthesis language released under the LGPL with many available unit generators

- Extempore, a live-coding environment which borrows a core foundation from the Impromptu environment

- FAUST, Functional Audio Stream, a functional compiled language for efficient real-time audio signal processing

- Hierarchical Music Specification Language (HMSL), optimized more for music than synthesis, developed in the 1980s in Forth

- Impromptu, a Scheme language environment for Mac OS X capable of sound and video synthesis, algorithmic composition, and 2D and 3D graphics programming

- jMusic

- JSyn

- Kyma (sound design language)

- Max/MSP The "lingua franca" for developing interactive music performance software

- Music Macro Language (MML), often used to produce chiptune music in Japan

- MUSIC-N, includes versions I, II, III, IV, IV-B, IV-BF, V, 11, and 360

- Nyquist

- OpenMusic

- Patchblocks

- Pure Data

- Reaktor

- Structured Audio Orchestra Language (SAOL), part of the MPEG-4 Structured Audio standard

- SuperCollider

- SynthEdit

- Vvvv

1.13.1 See also

- Comparison of audio synthesis environments

- List of music software

1.14 Module file

For other uses, see Module.

Module files (**MOD music**, **tracker music**) are a family of music file formats originating from the MOD file format on Amiga systems used in the late 1980s. Those who produce these files (using the software called trackers) and listen to them, form the worldwide **MOD scene**, a part of the demoscene subculture.

The mass interchange of "MOD music" or "tracker music" (music stored in module files created with trackers) evolves from early FIDO networks. Many websites host large numbers of these files, the most comprehensive of them being the Mod Archive.

Nowadays most module files, including ones in zipped form, are supported by most popular media players such as Winamp, VLC, Foobar2000, Amarok, Exaile and many others (mainly due to inclusion of common playback libraries such as libmodplug for gstreamer).

1.14.1 Structure

Module files store several "patterns" or "pages" of music data in a form similar to that of a spreadsheet. These patterns contain note numbers, instrument numbers, and controller messages.[1] The number of notes that can be played simultaneously depends on how many "tracks" there are per pattern. They also contain digitally recorded samples as well as coding for sequencing the samples in playback.[2] The programs that are used to create these files provide composers with the means to control and manipulate sound samples in almost limitless ways to produce music.

Module files are also referred to as "tracker modules", and the process of composing modules is known as tracking.

A disadvantage of module files is that there is no real standard specification in how the modules should be played back properly, which may result in modules sounding slightly different in different players. This is mostly due to effects that can be applied to the samples in the module file and how the authors of different players choose to implement them.[3]

1.14.2 History

The worldwide MOD scene, closely related to the Demoscene, started on the Commodore 64 with SID music used on video game cracks.[4][5] It spread to the Amiga and eventually to the PC.[6] Soon after Amiga computers with the Paula sound chip were introduced, Karsten Obarski wrote the sequencer software Ultimate Soundtracker in 1987 which was based on the tracker concept invented by Chris Hülsbeck.[7][8][9] Ultimate Soundtracker was a commercial product, but soon shareware clones such as NoiseTracker and ProTracker, being direct descendants from the original Soundtracker code, appeared as well. Protracker ran on newer versions of AmigaOS and was very stable to boot. Some trackers such as OctaMED took advantage of tricks like software mixing to give the artist more flexibility in song writing.[10] Modules were originally intended to be used in video games, but the demoscene and musicians started composing them for demos. Coincidentally the demoscene, being full of talented programmers and musicians, pushed trackers, and the MOD format quickly became one of the most popular music formats across the home computer platforms.[6] Among the reasons for the format's success was its comparably low CPU overhead (on the Amiga it was possible to process all the music in the video memory, skipping the CPU altogether), small file sizes and relatively good sound quality, which mostly depended on the amount of storage that could be used for the music, rather than the capabilities of the format itself.[11]

Many demosceners wrote their own trackers with features not present in Ultimate Soundtracker, and musicians took full advantage of these features, creating music as efficient as the code in demos. As technology advanced, computer audio matured and, with MS-DOS, PCs had even more capability. Many PCs used Sound Blaster and Gravis Ultrasound cards which allowed for many audio channels. As the demoscene moved onto these new computers, they would write new trackers for them. FastTracker 2 was one such program. Written by two members of the demogroup Triton, it introduced a new format called XM or extended module.[12][13] FT2 was able to use 32 channels at once and added many useful commands and other features. It was not alone however, Scream Tracker had a different layout that some preferred and had support for FM synthesis on cards that included an OPL 2/3/4 chip. Impulse Tracker, which based its interface off of Scream Tracker's, further advanced module composing adding filters and 64 channels of audio and introduced a new format called IT.[14]

1.14.3 Scene

Tracker music is characteristic in that it is made by hand, distributed as open source, and executed in real-time.[15][16] Composers adapt to the technical limitations as well as the cultural conditions, where resources were often reserved for the visual content.[17] The process of composing module files, known as tracking, is a highly creative and skillful activity that involves a much closer contact with musical sound than conventional composition, because every aspect of each sonic event is coded, from pitch and duration to exact volume, panning, and laying in numerous effects such as echo, tremolo and fades.[18] Once the module file is finished, it is released to the tracker community. The composer uploads the newly composition to one or more of several sites where module files are archived, making it available to his or her audience, who will download the file on their own computers. By encoding textual information within each module file, composers maintain contact with their audiences and with one another by including their email addresses, greetings to fans and other composers, and virtual signatures.[18]

Although trackers can be considered to have some technical limitations, it does not prevent a creative individual from producing music that is indiscernible from professionally created music.[19] Many tracker musicians gained international prominence within MOD software users and some of them went on to work for high-profile video game studios, or began to appear on record labels.[20][9] Notable artists include Andrew Sega, Jeroen Tel, Bjørn Lynne, Alexander Brandon, Skaven, Purple Motion, KFMF, 4mat, Jesper Kyd, Brothomstates, Elwood, Markus Kaarlonen, Michiel van den Bos and Dan Gardopée. Deadmau5 and Erez Eisen of Infected Mushroom have both used Impulse Tracker in their early career.[21][22]

1.14.4 Music disk

Music disk, or musicdisk, is a term used by the demoscene to describe a collection of songs made on a computer. They are essentially the computer equivalent of an album. A music disk is typically packaged in the form of a program with a custom user interface, so the listener does not need other software to play the songs.[23] The "disk" part of the term comes from the fact that music disks were once made to fit on a single floppy disk, so they could be easily distributed at demo parties. On modern platforms, music disks are usually downloaded to a hard disk drive.

Amiga music disks usually consist of MOD files, while PC music disks often contain multichannel formats such as XM or IT. Music disks are also common on the Commodore 64 and Atari ST, where they use their own native formats.

Related terms include *music pack*, which can refer to a demoscene music collection that does not include its own player, and *chipdisk*, a music disk containing only chiptunes, which have become popular on the PC given the large size of MP3 music disks.

1.14.5 Popular formats

Each module file format builds on concepts introduced in its predecessors.

Sound/Pro/Noisetracker module (file extension .mod, or mod. prefix on Amiga systems)
This is the original module format. Uses inverse-frequency note numbers. 4 voices, with up to 32 in later variations of the format. Pattern data is not packed. Instruments are simple volume levels; samples and instruments correspond one-to-one. 15 instruments in the original Soundtracker, 31 in later trackers. This format was originally created to be easily playable with the Amiga hardware, since it was equipped with a four-channel DAC. The CPU has to do very little work to play these modules on an Amiga. Many games utilize this format - often with small player programs included. In the early 1990s, usage of this format with games was widespread across platforms, with games on PC and Nintendo systems utilizing it, as well.

The original .mod extension is actually not a suffix on the Amiga, but a prefix; mod.* is the standard naming convention on the Amiga, and same prefix standard is used in basically all the other various sample/synth-trackers ever made for the Amiga - Art of Noise, AHX/THX, Musicline, Startrekker, FutureComposer, SidMon, Brian Postma's SoundMon etc. The majority of the "oldschool format"-players for Windows, Linux, Mac OS etc. will, when trying to load an "original" mod.*-file (or ahx.*, bp.*, fc14.* and so on), simply not play it due not analysing the file to determine the type - they **only** check for a filename extension as a **suffix**. Simply renaming the file from "mod.filename" to "filename.mod" is usually a sufficient workaround.

Oktalyzer (originated on Amiga computers) This was an early effort to bring 8 channel sound to the Amiga.

Later replayers have improved on the sound quality attainable from these modules by more demanding mixing technologies.

MED/OctaMED (originated on Amiga computers)
This format is very similar to sound/pro/noisetracker, but the way the data is stored is different. MED was not a direct clone of SoundTracker, and had different features and file formats. OctaMED was an 8-channel version of MED, which eventually evolved into OctaMED Soundstudio (which offers 128-channel sound, optional synth sounds, MIDI support and lots of other high-end features).

AHX (originated on Amiga computers) This format is a synth-tracker. There are no samples in the module file, rather descriptions of how to synthesize the required sound. This results in very small audio files (AHX modules are typically 1k-4k in size), and a very characteristic sound. AHX is designed for music with chiptune sound. The AHX tracker requires Kickstart 2.0 and 2 mb RAM memory.

.s3m (originated in ScreamTracker version 3 for PC)
Up to 16 or more voices. Samples can specify any playback frequency for middle C. Simple packing of pattern data. Introduction of several new controllers and a dedicated "volume column" in each voice to replace volume controllers. Predictable support for stereo panning and AdLib FM synthesis instruments (although the latter is rarely supported in playback software).[24]

.xm (originated in Fast Tracker) Introduction of instruments with volume and panning envelopes. Basic pattern compression, no sample compression. Added ping-pong loops to samples.[24]

.it (originated in Impulse Tracker) New Note Actions let the previous note in a track fade out on top of the next note (providing greater effective polyphony). Instruments can now share a sample. Adds some new effects such as a resonant filter. Better pattern compression. Added sample compression. Added sustain loops to samples.[24]

.mo3 Created by Ian Luck to use MP3/Ogg compressed samples

.mtm MultiTracker modules

.umx Unreal/Tournament music package. This is actually a standard Unreal package file that wraps one .mod, .s3m, .it or .xm file so it can be accessed from within the game.[25]

1.14.6 Software module file players and converters

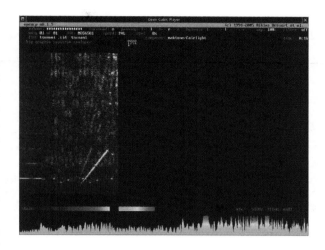

OpenCubic Player, *example of a typical MOD player with STFT spectrum audio visualization*

Main article: List of audio trackers

Many of the listed software use the modplug engine from the open source multimedia framework gstreamer.[26]

Players

- XMPlay (Windows), from Un4seen Developments, which also created the MO3 format

- OZMod (Java, cross-platform, free source code)

- Winamp (Windows)

- AIMP

- BZR Player (Windows)

- foobar2000 (Windows) (with foo_dumb plugin)

- Mod4Win (Windows), one of the first Windows Mod player

- K-Multimedia Player (Windows)

- Quintessential Player (Windows)

- Sonique (Windows)

- VLC (Linux, Mac OS X, Windows)

- Audacious (Linux)

- XMMS and XMMS2 (Linux/UNIX)

- Totem (Linux/UNIX)

- Music Player Daemon (Linux/UNIX)

- DeaDBeeF (Linux/UNIX, Android)

- MikMod (Linux/UNIX/DOS)

- Neutron Music Player[27] (Android OS, BlackBerry 10/PlayBook)

- Modo Computer Music Player (Android OS)

See also: list of Amiga music format players

Converters and trackers

- Cog (Mac OS X)

- Amarok (Linux/UNIX)

- Audacious (Linux/UNIX)

- ModPlug Tracker (Windows)

- TiMidity (Linux/UNIX)

- OctaMED (Amiga)

- Renoise (Windows)

- Unix Amiga Delitracker Emulator (Linux/UNIX)

1.14.7   See also

- Tracker

- Category:Tracker musicians

- Demoscene

- TraxWeekly

- Static Line

1.14.8   References

[1] Darren Irvine, Jeremy S Rice, Radix, SquareMeister, Kupan, Pulse, Ilpo Karkkainen, ToalNkor, Stereoman, Dan Nicholson, Greebo, MAZ, Barry Nathan, Rich "Akira" Pizor, Novus, Louis "Farmer" Gorenfeld, Dr. Avalance, Rubz, Toodeloo, Linus Walleji, Kosmos, Trinity, Ganja Man, Airon, Vitor Pinho, Spatulaman, Sir Garbagetruck, Bonehead, Kevin Krebs, T-Jay, MaXimizer, phume, Captain Paradox, Asatur V. Nazarian, XRQ, DNATrance. "The Tracker's Handbook". Archived from the original on 6 June 2015. Retrieved 5 June 2015.

[2] Williams, Perry; Vessey, Chris (21 October 1996). "MIDI and home computer music composition and performance". University of Prince Edward Island. Archived from the original on 23 May 2015. Retrieved 23 May 2015.

[3] Karen Collins; Bill Kapralos; Holly Tessler. *The Oxford Handbook of Interactive Audio*. Oxford. p. 624. ISBN 978-0-19-979722-6. Retrieved 2014-09-13.

[4] Weasel, Wild (9 November 2012). "Introduction to the Demoscene". Hardcore Gaming 101. Retrieved 6 December 2012.

[5] "The History of Sound Cards and Computer Game Music". MacGateWay. July 13, 2012. Retrieved 2014-09-08.

[6] "Tracker music". Giant Bomb. Retrieved 2014-09-08.

[7] Karen Collins (August 2008). *Game Sound: An Introduction to the History, Theory, and Practice of Video Game Music and Sound Design*. MIT Press. p. 216. ISBN 978-0-262-03378-7. Retrieved 6 December 2014.

[8] Olga Guriunova. *Art Platforms and Cultural Production on the Internet*. Routledge. p. 162. ISBN 978-0-415-89310-7. Retrieved 2014-09-13.

[9] Karen Collins (12 May 2008). *From Pac-Man to Pop Music: Interactive Audio in Games and New Media* (Kindle ed.). Ashgate Publishing. p. 250. ISBN 978-0-754-66200-6. Retrieved 6 December 2014.

[10] SOS (May 1997). "RBF Software Octamed Soundstudio. The release of this tracker is welcome news for Amiga users, but it's also a glimpse of things to come on the PC platform. Amiga expert PAUL OVERAA puts the package through its paces". Sound on Sound. Retrieved 6 December 2014.

[11] Sfetcu, Nicolae (7 May 2014). *The Music Sound*. Retrieved 17 December 2014.

[12] Triton Productions (1996). "Fast Tracker v2.08. "In a dream we are connected siamese twins at the wrist"" (PDF). Under World Digital Publishing. Retrieved 6 December 2014.

[13] Ranjan Parekh (2006). *Principles of Multimedia*. Tata McGraw-Hill. p. 727. ISBN 978-0-070-58833-2. Retrieved 6 December 2014.

[14] Lim, Jeffrey (22 March 2014). "20 Years of Impulse Tracker, Part 2". Jeffrey Lim's blog. Retrieved 6 December 2014.

[15] Peter Moormann. *Music and Game: Perspectives on a Popular Alliance*. Springer VS. p. 223. ISBN 978-3-531-18913-0. Retrieved 2014-09-13.

[16] Leonard, Andrew (29 April 1999). "Mod love. With their ears, their computers and a little code, "mod trackers" build their own worlds of sound". *Salon*. Salon Media Group. Archived from the original on 20 May 2015. Retrieved 20 February 2015.

[17] Weasel, Wild (6 November 2011). "Demoscene". Hardcoregaming101. Retrieved 2014-09-03.

[18] Rene T. A. Lysloff; Jr. Leslie C. Gay; Andrew Ross. *Music and Technoculture*. Wesleyan University Press. p. 352. ISBN 978-0819565143. Retrieved 2014-09-13.

[19] "Demoscene: Interview with Romeo Knight!". OpenBytes. 17 October 2010. Retrieved 2014-09-04.

[20] Kopstein, Joshua (10 April 2012). "A brief video history of the demoscene in memory of Commodore boss Jack Tramiel". *The Verge*. Vox Media. Retrieved 21 August 2014.

[21] Burns, Todd L. (September 30, 2008). "Deadmau5: It's complicated". *Resident Advisor*. Retrieved September 17, 2014.

[22] Levine, Mike (September 1, 2009). "Geeking Out With Infected Mushroom". *Electronic Musician*. Retrieved September 17, 2014.

[23] Driscoll, Kevin; Diaz, Joshua (2009). "Endless loop: A brief history of chiptunes". Transformative Works and Cultures. Archived from the original on 25 May 2015. Retrieved 23 May 2015.

[24] Matsuoka, Claudio (2007-11-04). "Tracker History Graphing Project". helllabs.org. Retrieved 2011-01-29. *Tracker History Graph*

[25] Composing Music for Unreal - Alexander Brandon, *epicgames.com* (1999)

[26] GStreamer Bad Plugins 0.10 Plugins Reference Manual

[27] "Neutron Music Player". Retrieved September 11, 2014.

1.14.9 Further reading

- Leonard, Andrew (29 April 1999). "Mod love — With their ears, their computers and a little code, "mod trackers" build their own worlds of sound". *Salon*. Salon Media Group.

- Rene T. A. Lysloff; Jr. Leslie C. Gay; Andrew Ross (29 October 2003). *Music and Technoculture*. Wesleyan University Press. p. 352. ISBN 978-0819565143.

- Ratliff, Brendan (September 2007). "Why did freely shared, tracked music in the 1990's computer demoscene survive the arrival of the MP3 age?" (PDF). University of Newcastle upon Tyne.

- Brandon, Alexander (9 May 2015). "From The Expert - MODs and the Demoscene". Original Sound Version.

1.14.10 External links

- The Mod Archive

- Amiga Music Preservation

- The Tracker's Handbook

1.15 MOS Technology SID

MOS Technology SIDs. The right chip is a 6581 from MOS Technology, known at the time as the Commodore Semiconductor Group (CSG.) The left chip is an 8580, also from MOS Technology. The numbers 0488 and 3290 are in WWYY form, i.e. the chips were produced week 4 1988 and week 32 1990. The last number is assumed to be a batch number.

The MOS Technology 6581/8580 **SID** (**Sound Interface Device**) is the built-in Programmable Sound Generator chip of Commodore's CBM-II, Commodore 64, Commodore 128 and Commodore MAX Machine home computers. It was one of the first sound chips of its kind to be included in a home computer prior to the digital sound revolution.

Together with the VIC-II graphics chip, the SID was instrumental in making the C64 the best-selling computer in history, and is partly credited for initiating the demoscene.

The SID has U.S. Patent 4,677,890, which was filed on February 27, 1983, and issued on July 7, 1987. The patent expired on July 7, 2004.

1.15.1 Design process

The SID was devised by engineer Robert "Bob" Yannes, who later co-founded the Ensoniq digital synthesizer company. Yannes headed a team that included himself, two technicians and a CAD operator, who designed and completed the chip in five months, in the latter half of 1981. Yannes was inspired by previous work in the synthesizer industry and was not impressed by the current state of computer sound chips. Instead, he wanted a high-quality instrument chip, which is the reason why the SID has features like the envelope generator, previously not found in home computer sound chips.[1][2]

> I thought the sound chips on the market, including those in the Atari computers, were primitive and obviously had been designed by people who knew nothing about music.[2]
>
> — Robert Yannes, *On the Edge: The Spectacular Rise and Fall of Commodore*

Emphasis during chip design was on high-precision frequency control, and the SID was originally designed to have 32 independent voices, sharing a common oscillator.[2] However these features could not be finished in time, so instead the mask work for a certain working oscillator was simply replicated three times across the chip's surface, creating three voices each with its own oscillator. Another feature that was not incorporated in the final design was a frequency look-up table for the most common musical notes, a feature that was dropped because of space limitations.[3] The support for an audio input pin was a feature Yannes added without asking, even though this had no practical use in a computer, although it enabled the chip to be used as a simple effect processor. The masks were produced in 7-micrometer technology to gain a high yield; the state of the art at the time was 6-micrometer technologies.[3]

The chip, like the first product using it (the Commodore 64), was finished in time for the Consumer Electronics Show in the first weekend of January 1982. Even though Yannes was partly displeased with the result, his colleague Charles Winterble said: "This thing is already 10 times better than anything out there and 20 times better than it needs to be."[4]

The specifications for the chip were not used as a blueprint. Rather, they were written as the development work progressed, and not all planned features made it into the final product. Yannes claims he had a feature-list of which three quarters made it into the final design. This is the reason why some of the specifications for the first version (6581) were accidentally incorrect. The later revision (8580) was revised to match the specification. For example, the 8580 expanded on the ability to perform a logical AND between two waveforms, something that the 6581 could only do in a somewhat limited and unintuitive manner. Another feature that differs between the two revisions is the filter: the 6581 version is far away from the specification.

1.15.2 Manufacturing, remarking, and forgery

Since 6581 and 8580 SID ICs are no longer produced, they have become highly sought after. In late 2007, various defective chips started appearing on eBay as supposedly "new".[5] All of these remarked SIDs have a defective filter, but some also have defective channels/noise generators, and some are completely dead. The remarked chips are assumed to either be factory rejects from back when the chip was still produced, or possibly 'reject pulls' from one of the chip pulling operations which were used to supply the chips used in the Elektron SIDStation and the HardSID cards. Fake SID chips have also been supplied to unwitting buyers from unscrupulous manufacturers in China; the supplied chips are laser-etched with completely bogus markings, and the chip inside the package is not a SID at all.[6]

1.15.3 Features

- three separately programmable independent audio oscillators (8 octave range, approximately 16 - 4000 Hz)

- four different waveforms per audio oscillator (sawtooth, triangle, pulse, noise)

- one multi mode filter featuring low-pass, high-pass and band-pass outputs with 6 dB/oct (bandpass) or 12 dB/octave (lowpass/highpass) rolloff. The different filter modes are sometimes combined to produce additional timbres, for instance a notch-reject filter.

- three attack/decay/sustain/release (ADSR) volume controls, one for each audio oscillator.

- three ring modulators.

- oscillator sync for each audio oscillator.

- two 8-bit A/D converters (typically used for game control paddles, but later also used for a mouse)

- external audio input (for sound mixing with external signal sources)

- random number/modulation generator

1.15.4 Technical details

The SID is a mixed-signal integrated circuit, featuring both digital and analog circuitry. All control ports are digital, while the output ports are analog. The SID features three-voice synthesis, where each voice may use one of at least five different waveforms: pulse wave (with variable duty

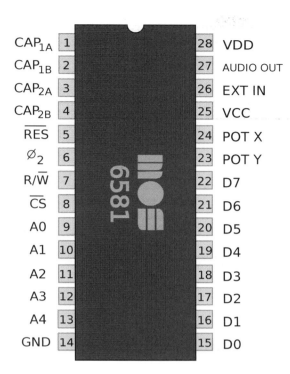

6581/6582/8580R5 Pin configuration

cycle), triangle wave, sawtooth wave, pseudorandom noise (called white noise in documentation), and certain complex/combined waveforms when multiple waveforms are selected simultaneously. A voice playing Triangle waveform may be ring-modulated with one of the other voices, where the triangle waveform's bits are inverted when the modulating voice's msb is set, producing a discontinuity and change of direction with the Triangle's ramp. Oscillators may also be hard-synced to each other, where the synced oscillator is reset whenever the syncing oscillator's msb raises.

Each voice may be routed into a common, digitally controlled analog 12 dB/octave multimode filter, which is constructed with aid of external capacitors to the chip. The filter has lowpass, bandpass and highpass outputs, which can be individually selected for final output amplification via master volume register. Using a combined state of lowpass and highpass results in a notch (or inverted bandpass) output.[7] The programmer may vary the filter's cut-off frequency and resonance. An external audio-in port enables external audio to be passed through the filter.

The ring modulation, filter, and programming techniques such as arpeggio (rapid cycling between 2 or more frequencies to make chord-like sounds) together produce the characteristic feel of SID music.

Due to imperfect manufacturing technologies of the time and poor separation between the analog and digital parts

of the chip, the 6581's output (before the amplifier stage) was always slightly biased from the zero level. By adjusting the amplifier's gain through the main 4-bit volume register, this bias could be modulated as PCM, resulting in a "virtual" fourth channel allowing 4-bit digital sample playback. The glitch was known and used from an early point on, first by Electronic Speech Systems to produce sampled speech in games such as Impossible Mission (1983, Epyx) and Ghostbusters (1984, Activision). The first instance of samples being used in actual musical compositions was by Martin Galway in Arkanoid (1987, Imagine), although he had copied the idea from an earlier drum synthesizer package called Digidrums. The length of sampled sound playback was limited first by memory and later technique. Kung Fu Fighting (1986), a popular early sample, has a playback length measured in seconds. c64mp3 (2010) and Cubase64 (2010) demonstrate playback lengths measured in minutes. Also, it was hugely CPU intensive - one had to output the samples very fast (in comparison to the speed of the 6510 CPU).

The better manufacturing technology in the 8580 used in the later revisions of Commodore 64C and the Commodore 128DCR caused the bias to almost entirely disappear, causing the digitized sound samples to become very quiet. Fortunately, the volume level could be mostly restored with either a hardware modification (biasing the audio-in pin), or more commonly a software trick involving using the Pulse waveform to intentionally recreate the required bias. The software trick generally renders one voice temporarily unusable, although clever musical compositions can make this problem less noticeable. An excellent example of this quality improvement noticeably reducing a sampled channel can be found in the introduction to Electronic Arts' game Skate or Die (1987). The guitar riff played is all but missing when played on the Commodore 64c or the Commodore 128.

At the X'2008 demo party, a completely new method of playing digitized samples was unveiled. The method allows for an unprecedented four (software-mixed) channels of 8-bit samples with optional filtering on top of all samples, as well as two ordinary SID sound channels.[8][9] The method works by resetting the oscillator using the waveform generator test bit, quickly ramping up the new waveform with the Triangle waveform selected, and then disabling all waveforms, resulting in the DAC continuing to output the last value---which is the desired sample. This continues for as long as two scanlines, which is ample time for glitch-free, arbitrary sample output. It is however more CPU-intensive than the 4-bit volume register DAC trick described above. Because the filtering in a SID chip is applied after the waveform generators, samples produced this way can be filtered normally.

The original manual for the SID mentions that if several waveforms are enabled at the same time, the result will be a binary AND between them. What happens in reality is that the input to the waveform DAC pins receive several waveforms at once. For instance, the Triangle waveform is made with a separate XOR circuit and a shift-to-left circuit. The top bit drives whether the XOR circuit inverts the accumulator value seen by the DAC. Thus, enabling triangle and sawtooth simultaneously causes adjacent accumulator bits in the DAC input to mix. (The XOR circuit does not come to play because it is always disabled whenever the sawtooth waveform is selected.) The pulse waveform is built by joining all the DAC bits together via a long strip of polysilicon, connected to the pulse control logic that digitally compares current accumulator value to the pulse width value. Thus, selecting the pulse waveform together with any other waveform causes every bit on the DAC to partially mix, and the loudness of the waveform is affected by the state of the pulse.

The noise generator is implemented as a 23-bit-length linear feedback shift register (Feedback polynomial: $x^{22}+x^{17}+1$).[10][11] When using noise waveform simultaneously with any other waveform, the pull-down via waveform selector tends to quickly reduce the XOR shift register to 0 for all bits that are connected to the output DAC. As the zeroes shift in the register when the noise is clocked, and no 1-bits are produced to replace them, a situation can arise where the XOR shift register becomes fully zeroed. Luckily, the situation can be remedied by using the waveform control test bit, which in that condition injects one 1-bit into the XOR shift register. Some musicians are also known to use noise's combined waveforms and test bit to construct unusual sounds.

The 6581 and 8580 differ from each other in several ways. The original 6581 was manufactured using the older NMOS process, which used 12V DC to operate. The 6581 is very sensitive to static discharge and if they weren't handled properly the filters would stop working, explaining the reason of the great quantity of dead 6581s in the market. The 8580 was made using the HMOS-II process, which requires less power (9V DC), and therefore makes the IC run cooler. The 8580 is thus far more durable than the 6581. Also, due to stabler waveform generators, the bit-mixing effects are less noticeable and thus the combined waveforms come close to matching the original SID specification (which stated that they will be combined as a binary AND). The filter is also very different between the two models, with the 6581 cutoff range being a relatively straight line on a log scale, while the cutoff range on the 8580 is a straight line on a linear scale, and is close to the designers' actual specifications. Additionally, a better separation between the analog and the digital circuits made the 8580's output less noisy and distorted. The noise in 6xxx-series systems can be reduced by disconnecting the audio-in pin.

The consumer version of the 8580 was rebadged the 6582, even though the die on the chip is identical to a stock 8580 chip, including the '8580R5' mark. Dr. Evil Laboratories used it in their SID Symphony expansion cartridge (sold to Creative Micro Designs in 1991), and it was used in a few other places as well, including one PC sound-card.

Despite its documented shortcomings, many SID musicians prefer the flawed 6581 chip over the corrected 8580 chip. The main reason for this is that the filter produces strong distortion that is sometimes used to produce simulation of instruments such as a distorted electric guitar. Also, the highpass component of the filter was mixed in 3 dB attenuated compared to the other outputs, making the sound more bassy. In addition to nonlinearities in filter, the D/A circuitry used in the waveform generators produces yet more additional distortion that made its sound richer in character.

Revisions

6581R1 produced in 1982

6581 produced in 1982

No instances reading "6581 R1" ever reached the market. In fact, Yannes has stated that "[the] SID chip came out pretty well the first time, it made sound. Everything we needed for the show was working after the second pass." High-resolution photos of Charles Winterble's prototype C64 show the markings "MOS 6581 2082", the last number being a date code indicating that his prototype SID chip was produced during the 20th week of 1982, which would be within 6 days of May 17, 1982.

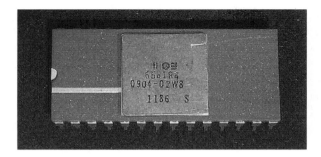

6581R4 CDIP produced in 1986

6582 produced in 1986

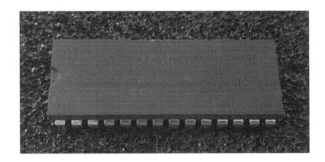

6582A produced in 1989

6582A produced in 1992

These are the known revisions of the various SID chips: (datecodes are in WWYY w=week y=year format)

- 6581 R1 - Prototype, only appeared on the CES machines and development prototypes, has a datecode of

8580R5 produced 1986 in the U.S.

4981 to 0882 or so. Has the full 12 bit filter cutoff range. An unknown number were produced, probably between 50 and 100 chips. All are ceramic packages.

- 6581 R2 - Will say "6581" only on the package. Filter cutoff range was reduced to 11 bits and the MSB bit disconnected/forced permanently on, but is still on the die.The filter is leaky at some ranges and they tend to run hotter than other sid revisions. Made from 1182 until at least 1483. First 10 weeks or so of chips have ceramic packages (these usually appear on engineering prototypes but a few are on sold machines), the rest have plastic packages.

- 6581 R3 - Will say "6581" only, "6581 R3" or "6581 CBM" on the package. Had a minor change to the protection/buffering of the input pins. No changes were made to the filter section. Made from before 2083 until 1386 or so. The 6581R3 since around the week 47 of 1985 made in the Phillipines use the HMOS HC-30 degree silicon though the manufacturing process remained NMOS.

- 6581 R4 - Will say "6581 R4" on the package. Silicon grade changed to HMOS-II "HC-30" grade, though the manufacturing process for the chip remained NMOS. Produced from 4985 until at least 2590.

- 6581 R4 AR - Will say "6581 R4 AR" on the package. Minor adjustment to the silicon grade, no die change from R4. Produced from around 1986 (week 22) until at least the year 1992.

- 6582 - Will say "6582" on the package. Typically produced around the year 1986 in Hong Kong.

- 6582 A - Will say "6582A" (or "6582 A") on the package. Typically produced around the years 1989, 1990 and 1992 in the Philippines.

- 8580 R5 - Will say "8580R5" on the package. Produced from the years 1986 to 1993 in the Philippines, Hong Kong and in the US.

Some of these chips are marked "CSG" ("Commodore Semiconductor Group") and the Commodore Logo, while others are marked with "MOS". This includes chips produced during the same week (and thus, receiving the same date code), indicating that at least two different factory lines were in operation during that week. The markings of chips varied by factory and even by line within a factory throughout most of the manufacturing run of the chip.

1.15.5 Game audio

The majority of games produced for the Commodore 64 made use of the SID chip, with sounds ranging from simply clicks and beeps to complex musical extravaganzas or even entire digital audio tracks.

Well known composers of game music for this chip are Martin Galway, known for many titles, including *Wizball*, and Rob Hubbard, known for titles such as *ACE 2*, *Commando*, *Delta*, *International Karate*, *IK+*, and *Monty on the Run*. Other noteworthies include Jeroen Tel (*Cybernoid* and *Myth*), David Dunn (*Finders Keepers* and *Flight Path 737*) and Chris Hülsbeck, whose composition career started with the SID but has spanned nearly every kind of computer music and other synthesizers since.

1.15.6 Emulation

The fact that many enthusiasts prefer the real chip sound over software emulators has led to several recording projects aiming to preserve the authentic sound of the SID chip for modern hardware.

The sid.oth4 project[12] has over 380 songs of high quality MP3 available recorded on hardsid hardware and the SOASC= project[13] have the entire High Voltage SID Collection release 49 (over 35,000 songs) recorded in from real Commodore 64s in high quality mp3. Both projects emphasize the importance of preserving the authentic sound of the SID chip.

1.15.7 Software emulation

- In 1989 on the Amiga computer, the demo "The 100 Most Remembered C64 Tunes" and later the PlaySID application was released, developed by Per Håkan Sundell and Ron Birk. This was one of the first attempts to emulate the SID in software only, and also introduced the file format for representing songs made on the C64 using the SID chip. This later spawned the creation of similar applications for other platforms as well as the creation of a community of people fascinated by SID music, resulting in *The High Voltage SID Collection* which contains over 45,000 SID tunes.

A SID file contains the 6510 program code and associated data needed to replay the music on the SID. The SID files have the MIME media type audio/prs.sid.

The actual file format of a SID file has had several versions. The older standard is PSID (current version V3). The newer standard, RSID, is intended for music that requires a more complete emulation of the Commodore 64 hardware.

The SID file format is not a native format used on the Commodore 64 or 128, but a format specifically created for emulator-assisted music players such as *PlaySID* , *Sidplay* and JSidplay2. However, there are loaders like *RealSID-Play* and converters such as PSID64 that make it possible to play a substantial portion of SID files on original Commodore computers.

- SIDPlayer, developed by Christian Bauer and released in 1996 for the BeOS operating system, was the first SID emulator to replicate the filter section of the SID chip using a second-order Infinite impulse response filter as an approximation.

- In June 1998, a cycle-based SID emulator engine called reSID became available. The all-software emulator, available with C++ source code, is licensed under the GPL by the author, Dag Lem. In 2008, Antti Lankila significantly improved the filter and distortion simulation in reSID.[14] The improvements were included in VICE version 2.1 as well.

- In 2007 the JSidplay2 project was released, a pure Java based SID player developed by Ken Händel.

1.15.8 Hardware reimplementations

- In 2008 the HyperSID project is released. HyperSID is a VSTi which acts like a MIDI controller for HyperSID hardware unit (synthesizer based on SID chip) and developed by HyperSynth company.

Hardware Implementations using the SID chip

- In 1989 Innovation Computer developed the Innovation Sound Standard, an IBM PC compatible sound card with a SID chip and a game port. MicroProse promised software support for the card, and Commodore BASIC programs that used SID required little conversion to run on GW-BASIC.[15]

- In 1997, an electronic musical instrument utilizing the SID chip as its synthesis engine was released. It is called the SidStation, built around the 6581 model SID chip (as opposed to the newer 8580),[16] and it's produced by Swedish company Elektron. As the SID chip had been discontinued for years, Elektron allegedly bought up almost all of the remaining stock. In 2004, Elektron released the Monomachine pattern-based sequencer with optional keyboard. The Monomachine contains several synthesis engines, including an emulated 6581 oscillator using a DSP.

- In 1999 HardSID, another PC sound card, was released. The card uses from one to four SID chips and allows a PC to utilize the sound capabilities of the chip directly, instead of by emulation via generic sound cards (e.g. SoundBlaster).

- The Catweasel from German company Individual Computers, a PCI + Zorro multiformat floppy disk controller and digital joystick adapter for PCs, Macs, and Amigas, includes a hardware SID option, i.e. an option to insert one or two real SID chips in a socket for use when playing .MUS files.

- The MIDIbox SID is a MIDI-controlled synthesizer which can contain up to eight SID chips. It is a free open source project using a PIC microcontroller. Control of the synthesizer is realized with software or via a control panel with knobs, LEDs, LCD, etc., which may optionally be mounted on a keyboardless Commodore 64 body.

- The Prophet64 is a cartridge for the Commodore 64. It features four separate music applications, mimicking everything from modern sequencers to the Roland 303/909 series. With an optional User Port peripheral, the Prophet64 may synchronized to other equipment using DIN Sync standard (SYNC 24). The website now states "Prophet64 has been replaced with the MSSIAH."

- The MSSIAH is a cartridge for the Commodore 64 that replaces the Prophet64.

- Artist/Hacker Paul Slocum developed the Cynthcart cartridge that enables you to turn your C64 into an analogue synthesizer. The Cynthcart is available through atariage.com.

- The Parallel Port SID Interface allows those with very slim budgets to connect the SID chip to a PC.

- In May 2009 the SID chip was interfaced to the BBC Micro and BBC Master range of computers via the 1 MHz bus allowing music written for the SID chip on the Commodore 64 to be ported and played on the BBC Micro.

- In October 2009 thrashbarg's project interfaced an SID chip to an ATmega8 to play MIDI files on a MOS 6581 SID.

- In March 2010 STG published the SIDBlaster/USB - an open source, open hardware implementation of the SID that connects to (and is powered by) a USB port, using an FTDI chip for the USB interface and a PIC to interface the SID.

- In August 2010 SuperSoniqs published the Playsoniq, a cartridge for MSX computers, with (in addition to other features) a real SID on it, ready to use on any MSX machine.

SID hardware clones

- The SwinSID is hardware emulation of the SID using an Atmel AVR processor, also featuring a real SID player based on the Atmel AVR processor.

- The V-SID 1.0 project (code name SID 6581D, 'D' for digital) from David Amoros was born in 2005. This project is a hardware emulation of the SID chip from the Bob Yannes's interview, datasheets. The V-SID 1.0 engine had been implemented in a FPGA EP1C12 Cyclone from ALTERA, on an ALTIUM development board, and emulates all the characteristics of the original SID, except the filter which is a digital version (IIR filter controlled by a CPU).

- The PhoenixSID 65X81 project (2006) aimed to faithfully create the SID sound using modern hardware. The workings of a SID chip were recreated on an FPGA, based on interviews with the SID's creator, original datasheets, and comparisons with real SID chips. It was distinguished from similar attempts by its use of real analog circuitry instead of emulation for the legendary SID filter. However, the project was discontinued, because George Pantazopoulos, who was the head of this project, died on April 23, 2007, at the age of 29.

- The C64 Direct-to-TV emulates large portions the SID hardware, minus certain features such as (most notably) the filters. It reduces the entire C64 to a small circuit that fits into a joystick while sacrificing some compatibility.

1.15.9   Conventional music

SID sounds and snippets of SID music has been introduced into mainstream music at several occasions:

- In the spring of 1999 Zombie Nation released a remix of game musician David Whittaker's *Lazy Jones* (originally written for the SID in 1984) under the title *Kernkraft 400*. They used an Elektron SidStation for the sound.

- In 2000 8 Bit Weapon acquired a SidStation used on the track "Femmachine SID Mix" as well as for their work for Kraftwerk's "Space Lab" remix on astralwerks records. By 2009 they also added the MSSIAH c64 music workstation cart and began using the MOS 6581R4 & 8580 SID Chips in their music for remixes, TV scores, Video Game Scores, and their own album releases as well as the Sony released ACID loop library "8 Bit Weapon: A Chiptune Odyssey."

- In 2001 Bas Bron sampled the drums from Jeroen Tel's and Reyn Ouwehand's song made for the Rubicon game in the song *You've got my love*.

- In 2007 Timbaland's extensive use of the SidStation led to the 2007 Timbaland plagiarism controversy around his tracks *Block Party* and *Do It* (written for Nelly Furtado).

- SidStation is essential to the sound of Swedish band Machinae Supremacy. The band defines itself as SID metal.

- The Swedish acid ambient artist Carbon Based Lifeforms features a song called MOS 6581 on their 2003 album Hydroponic Garden.

1.15.10   See also

- Commodore 64 Games that Talk - A web page devoted to all the c64 games that contain Voice or Digitized speech, that demonstrates the SID chips ability to speak, as clearly as a real person.

- MOS Technology VIC - the combined graphics and sound chip of the VIC-20

- Atari POKEY

- MOS Technology 8364 "Paula"

- Chiptune

- Sound chip

- The High Voltage SID Collection

- Press Play on Tape, a C64 revival band

- Machinae Supremacy

- 8 Bit Weapon

1.15.11   References

[1] Perry, Tekla S.; Wallich, Paul (March 1985). "Design case history: the Commodore 64" (PDF). *IEEE Spectrum*: 48–58. ISSN 0018-9235. Retrieved 2011-11-12.

[2] Bagnall, Brian (2005). "The Secret Project 1981". *On the Edge - The Spectacular Rise and Fall of Commodore* (1 ed.). Winnipeg, Manitoba: Variant Press. p. 235. ISBN 0-9738649-0-7.

[3] Bagnall, Brian (2005). "The Secret Project 1981". *On the Edge - The Spectacular Rise and Fall of Commodore* (1 ed.). Winnipeg, Manitoba: Variant Press. p. 236. ISBN 0-9738649-0-7.

[4] Bagnall, Brian (2005). "The Secret Project 1981". *On the Edge - The Spectacular Rise and Fall of Commodore* (1 ed.). Winnipeg, Manitoba: Variant Press. p. 237. ISBN 0-9738649-0-7.

[5] http://kevtris.org/Projects/sid/remarked_sids.html   re-marked SIDs

[6] http://www.lemon64.com/forum/viewtopic.php?t=27739. Retrieved 31 January 2014. Missing or empty |title= (help)

[7] "MIDIbox SID V2-User manual".

[8] "New revolutionary C64 music routine unveiled".

[9] "Mixer-SounDemon".

[10] "Sound Interface Device reference".

[11] "Examination of SID noise waveform".

[12] sid.oth4 project, sid.oth4 project

[13] SOASC= project, SOASC= project

[14] "JSIDPlay2: a cross-platform SID player and C64 emulator".

[15] Latimer, Joey (August 1989). "Innovation Sound Standard". *Compute!*. p. 68. Retrieved 11 November 2013.

[16] Revision as of 20:29, 19 May 2009 of "Commodore 64" wikipage

1.15.12   Notes

- Appendix O, "6581 Sound Interface Device (SID) Chip Specifications", of the *Commodore 64 Programmer's Reference Guide* (see the C64 article).

- Bagnall, Brian. *On The Edge: The Spectacular Rise and Fall of Commodore*, pp. 231–238,370–371. ISBN 0-9738649-0-7.

- Commodore 6581 Sound Interface Device (SID) datasheet. October, 1982.

1.15.13   Further reading

- Karen Collins, *"Loops and bloops". Music of the Commodore 64 games*, soundscapes, volume 8, Feb 2006

1.15.14   External links

SID information

- SID in-depth information page

- SID at DMOZ

- The 6581 SID Datasheet

- SID programming info

- MOS 8580 SID die shots

1.16   Music tracker

Music trackers (usually referred to simply as **trackers**) are a type of music sequencer software used to create music. They represent music tracks as an arrangement of discrete musical notes positioned in one of several channels, at discrete chronological positions on a timeline. The file format used for saving songs is called a module file.

A music tracker's musical interface is traditionally numeric: both notes and parameter changes, effects and other commands are entered with the keyboard into a grid of fixed time slots as codes consisting of letters, numbers and hexadecimal digits.[1] Separate *patterns* have independent timelines; a complete song consists of a master list of repeated and concatenated patterns.

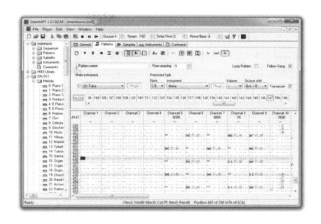

OpenMPT, a modern tracker with a graphical user interface

Later trackers departed from module file limitations and advantages, adding other options both to the sound synthesis (hosting generic synthesizers and effects or MIDI output) and to the sequencing (MIDI input and recording), effectively becoming general purpose sequencers with a different user interface.

1.16.1   History

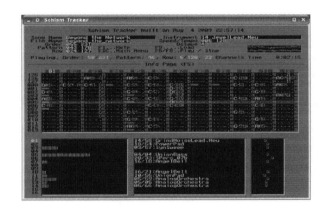

Schism Tracker with a classical ASCII based GUI, typical for trackers of the 1980s and 1990s, playing a module from the video game Bejeweled *by Finnish composer Skaven*

1987: origins on the Amiga

The term tracker derives from *Ultimate Soundtracker*; the first tracker software. *Ultimate Soundtracker* was written by Karsten Obarski and released in 1987 by EAS Computer Technik for the Commodore Amiga.[2] *Ultimate Soundtracker* was a commercial product, but soon shareware clones such as *NoiseTracker* appeared as well. The general concept of step-sequencing samples numerically, as used in trackers, is also found in the Fairlight CMI sampling workstation of the early 1980s. Some early tracker-like programs appeared for the Commodore 64, such as *Sound Monitor*, but these did not feature sample playback, instead playing notes on the computer's internal synthesizer.

The first trackers supported four pitch and volume modulated channels of 8-bit PCM samples, a limitation derived from the Amiga's Paula audio chipset and the commonplace 8SVX format used to store sampled sound. However, since the notes were samples, the limitation was less important than those of synthesizing music chips.[3]

1990s: MS-DOS PC versions

During the 1990s, tracker musicians gravitated to the PC as software production in general from C64 and Amiga platforms to the PC. Although the IBM and compatibles initially lacked the hardware sound processing capabilities of the Amiga, with the advent of the Sound Blaster line from Creative, PC audio slowly began to approach CD Quality (44.1 kHz/16 bit/Stereo) with the release of the SoundBlaster 16.

Another sound card popular on the PC tracker scene was the Gravis Ultrasound, which continued the hardware mixing tradition, with 32 internal channels and onboard memory for sample storage. For a time, it offered unparalleled sound quality and became the choice of discerning tracker musicians. Understanding that the support of tracker music would benefit sales, Gravis gave away some 6000 GUS cards to participants. Coupled with excellent developer documentation, this gesture quickly prompted the GUS to become an integral component of many tracking programs and software. Inevitably, the balance was largely redressed with the introduction of the Sound Blaster AWE32 and its successors, which also featured on-board RAM and wavetable (or sample table) mixing.

Screenshot of Scream Tracker 3.21, a popular Tracker for the PC during the 1990s

The responsibility for audio mixing passed from hardware

to software (the main CPU), which gradually enabled the use of more and more channels. From the typical 4 MOD channels of the Amiga, the limit had moved to 7 with TFMX players and 8, first with Oktalyzer and later with the vastly more popular OctaMED (all Amiga programs), then 32 with ScreamTracker 3 and FastTracker 2 on the PC and on to 64 with Impulse Tracker (PC) and MED SoundStudio (Amiga and later PC).

As such, hardware mixing did not last. As processors got faster and acquired special multimedia processing abilities (e.g. MMX) and companies began to push Hardware Abstraction Layers, like DirectX, the AWE and GUS range became obsolete. DirectX, WDM and, now more commonly, ASIO, deliver high-quality sampled audio irrespective of hardware brand.

There was also a split off from the sample based trackers taking advantage of the OPL2/OPL3 chips of the Sound Blaster series. Adlib Tracker II and many others survive to this day. All Sound Tracker was able to combine both the FM synthesis of the OPL chips and the sample based synthesis of the EMU-8000 chips in the Sound Blaster AWE series of cards as well as MIDI output to any additional hardware of choice.

2000s: Multiple platforms

Tracker music could be found in computer games of the late 1990s and early 2000s, such as the *Unreal series*, *Deus Ex*, *Jazz Jackrabbit* and *Hitman: Codename 47*. Tracker software continues to develop. Some of the early Amiga trackers such as ProTracker, OctaMED have received various updates, mostly for porting to other platforms. ProTracker having resumed development in 2004, with plans for releasing version 5 to Windows and AmigaOS, but only version 4.0 beta 2 for AmigaOS has been released. Other cross-platform trackers include Renoise, MilkyTracker and SunVox.

Buzz, ModPlug Tracker, Renoise, Psycle, and others offer features undreamed-of back in the day (improved signal-to-noise ratios, automation, VST support, internal DSPs and multi-effects, multi I/O cards support etc.).

In 2005, FamiTracker, a tracker for the NES and Famicom, was officially released. As of version 0.5 beta, it is so far the only tracker for the system with full expansion audio support including the Sunsoft5B.

During 2007, Renoise and Modplug Tracker (OpenMPT) were presented in the *Computer Music Magazine* as professional and inexpensive alternative to other music production software.[4]

Adlib Tracker II has been steadily updated since the late 1990s and has become GPL'd on the Google Code Project.

Renoise, a popular tracker in the 2000s and 2010s.

2010s: Current state

Jeskola Buzz Modular is being regularly updated as of September 2012.[5]

As of 2010, Renoise and Modplug Tracker (OpenMPT) are probably the most actively developed tracker and the most long-living project of this kind, started in 2000 and 1997, respectively.

In 2011, DefleMask was released. It is a multi-system Chip-music Tracker, supporting SEGA Genesis, SEGA Master System, Nintendo Game Boy, YAMAHA's SMAF, among other systems, developed by Delek.[6]

In June 2011, an on-line software synthesizer-based tracker called Sonant Live[7] was released. It is different from other trackers in that it runs completely in a web browser.

In January 2015, Adlib Tracker II released its most robust update to date with many new features to control the FM synthesizer chip.

1.16.2 Terminology

See also: Module file

There are several elements common to any tracker program: samples, notes, effects, tracks (or channels), patterns, and orders.

A **sample** is a small digital sound file of an instrument, voice, or other sound effect. Most trackers allow a part of the sample to be looped, simulating a sustain of a note.

A **note** designates the frequency at which the sample is played back. By increasing or decreasing the playback speed of a digital sample, the pitch is raised or lowered, simulating instrumental notes (e.g. C, C#, D, etc.).

An **effect** is a special function applied to a particular note. These effects are then applied during playback through ei-

ther hardware or software. Common tracker effects include volume, portamento, vibrato, retrigger, and arpeggio.

A **track** (or **channel**) is a space where one sample is played back at a time. Whereas the original Amiga trackers only provided four tracks, the hardware limit, modern trackers can mix a virtually unlimited number of channels into one sound stream through software mixing. Tracks have a fixed number of "rows" on which notes and effects can be placed (most trackers lay out tracks in a vertical fashion). Tracks typically contain 64 rows and 16 beats, although the beats and tempo can be increased or decreased to the composer's taste.

A basic drum set could thus be arranged by putting a bass drum at rows 0, 4, 8, 12 etc. of one track and putting some hihat at rows 2, 6, 10, 14 etc. of a second track. Of course bass and hats could be interleaved on the same track, if the samples are short enough. If not, the previous sample is usually stopped when the next one begins. Some modern trackers simulate polyphony in a single track by setting the "new note action" of each instrument to cut, continue, fade out, or release, opening new mixing channels as necessary.

A **pattern** is a group of simultaneously played tracks that represents a full section of the song. A pattern usually represents an even number of measures of music composition.

An **order** is part of a sequence of patterns which defines the layout of a song. Patterns can be repeated across multiple orders to save tracking time and file space.

There are also some tracker-like programs that utilize tracker-style sequencing schemes, while using real-time sound synthesis instead of samples. Many of these programs are designed for creating music for a particular synthesizer chip such as the OPL chips of the Adlib and Sound-Blaster sound cards, or the sound chips of classic home computers.

Tracker music is typically stored in module files where the song data and samples are encapsulated in a single file. Several module file formats are supported by popular music player programs such as Winamp or XMMS. Well-known formats include MOD, MED, S3M, XM and IT.

1.16.3 Use in professional music

The hardcore techno scene has had many releases originally written using trackers and released on CD and vinyl.[8] Notable artists include Nasenbluten, Noisekick and Deadmau5.[9][10][11]

1.16.4 List of music trackers

This is a selected list of music trackers sorted by computer platform.

Windows, Mac OS X, and Linux

Interpreted platforms

These trackers run in JITed virtual machines, such as the Java.

- **MikMod** (Jean-Paul Mikkers, 1992) - Java[15]

- **Jeskola Buzz** - .NET Framework

- **PulseBoy** - Adobe Flash[16]

Atari ST / STE / Falcon

- **ST SoundTracker** (Equinox, 1990)

- **Audio Sculpture** (Synchron Assembly, 1990)

- **Protracker STE** (Equinox, 1991)

- **Octalyser** (Code & Alan F, 1992)

- **Megatracker** (Simplet & Axel Follet, 1994)

- **DBE-Tracker** (ST-Ghost, 1995)

- **Digital Tracker** (Emmanuel Jaccard, 1996)

- **Graoumf Tracker** (Laurent de SORAS, 1996)

- **Digital Home Studio** (Emmanuel Jaccard, 1997)

- **FlexTrax** [17] (Thomas Bergström, 2000)

- **ACE Tracker** [18] (Thomas Bergström, 2002)

- **maxYMiser** (Gareth Morris, 2005)

- **Hextracker** (Paulo Simoes, 2011)

Amiga

- **Ultimate Soundtracker** (Karsten Obarski, 1987)

- **Protracker** (Lars Hamre, Anders Hamre, Sven Vahsen, Rune Johnsrud, 1990)

- **OctaMED** (1989, Teijo Kinnunen)

- **NoiseTracker** (Pex Tufvesson, Anders Berkeman, 1989)

- **Audio Sculpture**

- **Radium**[14]

DOS

- **Scream Tracker** (Sami Tammilehto, 1990)

- **Modedit**

- **Fast Tracker** (Triton Demo-Crew, 1995)

- **Impulse Tracker** (Jeffrey Lim, 1995)

- **Sound Club** (Priit Kasesalu, Ahti Heinla, Jaan Tallinn: Estonia, 1993) .SN .MOD .MIDI modules

Other operating systems

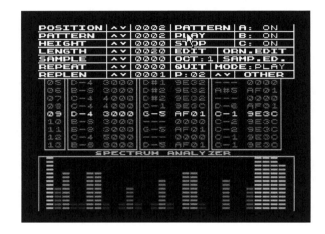

Soundtracker

Allows users to create music for one system on another. Usually uses emulation to produce sound, some of trackers also can use real sound chips connected to host system.

- **ChibiTracker** (2006, Juan Linietsky) - ChibiTracker has a GNU open-source license and runs on FreeBSD, BeOS and Nintendo DS.[13]

- **LittleGPTracker** (2009) - LittleGPTracker is aimed at the GP2X hand-held console, but also runs on PSP, Windows, Mac OS X and Linux.[19]

- **Little Sound Dj** (Johan Kotlinski) - Game Boy.

- **MilkyTracker** (2008, pailes et al.) - MilkyTracker has a GPL open-source license and runs on Linux, FreeBSD, Windows, Windows CE, Mac OS X, Xbox 360, AROS and AmigaOS 4.[12] It supports .MOD and .XM module files, and attempts to recreate the user experience of *Fasttracker II.*

- **NitroTracker** (Tobias Weyland, 2006, GPL) - Nintendo DS[20]

- **Schism Tracker**
  2003, Mrs. Brisby, Storlek et al. - GPL licensed for Windows, Mac OS X, Linux, FreeBSD, Wii, Pandora (console) (and further platforms with GCC4 and SDL support). Based like the *OpenMPT* on *ModPlug* source code,[21] but with focus on Look and Feel and compatibility to the Impulse Tracker.[22]

- **Soundtracker** (Jarosław Burczyński, 1990, public domain) – Soundtracker sequenced the three channels of the AY-3-8910 audio chip on the 128K models of ZX Spectrum. Though the instruments were referred to as samples, they were chip-generated sounds. The user is able to modify each sample via use of amplitude envelopes, noise frequency envelopes and pitch modifications. When these "samples" were played in the tracker they could also be modified by arpeggios (referred to as ornaments).[23] A second program, *ST Compiler*, allowed *Soundtracker* songs to be integrated into other code.[24]

- **SunVox** (2011, Alex Zolotov) - SunVox is freeware for Windows, Linux, Mac OS X, Palm OS and Windows Mobile; and available commercially for the iPhone/iPod touch/iPad and Android.

1.16.5   See also

- Category:Tracker musicians

- Computer game music

- Modular software music studio

- List of music software

1.16.6   References

[1] Gallagher, Mitch (2009). *The Music Tech Dictionary: A Glossary of Audio-Related Terms and Technologies.* Course Technology. Retrieved September 10, 2014.

[2] Matsuoka, Claudio (2007-11-04). "Tracker History Graphing Project". helllabs.org. Retrieved 2011-01-29. *Tracker History Graph*

[3] Commodore's SID or General Instruments' venerable AY-3-8912 and Yamaha's compatible YM2149.

[4] "Top Trackers". *Computer Music Magazine* (Future Publishing Ltd) (113). June 2007. Retrieved 2007. *Tracker! The amazing free music software giving the big boys a run for their money.*

[5] Buzz changelog

[6] DefleMask's Website, Delek's website for his Multi-System Tracker. DefleMask Tracker.

[7] Sonant Live, an on line music tracker.

[8] Index of /deadnoise/MOD FILES

[9] Energy Flash: A Journey Through Rave Music and Dance Culture by Simon Reynolds

[10] Noisekick Interview

[11] Burns, Todd L. (2008-09-30). "Deadmau5: It's complicated". residentadvisor.net. Retrieved 2014-09-03. *I was in my Mom's basement tooling away on Impulse Tracker on a 386 just doing Nintendo music until some Loop Library company hired me as a producer.*

[12] Kirn, Peter (2008-03-14). "MilkyTracker Pan-Platform Tracker Now Open Source, with New Features". *Create Digital Music.* Retrieved 2010-05-17.

[13] Kirn, Peter (2008-04-11). "Chibitracker on DS; Favorite Trackers on the Road?". *Create Digital Music.* Retrieved 2010-05-17.

[14] Matheussen, Kjetil (3 May 2014). *Radium: A music editor inspired by the music tracker* (pdf). Linux Audio Conference. Karlsruhe. pp. 1–8. Retrieved 24 May 2015.

[15] Phillips, Dave (2000-12-01). "About the Mod: Part One". *Linux Journal.* Retrieved 2011-06-13.

[16] Hamilton, Kirk (2012-10-04). "Make Chiptunes In Your Browser With This Awesome, Simple Sequencer". *Kotaku.* Retrieved 2013-06-09.

[17] New Beat Homepage

[18] New Beat Homepage

[19] "LittleGPTracker Hits 1.0; Free, GP2x, Linux, Mac, Windows, Does Lots of Stuff". *Create Digital Music.* 2008-05-29. Retrieved 2010-05-21.

[20] NitroTracker, DS Music Tool, Now Open Source - Create Digital Music

[21] storlek (2011-02-01). "Modplug". schismtracker.org. Retrieved 2011-02-05. *Schism Tracker uses a highly customized version of the Modplug library, [...]. Many of Schism's fixes have since been back-ported to OpenMPT [...]*

[22] "Player abuse tests". schismtracker.org. 2009-08-01. Retrieved 2011-02-06.

[23] "Your Sinclair" (83). Future. November 1992. pp. 6 and 22.

[24] "Your Sinclair" (84). Future. December 1992. p. 5.

1.16.7   Further reading

- René T. A. Lysloff, Leslie C. Gay (2003). *Music and technoculture* (illustrated ed.). Wesleyan University Press. pp. 37–38,50 58. ISBN 978-0-8195-6513-6.

1.16.8   External links

- Andrew 'Necros' Sega: Taking Tracking Mainstream Part 1, Part 2, Part 3, Part 4, Part 5 Tracker history presentation on the *Notacon* April 27, 2007

- Tracker History Graphing Project lineage of music trackers by Claudio Matsuoka (accessed April 2013)

- The Tracker's Handbook, an introduction to tracking

1.17   Nintendocore

Not to be confused with the hip hop subgenre, Nerdcore.

Nintendocore (also known as **Nintendo rock**,[1] **video rock**,[2] and **nerdcore**)[3][4] is a music genre that fuses aggressive styles of modern rock with chiptune and video game music. Pioneered by Horse the Band, The Advantage, and Minibosses, Nintendocore emerged from various styles of hardcore punk and heavy metal, and has been influenced by many other musical genres.

1.17.1   Characteristics

Nintendocore frequently features the use of electric guitars, drum kits, and typical rock instrumentation alongside synthesizers,[5] chiptunes, 8-bit sounds, and electronically produced beats.[1][3][6] It originated out of a very diverse range of musical styles, including hardcore punk,[3][5][7] post-hardcore,[6][8] melodic metalcore,[5][8] and heavy metal.[9] In addition to these origins, it has been influenced by a variety of other genres, such as electro,[3] noise rock,[1][10] post-rock,[8][11] and screamo.[3][12] Thus, Nintendocore groups vary stylistically. Horse the Band, combines metalcore, heavy metal, thrash metal, and post-hardcore with post-rock passages.[3][8][12] "The Black Hole" from Horse the Band's third album, *The Mechanical Hand*, is an example of Nintendocore, featuring screamed vocals, heavy "Nintendo riffs," and "sound effects from numerous games."[13] Math the Band includes electro and dance-punk styles.[14] Minibosses use Kyuss-inspired heavy metal riffing,[15] and The Advantage is associated with styles such as noise rock and post-rock.[16] The Depreciation Guild was an indie band that incorporated 8-bit sounds, video game music, and elements of shoegaze.[17]

Some bands feature singing, such as The Depreciation Guild, whose frontman Kurt Feldman provides "ethereal" and "tender vocals,"[17] and The Megas, who write lyrics that mirror video game storylines.[18] Others, such as Horse the Band and Math the Band, add screamed vocals into the mix.[3][4][8][12][19] But yet other groups are strictly instrumental, such as Minibosses,[15] and The Advantage.[1][11] While otherwise diverse, all Nintendocore groups "use specific instruments to mimic the sounds of Nintendo games."[6]

1.17.2   History and notable artists (Early 1990s-present)

The Minibosses at Penny Arcade Expo 2005.

Although video game music started much earlier in genres like chiptune and bitpop, the first known band to cover a video game song was the all-female indie rock group Autoclave with their cover of the theme song from the popular video game *Paperboy* off of their self-titled debut 1991 album.[20] The second group in existence to be known to cover a video game song was the band Mr. Bungle, with their live cover of the *Super Mario Bros.* theme song, which was a regular staple throughout their 1990's live concert setlist.[21] Mr. Bungle also sampled sounds from video games off their debut album from 1991.[22] The term Nintendocore was later initiated by the metalcore group Horse the Band,[5] whose frontman originally coined the term "Nintendocore" as a joke.[23] At present, the group has released five studio albums in the Nintendocore style, starting with 2000's *Secret Rhythm of the Universe*.[5][18]

Another Nintendocore pioneer is The Advantage,[24] whom *The New York Times* praises as one of the groups who brought video game music into the mainstream modern music spotlight.[2] The Advantage is an instrumental rock band formed by two students attending Nevada Union High School.[2] The group "plays nothing but music from the original Nintendo console games."[2] By creating rock cover versions of video game sound tracks, they have "brought legitimacy to a style of music dubbed Nintendocore."[1]

The rock group Minibosses "are one of the most well-established bands in the Nintendocore genre, with an impressive roster of covers including *Contra*, *Double Dragon*, *Excitebike*," and other video game themes.[18] The band is from Phoenix, Arizona, and is known as one of the primary representatives of Nintendo rock,[25] performing at various video game expositions.[18] In addition to covers, the band has also produced original work.[18] *The Harvard Crimson* refers to Minibosses as "sworn rivals" of The NESkimos,[1] another Nintendocore practitioner.[18]

The 2007 debut album by The Depreciation Guild, *In Her Gentle Jaws* has been referred to as Nintendocore by Pitchfork Media. The website wrote that "*In Her Gentle Jaws* sticks its neck out further than Nintendocore staples like The Advantage or Minibosses", and that the album's instrumental title track "could plausibly come from an NES cartridge."[17]

Other bands known to represent the genre include Math the Band,[4] Karate High School on its debut album,[26] The Megas,[18] The Octopus Project,[27] An Albatross,[28] Rolo Tomassi,[29] Crystal Castles,[30] Powerglove, and Hella, a project featuring The Advantage drummer Spencer Seim on guitar.[31] Sky Eats Airplane has labeled itself under the genre, though Canadian magazine *Exclaim!* has disputed this labeling.[32]

1.17.3 See also

- Game Boy music

- Nerdcore hip hop

- Nintendocore musical groups

- Video game music cover bands

- Video game music culture

1.17.4 References

[1] Payne, Will B. (2006-02-14). "Nintendo Rock: Nostalgia or Sound of the Future". The Harvard Crimson. Retrieved 2011-03-14.

[2] Weingarten, Marc (29 April 2004). "Resurrecting the Riffs, A Nintendo Rock Band". The New York Times. Retrieved 21 March 2011.

[3] Wright (2010-12-09). "Subgenre(s) of the Week: Nintendocore (feat. Holiday Pop)". The Quest. Retrieved 2 January 2015.

[4] Yun, Elizabeth (4 January 2011). "Math the Band Strive to 'Take Fun Seriously' -- Exclusive Video". *Spinner.com*. AOL. Archived from the original on 17 November 2011. Retrieved 30 March 2011.

[5] Greer, Nick (2005-01-24). "HORSE the band R. Borlax". Sputnikmusic. Retrieved 2011-03-14.

[6] Loftus, Johnny. "HORSE the Band". *Allmusic*. Rovi Corporation. Retrieved 2011-03-14.

[7] Sutherland, Sam (December 2006). "Horse the Band - Pizza EP". Exclaim!.

[8] "Horse The Band, Super 8 Bit Brothers, Endless Hallway ,and Oceana". *The A. V. Club*. The Onion. 8 November 2010. Archived from the original on 15 March 2012. Retrieved January 2, 2015.

[9] Turull, Alisha (6 October 2009). "New Releases: Lita Ford, the Fall of Troy, Horse the band, Immortal, Inhale Exhale". *Noisecreep*. AOL. Retrieved 30 March 2011.

[10] Leahey, Andrew. "A Natural Death". *Allmusic*. Rovi Corporation. Retrieved 8 May 2011.

[11] Loftus, Johnny. "The Mechanical Hand". *Allmusic*. Rovi Corporation. Retrieved 10 April 2011.

[12] Loftus, Johnny. "R. Borlax [Bonus Tracks]". *Allmusic*. Rovi Corporation. Retrieved 10 April 2011.

[13] Weber, Scott (Site moderator). "Horse the Band - The Mechanical Hand". AbsolutePunk. Retrieved 2011-05-07.

[14] Trivett, Ben (21 October 2010). "Math the Band Play Blistering Set at CMJ -- Exclusive Photos". *Spinner.com*. AOL. Retrieved 30 March 2011.

[15] Borges, Mario Mesquita. "Minibosses". *Allmusic*. Rovi Corporation. Retrieved 10 April 2011.

[16] Trivett, Ben (21 October 2010). "Math the Band Play Blistering Set at CMJ -- Exclusive Photos". *Spinner.com*. AOL. Archived from the original on 1 January 2011. Retrieved 30 March 2011.

[17] Moerder, Adam (Staff member). "The Depreciation Guild - In Her Gentle Jaws". Pitchfork Media. Retrieved 2011-05-09.

[18] Bayer, Jonah (2009-03-05). "Like Video Games? You'll Love Nintendocore". Gibson Guitar Corporation. Retrieved 2011-03-15.

[19] Synyard, Dave (September 2007). "Horse the Band - A Natural Death". Exclaim!. Retrieved 10 July 2011.

[20] Autoclave (album)

[21] http://www.bunglefever.com/faq.html#VII.1

[22] Mr. Bungle (album)

[23] Willschick, Aaron (2007-06-03). "Interview with HORSE The Band bassist Dash Arkenstone". *PureGrainAudio*. ProtogenLabs. Retrieved 2011-03-14.

[24] Hughes, Josiah (August 2008). "Hella guitarist Spencer Seim releases solo album as sBACH". Exclaim!. Retrieved 10 July 2011.

[25] Rene Gutel (August 26, 2004). "The Rise of Nintendo Rock". NPR. KJZZ 91.5. Retrieved 10 April 2011. Missing or empty |series= (help)

[26] Pertola, Petteri (28 May 2009). "Karate High School - Invaders". Rockfreaks.net. Retrieved 2 January 2015.

[27] Moerder, Adam (25 October 2007). "Album Reviews: The Octopus Project - Hello, Avalanche". Pitchfork Media. Retrieved 10 July 2011.

[28] Moerder, Adam (14 July 2006). "Album Review: An Albatross - Blessphemy (of the Peace-Beast Feastgiver and the Bear-Warp Kumite)". Pitchfork Media. Retrieved 10 July 2011.

[29] Sean Reid (19 May 2010). "Alter The Press!:Album Review:Rolo Tomassi - Cosmology". Alter The Press!. Retrieved 15 June 2011.

[30] "Crystal Castles". *SPIN Magazine* (SPIN Media) **23** (12): 26. December 2007. ISSN 0886-3032.

[31] Moerder, Adam (23 March 2005). "Album Reviews: Hella - Church Gone Wild/Chripin' Hard". Pitchfork Media. Retrieved 10 July 2011.

[32] Synyard, Dave (March 2008). "Sky Eats Airplane Everything Perfect On The Wrong Day". Exclaim!. Retrieved 10 July 2011.

An illustration of a contemporary personal desktop computer

1.18 Personal computer

A **personal computer** is a general-purpose computer whose size, capabilities and original sale price make it useful for individuals, and is intended to be operated directly by an end-user with no intervening computer operator. This contrasts with the batch processing or time-sharing models that allowed larger, more expensive minicomputer and mainframe systems to be used by many people, usually at the same time. A related term is "**PC**" that was initially an acronym for "personal computer", but later became used primarily to refer to the ubiquitous Wintel platform.

Software applications for most personal computers include, but are not limited to, word processing, spreadsheets, databases, web browsers and e-mail clients, digital media playback, games and many personal productivity and special-purpose software applications. Modern personal computers often have connections to the Internet, allowing access to the World Wide Web and a wide range of other resources. Personal computers may be connected to a local area network (LAN), either by a cable or a wireless connection. A personal computer may be a desktop computer or a laptop, netbook, tablet or a handheld PC.

Early computer owners usually had to write their own programs to do anything useful with the machines, which even did not include an operating system. The very earliest microcomputers, equipped with a front panel, required hand-loading of a bootstrap program to load programs from external storage (paper tape, cassettes, or eventually diskettes). Before very long, automatic booting from permanent read-only memory became universal. Today's users have access to a wide range of commercial software, freeware and free and open-source software, which are provided in ready-to-run or ready-to-compile form. Software for personal computers, such as applications and video games, are typically developed and distributed independently from the hardware or OS manufacturers, whereas software for many mobile phones and other portable systems is approved and distributed through a centralized online store.[1][2]

Since the early 1990s, Microsoft operating systems and Intel hardware have dominated much of the personal computer market, first with MS-DOS and then with Windows. Popular alternatives to Microsoft's Windows operating systems include Apple's OS X and free open-source Unix-like operating systems such as Linux and BSD. AMD provides the major alternative to Intel's processors.

1.18.1 History

Main article: History of personal computers

The Programma 101 was the first commercial "desktop personal computer", produced by the Italian company Olivetti and invented by the Italian engineer Pier Giorgio Perotto, inventor of the magnetic card system. The project started in 1962. It was launched at the 1964 New York World's Fair, and volume production began in 1965, the computer retailing for $3,200.[3]

NASA bought at least ten Programma 101s and used them for the calculations for the 1969 Apollo 11 Moon landing. Then ABC used the Programma 101 to predict the presidential election of 1969, and the U.S. military used the machine to plan their operations in the Vietnam War. The Programma 101 was also used in schools, hospitals, government offices. This marked the beginning of the era of the personal computer.

In 1968, Hewlett-Packard was ordered to pay about $900,000 in royalties to Olivetti after their Hewlett-Packard 9100A was ruled to have copied some of the solutions adopted in the Programma 101, including the magnetic card, the architecture and other similar components.[3]

The Soviet MIR series of computers was developed from 1965 to 1969 in a group headed by Victor Glushkov. It was designed as a relatively small-scale computer for use in engineering and scientific applications and contained a hardware implementation of a high-level programming language. Another innovative feature for that time was the user interface combining a keyboard with a monitor and light pen for correcting texts and drawing on screen.[4]

In what was later to be called the Mother of All Demos, SRI researcher Douglas Engelbart in 1968 gave a preview of what would become the staples of daily working life in the 21st century: e-mail, hypertext, word processing, video conferencing and the mouse. The demonstration required technical support staff and a mainframe time-sharing computer that were far too costly for individual business use at the time.

By the early 1970s, people in academic or research institutions had the opportunity for single-person use of a computer system in interactive mode for extended durations, although these systems would still have been too expensive to be owned by a single person.

In 1973 the IBM Los Gatos Scientific Center developed a portable computer prototype called SCAMP (Special Computer APL Machine Portable) based on the IBM PALM processor with a Philips compact cassette drive, small CRT and full function keyboard. SCAMP emulated an IBM 1130 minicomputer in order to run APL\1130.[5] In 1973

Commodore PET in 1983 (at American Museum of Science and Energy)

APL was generally available only on mainframe computers, and most desktop sized microcomputers such as the Wang 2200 or HP 9800 offered only BASIC. Because SCAMP was the first to emulate APL\1130 performance on a portable, single user computer, *PC Magazine* in 1983 designated SCAMP a "revolutionary concept" and "the world's first personal computer".[5][6] This seminal, single user portable computer now resides in the Smithsonian Institution, Washington, D.C.. Successful demonstrations of the 1973 SCAMP prototype led to the IBM 5100 portable microcomputer launched in 1975 with the ability to be programmed in both APL and BASIC for engineers, analysts, statisticians and other business problem-solvers. In the late 1960s such a machine would have been nearly as large as two desks and would have weighed about half a ton.[5]

Another seminal product in 1973 was the Xerox Alto, developed at Xerox's Palo Alto Research Center (PARC), it had a graphical user interface (GUI) which later served as inspiration for Apple Computer's Macintosh, and Microsoft's Windows operating system. Also in 1973 Hewlett Packard introduced fully BASIC programmable microcomputers that fit entirely on top of a desk, including a keyboard, a small one-line display and printer. The Wang 2200 microcomputer of 1973 had a full-size cathode ray tube (CRT) and cassette tape storage.[7] These were generally expensive specialized computers sold for business or scientific uses. The introduction of the microprocessor, a single chip with all the circuitry that formerly occupied large cabinets, led to the proliferation of personal computers after 1975.

Early personal computers—generally called microcomputers—were often sold in a kit form and in limited volumes, and were of interest mostly to hobbyists and technicians. Minimal programming was done with

IBM Personal Computer XT in 1988

The 8-bit PMD 85 personal computer produced in 1985-1990 by the Tesla company in the former socialist Czechoslovakia. This computer was produced locally (in Piešťany) due to a lack of foreign currency with which to buy systems from the West.

toggle switches to enter instructions, and output was provided by front panel lamps. Practical use required adding peripherals such as keyboards, computer displays, disk drives, and printers. Micral N was the earliest commercial, non-kit microcomputer based on a microprocessor, the Intel 8008. It was built starting in 1972 and about 90,000 units were sold.

In 1976 Steve Jobs and Steve Wozniak sold the Apple I computer circuit board, which was fully prepared and contained about 30 chips. The Apple I computer differed from the other hobby computers of the time at the beckoning of Paul Terrell owner of the Byte Shop who gave Steve Jobs his first purchase order for 50 Apple I computers only if the computers were assembled and tested and not a kit computer so he would have computers to sell to everyone, not just people that could assemble a computer kit. The Apple I as delivered was still a kit computer as it did not have a power supply, case, or keyboard as delivered to the Byte Shop.

The first successfully mass marketed personal computer was the Commodore PET introduced in January 1977, but back-ordered and not available until later in the year.[8] At the same time, the Apple II (usually referred to as the "Apple") was introduced[9] (June 1977), and the TRS-80 from Tandy Corporation / Tandy Radio Shack in summer 1977, delivered in September in a small number. Mass-market ready-assembled computers allowed a wider range of people to use computers, focusing more on software applications and less on development of the processor hardware.

During the early 1980s, home computers were further developed for household use, with software for personal productivity, programming and games. They typically could be used with a television already in the home as the computer display, with low-detail blocky graphics and a limited color range, and text about 40 characters wide by 25 characters tall. Sinclair Research,[10] a UK company, produced the ZX Series - the ZX80 (1980), ZX81 (1981), and the ZX Spectrum; the latter was introduced in 1982, and to-

IBM 5150, released in 1981

taled 8 million unit sold. Following came the Commodore 64, totaled 17 million units sold.[11][12]

In the same year, the NEC PC-98 was introduced, which was a very popular personal computer that sold in more than 18 million units.[13] Another famous personal computer, the revolutionary Amiga 1000, was unveiled by Commodore on July 23, 1985. The Amiga 1000 featured a multitasking, windowing operating system, color graphics with a 4096-color palette, stereo sound, Motorola 68000 CPU, 256 kB RAM, and 880 kB 3.5-inch disk drive, for US$1,295.[14]

Somewhat larger and more expensive systems (for example, running CP/M), or sometimes a home computer with additional interfaces and devices, although still low-cost compared with minicomputers and mainframes, were aimed at office and small business use, typically using "high resolution" monitors capable of at least 80 column text display, and often no graphical or color drawing capability.

Workstations were characterized by high-performance processors and graphics displays, with large-capacity local disk storage, networking capability, and running under a multitasking operating system.

Eventually, due to the influence of the IBM PC on the personal computer market, personal computers and home computers lost any technical distinction. Business computers acquired color graphics capability and sound, and home computers and game systems users used the same processors and operating systems as office workers. Mass-market computers had graphics capabilities and memory comparable to dedicated workstations of a few years before. Even local area networking, originally a way to allow business computers to share expensive mass storage and peripherals, became a standard feature of personal computers used at home.

In 1982 "The Computer" was named Machine of the Year by *Time* Magazine.

In the 2010s, several companies such as Hewlett-Packard and Sony sold off their PC and laptop divisions. As a result, the personal computer was declared dead several times during this time.[15]

Market and sales

See also: Market share of personal computer vendors

In 2001, 125 million personal computers were shipped in comparison to 48,000 in 1977.[16] More than 500 million personal computers were in use in 2002 and one billion personal computers had been sold worldwide from the mid-1970s up to this time. Of the latter figure, 75% were professional or work related, while the rest were sold for personal or home use. About 81.5% of personal computers shipped had been desktop computers, 16.4% laptops and 2.1% servers. The United States had received 38.8% (394 million) of the computers shipped, Europe 25% and 11.7% had gone to the Asia-Pacific region, the fastest-growing market as of 2002. The second billion was expected to be sold by 2008.[17] Almost half of all households in Western Europe had a personal computer and a computer could be found in 40% of homes in United Kingdom, compared with only 13% in 1985.[18]

The global personal computer shipments were 350.9 million units in 2010,[19] 308.3 million units in 2009[20] and 302.2 million units in 2008.[21][22] The shipments were 264 million units in the year 2007, according to iSuppli,[23] up 11.2% from 239 million in 2006.[24] In 2004, the global shipments were 183 million units, an 11.6% increase over 2003.[25] In 2003, 152.6 million computers were shipped, at an estimated value of $175 billion.[26] In 2002, 136.7 million PCs were shipped, at an estimated value of $175 billion.[26] In 2000, 140.2 million personal computers were

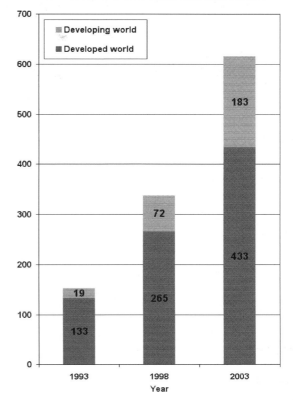

Personal computers (million), source: ITU

Personal computers worldwide in million distinguished by developed and developing world

shipped, at an estimated value of $226 billion.[26] Worldwide shipments of personal computers surpassed the 100-million mark in 1999, growing to 113.5 million units from 93.3 million units in 1998.[27] In 1999, Asia had 14.1 million units shipped.[28]

As of June 2008, the number of personal computers in use worldwide hit one billion,[29] while another billion is expected to be reached by 2014. Mature markets like the United States, Western Europe and Japan accounted for 58% of the worldwide installed PCs. The emerging markets were expected to double their installed PCs by 2012 and to take 70% of the second billion PCs. About 180 million computers (16% of the existing installed base) were expected to be replaced and 35 million to be dumped into landfill in 2008. The whole installed base grew 12% annually.[30][31]

Based on International Data Corporation (IDC) data for Q2 2011, for the first time China surpassed US in PC shipments by 18.5 million and 17.7 million respectively. This trend reflects the rising of emerging markets as well as the relative stagnation of mature regions.[32]

In the developed world, there has been a vendor tradition to keep adding functions to maintain high prices of personal computers. However, since the introduction of the One Laptop per Child foundation and its low-cost XO-1 laptop, the computing industry started to pursue the price too. Although introduced only one year earlier, there were 14 million netbooks sold in 2008.[33] Besides the regular computer manufacturers, companies making especially rugged versions of computers have sprung up, offering alternatives for people operating their machines in extreme weather or environments.[34]

Deloitte consulting firm predicted that in 2011, smartphones and tablet computers as computing devices would surpass the PCs sales.[37] As of 2013, worldwide sales of PCs had begun to fall as many consumers moved to tablets and smartphones for gifts and personal use. Sales of 90.3 million units in the 4th quarter of 2012 represented a 4.9% decline from sales in the 4th quarter of 2011.[38] Global PC sales fell sharply in the first quarter of 2013, according to IDC data. The 14% year-over-year decline was the largest on record since the firm began tracking in 1994, and double what analysts had been expecting.[39][40] The decline of Q2 2013 PC shipments marked the fifth straight quarter of falling sales.[41] "This is horrific news for PCs," remarked an analyst. "It's all about mobile computing now. We have definitely reached the tipping point."[39] Data from Gartner Inc. showed a similar decline for the same time period.[39] China's Lenovo Group bucked the general trend as strong sales to first time buyers in the developing world allowed the company's sales to stay flat overall.[39] Windows 8, which was designed to look similar to tablet/smartphone software, was cited as a contributing factor in the decline of new PC sales. "Unfortunately, it seems clear that the Windows 8 launch not only didn't provide a positive boost to the PC market, but appears to have slowed the market," said IDC Vice President Bob O'Donnell.[40]

In August 2013, Credit Suisse published research findings that attributed around 75% of the operating profit share of the PC industry to Microsoft (operating system) and Intel (semiconductors).[42]

According to IDC, in 2013 PC shipments dropped by 9.8% as the greatest drop-ever in line with consumers trends to use mobile devices.[43]

Average selling price

Selling prices of personal computers steadily declined due to lower costs of production and manufacture, while the capabilities of computers increased. In 1975, an Altair kit sold for only around US $400, but required customers to solder components into circuit boards; peripherals required

to interact with the system in alphanumeric form instead of blinking lights would add another $2,000, and the resultant system was only of use to hobbyists.[44]

At their introduction in 1981, the US $1,795 price of the Osborne 1 and its competitor Kaypro was considered an attractive price point; these systems had text-only displays and only floppy disks for storage. By 1982, Michael Dell observed that a personal computer system selling at retail for about $3,000 US was made of components that cost the dealer about $600; typical gross margin on a computer unit was around $1,000.[45] The total value of personal computer purchases in the US in 1983 was about $4 billion, comparable to total sales of pet food. By late 1998, the average selling price of personal computer systems in the United States had dropped below $1,000.[46]

For Microsoft Windows systems, the average selling price (ASP) showed a decline in 2008/2009, possibly due to low-cost netbooks, drawing $569 for desktop computers and $689 for laptops at U.S. retail in August 2008. In 2009, ASP had further fallen to $533 for desktops and to $602 for notebooks by January and to $540 and $560 in February.[47] According to research firm NPD, the average selling price of all Windows portable PCs has fallen from $659 in October 2008 to $519 in October 2009.[48]

1.18.2 Terminology

"PC" is an initialism for "personal computer". However, it is sometimes used in a different sense, referring to a personal computer with an Intel x86-compatible processor, very often running (but not necessarily limited to) Microsoft Windows, which is a combination sometimes also called Wintel, although large portion of PCs are not shipped with preinstalled Windows operating systems. Some PCs, including the OLPC XOs, are equipped with x86 or x64 processors but not designed to run Microsoft Windows. "PC" is used in contrast with "Mac", an Apple Macintosh computer.[49][50][51][52] This sense of the word is used in the *Get a Mac* advertisement campaign that ran between 2006 and 2009, as well as its rival, *I'm a PC* campaign, that appeared in 2008. Since Apple's transition to Intel processors starting 2005, all Macintosh computers are now PCs.[53]

1.18.3 Types

Stationary

Workstation Main article: Workstation

A workstation is a high-end personal computer designed for technical, mathematical, or scientific applications. In-

Sun SPARCstation 1+ from the early 1990s, with a 25 MHz RISC processor

A Dell OptiPlex desktop computer

tended primarily to be used by one person at a time, they are commonly connected to a local area network and run multi-user operating systems. Workstations are used for tasks such as computer-aided design, drafting and modeling, computation-intensive scientific and engineering calculations, image processing, architectural modeling, and computer graphics for animation and motion picture visual effects.[54]

Desktop computer　Main article: Desktop computer
Prior to the widespread usage of PCs, a computer that could fit on a desk was remarkably small, leading to the "desktop" nomenclature. More recently, the phrase usually indicates a particular style of computer case. Desktop computers come in a variety of styles ranging from large vertical tower cases to small models which can be tucked behind an LCD monitor. In this sense, the term "desktop" refers specifically to a horizontally oriented case, usually intended to have the display screen placed on top to save desk space. Most modern desktop computers have separate screens and keyboards.

Gaming computer　Main article: Gaming computer

A gaming computer is a standard desktop computer that typically has high-performance hardware, such as a more powerful video card, processor and memory, in order to handle the requirements of demanding video games, which are often simply called "PC games".[55] A number of com-

panies, such as Alienware, manufacture prebuilt gaming computers, and companies such as Razer and Logitech market mice, keyboards and headsets geared toward gamers.

Single unit　Further information: All-in-one computer

Single-unit PCs (also known as all-in-one PCs) are a subtype of desktop computers that combine the monitor and case of the computer within a single unit. The monitor often utilizes a touchscreen as an optional method of user input, but separate keyboards and mice are normally still included. The inner components of the PC are often located directly behind the monitor and many of such PCs are built similarly to laptops.

Nettop　Main article: Nettop

A subtype of desktops, called nettops, was introduced by Intel in February 2008, characterized by low cost and lean functionality. A similar subtype of laptops (or notebooks) is the netbook, described below. The product line features the new Intel Atom processor, which specifically enables nettops to consume less power and fit into small enclosures.

Home theater PC   Main article: Home theater PC

A home theater PC (HTPC) is a convergence device that

A modern laptop computer

An Antec Fusion V2 home theater PC, with a keyboard placed on top of it.

combines the functions of a personal computer and a digital video recorder. It is connected to a TV set or an appropriately sized computer display, and is often used as a digital photo viewer, music and video player, TV receiver, and digital video recorder. HTPCs are also referred to as media center systems or media servers. The general goal in a HTPC is usually to combine many or all components of a home theater setup into one box. More recently, HTPCs gained the ability to connect to services providing on-demand movies and TV shows.

HTPCs can be purchased pre-configured with the required hardware and software needed to add television programming to the PC, or can be cobbled together out of discrete components, what is commonly done with software support from MythTV, Windows Media Center, GB-PVR, SageTV, Famulent or LinuxMCE.

Portable

Laptop   Main article: Laptop

A laptop computer, also called a notebook, is a small personal computer designed for portability. Usually, all of the hardware and interfaces needed to operate a laptop, such as the graphics card, audio devices or USB ports (previously parallel and serial ports), are built into a single unit. Laptops contain high-capacity batteries that can power the device for extensive periods of time, enhancing portability. Once the battery charge is depleted, it will have to be recharged through a power outlet. In the interests of saving power, weight and space, laptop graphics cards are in many cases integrated into the CPU or chipset and use system RAM, resulting in reduced graphics performance when compared to an equivalent desktop machine. For this reason, desktop

or gaming computers are usually preferred to laptop PCs for gaming purposes.

One of the drawbacks of laptops is that, due to the size and configuration of components, usually relatively little can be done to upgrade the overall computer from its original design. Internal upgrades are either not manufacturer-recommended, can damage the laptop if done with poor care or knowledge, or in some cases impossible, making the desktop PC more modular. Some internal upgrades, such as memory and hard disk drive upgrades are often easily performed, while a display or keyboard upgrade is usually impossible. Just as desktops, laptops also have the same possibilities for connecting to a wide variety of devices, including external displays, mice, cameras, storage devices and keyboards, which may be attached externally through USB ports and other less common ports such as external video.

A subtype of notebooks, called subnotebook, has most of the features of a standard laptop computer, but with smaller physical dimensions. Subnotebooks are larger than hand-held computers, and usually run full versions of desktop or laptop operating systems. Ultra-Mobile PCs (UMPC) are usually considered subnotebooks, or more specifically, sub-notebook tablet PCs, which are described below. Netbooks are sometimes considered to belong to this category, though they are sometimes separated into a category of their own (see below).

Desktop replacement   Main article: Desktop replacement computer

A desktop replacement computer (DTR) is a personal computer that provides the full capabilities of a desktop computer while remaining mobile. Such computers are often actually larger, bulkier laptops. Because of their increased size, this class of computers usually includes more power-

An Acer Aspire desktop replacement laptop

ful components and a larger display than generally found in smaller portable computers, and can have a relatively limited battery capacity or none at all in some cases. Some use a limited range of desktop components to provide better performance at the expense of battery life. Desktop replacement computers are sometimes called *desknotes*, as a portmanteau of words "desktop" and "notebook," though the term is also applied to desktop replacement computers in general.[56]

Netbook   Main article: Netbook
Netbooks, also called mini notebooks or subnotebooks,

An HP netbook

are a subgroup of laptops[57] acting as a category of small, lightweight and inexpensive laptop computers suited for general computing tasks and accessing web-based applications. They are often marketed as "companion devices",

with an intention to augment other ways in which a user can access computer resources.[57] Walt Mossberg called them a "relatively new category of small, light, minimalist and cheap laptops."[58] By August 2009, CNET called netbooks "nothing more than smaller, cheaper notebooks."[57]

Initially, the primary defining characteristic of netbooks was the lack of an optical disc drive, requiring it to be a separate external device. This has become less important as flash memory devices have gradually increased in capacity, replacing the writable optical disc (e.g. CD-RW, DVD-RW) as a transportable storage medium.

At their inception in late 2007—as smaller notebooks optimized for low weight and low cost[59]—netbooks omitted key features (e.g., the optical drive), featured smaller screens and keyboards, and offered reduced specifications and computing power. Over the course of their evolution, netbooks have ranged in their screen sizes from below five inches[60] to over 13 inches,[61] with weights around ~1 kg (2-3 pounds). Often significantly less expensive than other laptops,[62] by mid-2009 netbooks had been offered to users "free of charge", with an extended service contract purchase of a cellular data plan.[63]

In the short period since their appearance, netbooks have grown in size and features, converging with new smaller and lighter notebooks. By mid-2009, CNET noted that "the specs are so similar that the average shopper would likely be confused as to why one is better than the other," noting "the only conclusion is that there really is no distinction between the devices."[57]

Tablet   Main article: Tablet computer
A tablet is a type of portable PC that de-emphasizes the use of traditional input devices (such as a mouse or keyboard) by using a touchscreen display, which can be controlled using either a stylus pen or finger. Some tablets may use a "hybrid" or "convertible" design, offering a keyboard that can either be removed as an attachment, or a screen that can be rotated and folded directly over top the keyboard.

Some tablets may run a traditional PC operating system such as Windows or Linux; Microsoft attempted to enter the tablet market in 2002 with its Microsoft Tablet PC specifications, for tablets and convertible laptops running Windows XP. However, Microsoft's early attempts were overshadowed by the release of Apple's iPad; following in its footsteps, most modern tablets use slate designs and run mobile operating systems such as Android and iOS, giving them functionality similar to smartphones. In response, Microsoft built its Windows 8 operating system to better accommodate these new touch-oriented devices.[64]

HP Compaq tablet PC with rotating/removable keyboard

Ultra-mobile PC   Main article: Ultra-mobile PC
The ultra-mobile PC (UMPC) is a specification for small-

A Samsung Q1 ultra-mobile PC

configuration tablet PCs. It was developed as a joint development exercise by Microsoft, Intel and Samsung, among others. Current UMPCs typically feature the Windows XP, Windows Vista, Windows 7, or Linux operating system, and low-voltage Intel Atom or VIA C7-M processors.

Pocket PC   Main article: Pocket PC
A pocket PC is a hardware specification for a handheld-sized computer (personal digital assistant, PDA) that runs the Microsoft Windows Mobile operating system. It may have the capability to run an alternative operating system like NetBSD or Linux. Pocket PCs have many of the capabilities of modern desktop PCs.

Numerous applications are available for handhelds adher-

An O₂ pocket PC

ing to the Microsoft Pocket PC specification, many of which are freeware. Some of these devices also include mobile phone features, actually representing a smartphone. Microsoft-compliant Pocket PCs can also be used with many other add-ons like GPS receivers, barcode readers, RFID readers and cameras. In 2007, with the release of Windows Mobile 6, Microsoft dropped the name Pocket PC in favor of a new naming scheme: devices without an integrated phone are called Windows Mobile Classic instead of Pocket PC, while devices with an integrated phone and a touch screen are called Windows Mobile Professional.[65]

1.18.4   Hardware

Main article: Personal computer hardware

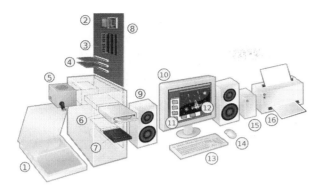

An exploded view of a modern personal computer and peripherals:

1. Scanner

2. CPU (Microprocessor)

3. Memory (RAM)

4. Expansion cards (graphics cards, etc.)

5. Power supply

6. Optical disc drive

7. Storage (Hard disk or SSD)

8. Motherboard

9. Speakers

10. Monitor

11. System software

12. Application software

13. Keyboard

14. Mouse

15. External hard disk

16. Printer

Computer hardware is a comprehensive term for all physical parts of a computer, as distinguished from the data it contains or operates on, and the software that provides instructions for the hardware to accomplish tasks. The boundary between hardware and software might be slightly blurry, with the existence of firmware that is software "built into" the hardware.

Mass-market consumer computers use highly standardized components and so are simple for an end user to assemble into a working system. A typical desktop computer consists of a computer case that holds the power supply, motherboard, hard disk drive, and often an optical disc drive. External devices such as a computer monitor or visual display unit, keyboard, and a pointing device are usually found in a personal computer.

The motherboard connects all processor, memory and peripheral devices together. The RAM, graphics card and processor are in most cases mounted directly onto the motherboard. The central processing unit (microprocessor chip) plugs into a CPU socket, while the memory modules plug into corresponding memory sockets. Some motherboards have the video display adapter, sound and other peripherals integrated onto the motherboard, while others use expansion slots for graphics cards, network cards, or other I/O devices. The graphics card or sound card may employ a break out box to keep the analog parts away from the electromagnetic radiation inside the computer case. Disk drives, which provide mass storage, are connected to the motherboard with one cable, and to the power supply through another cable. Usually, disk drives are mounted in the same case as the motherboard; expansion chassis are also made for additional disk storage. For extended amounts of data, a tape drive can be used or extra hard disks can be put together in an external case.

The keyboard and the mouse are external devices plugged into the computer through connectors on an I/O panel on the back of the computer case. The monitor is also connected to the I/O panel, either through an onboard port on the motherboard, or a port on the graphics card.

Capabilities of the personal computers hardware can sometimes be extended by the addition of expansion cards connected via an expansion bus. Standard peripheral buses often used for adding expansion cards in personal computers include PCI, PCI Express (PCIe), and AGP (a high-speed PCI bus dedicated to graphics adapters, found in older computers). Most modern personal computers have multiple physical PCI Express expansion slots, with some of the having PCI slots as well.

Computer case

Main article: Computer case

A computer case is an enclosure that contains the main

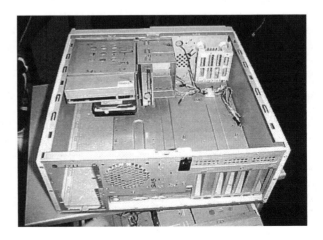

A stripped ATX case lying on its side.

components of a computer. They are usually constructed from steel or aluminum combined with plastic, although other materials such as wood have been used. Cases are available in different sizes and shapes; the size and shape of a computer case is usually determined by the configuration of the motherboard that it is designed to accommodate, since this is the largest and most central component of most computers.

The most popular style for desktop computers is ATX, although microATX and similar layouts became very popular for a variety of uses. Companies like Shuttle Inc. and AOpen have popularized small cases, for which FlexATX is the most common motherboard size.

Power supply unit

Main article: Power supply unit (computer)
The power supply unit (PSU) converts general-purpose

Computer power supply unit with top cover removed.

mains AC electricity to direct current (DC) for the other components of the computer. The rated output capacity of a PSU should usually be about 40% greater than the calculated system power consumption needs obtained by adding up all the system components. This protects against overloading the supply, and guards against performance degradation.

Processor

Main article: Central processing unit
The central processing unit, or CPU, is a part of a computer that executes instructions of a software program. In newer

AMD Athlon 64 X2 CPU.

PCs, the CPU contains over a million transistors in one integrated circuit chip called the microprocessor. In most cases, the microprocessor plugs directly into the motherboard. The chip generates so much heat that the PC builder is required to attach a special cooling device to its surface; thus, modern CPUs are equipped with a fan attached via heat sink.

IBM PC compatible computers use an x86-compatible microprocessor, manufactured by Intel, AMD, VIA Technologies or Transmeta. Apple Macintosh computers were initially built with the Motorola 680x0 family of processors, then switched to the PowerPC series; in 2006, they switched to x86-compatible processors made by Intel.

Motherboard

Main article: Motherboard
The motherboard, also referred to as system board or main

A motherboard without processor, memory and expansion cards, cables

board, is the primary circuit board within a personal computer, and other major system components plug directly into it or via a cable. A motherboard contains a microprocessor, the CPU supporting circuitry (mostly integrated circuits) that provide the interface between memory and input/output peripheral circuits, main memory, and facilities for initial setup of the computer immediately after power-on (often called boot firmware or, in IBM PC compatible computers, a BIOS or UEFI).

In many portable and embedded personal computers, the motherboard houses nearly all of the PC's core components. Often a motherboard will also contain one or more peripheral buses and physical connectors for expansion purposes. Sometimes a secondary daughter board is connected to the motherboard to provide further expandability or to satisfy space constraints.

Main memory

Main article: Primary storage
A PC's main memory is a fast primary storage device that

1GB DDR SDRAM PC-3200 module

is directly accessible by the CPU, and is used to store the currently executing program and immediately needed data. PCs use semiconductor random access memory (RAM) of various kinds such as DRAM, SDRAM or SRAM as their primary storage. Which exact kind is used depends on cost/performance issues at any particular time.

Main memory is much faster than mass storage devices like hard disk drives or optical discs, but is usually volatile, meaning that it does not retain its contents (instructions or data) in the absence of power, and is much more expensive for a given capacity than is most mass storage. As a result, main memory is generally not suitable for long-term or archival data storage.

Hard disk

Main article: Hard disk drive
Mass storage devices store programs and data even when the power is off; they do require power to perform read and write functions during usage. Although flash memory has dropped in cost, the prevailing form of mass storage in personal computers is still the hard disk drive.

A Western Digital 250 GB hard disk drive

If the mass storage controller provides additional ports for expandability, a PC may also be upgraded by the addition of extra hard disk or optical disc drives. For example, BD-ROMs, DVD-RWs, and various optical disc recorders may all be added by the user to certain PCs. Standard internal storage device connection interfaces are PATA, Serial ATA and SCSI.

Solid state drives (SSDs) are a much faster replacement for traditional mechanical hard disk drives, but are also more expensive in terms of cost per gigabyte.

Visual display unit

Main article: Visual display unit

A visual display unit, computer monitor or just display, is a piece of electrical equipment, usually separate from the computer case, which displays visual images without producing a permanent computer record. A display device is usually either a CRT or some form of flat panel such as a TFT LCD. Multi-monitor setups are also quite common.

The display unit houses an electronic circuitry that generates its picture from signals received from the computer. Within the computer, either integral to the motherboard or plugged into it as an expansion card, there is pre-processing circuitry to convert the microprocessor's output data to a format compatible with the display unit's circuitry. The images from computer monitors originally contained only text, but as graphical user interfaces emerged and became common, they began to display more images and multimedia content.

The term "monitor" is also used, particularly by technicians in broadcasting television, where a picture of the broadcast data is displayed to a highly standardized reference monitor for confidence checking purposes.

Video card

Main article: Video card

The video card—otherwise called a graphics card, graph-

An ATI Radeon video card

ics adapter or video adapter—processes the graphics output from the motherboard and transmits it to the display. It is an essential part of modern multimedia-enriched computing. On older models, and today on budget models, graphics circuitry may be integrated with the motherboard, but for modern and flexible machines, they are connected by the PCI, AGP, or PCI Express interface.

When the IBM PC was introduced, most existing business-oriented personal computers used text-only display adapters and had no graphics capability. Home computers at that time had graphics compatible with television signals, but with low resolution by modern standards owing to the limited memory available to the eight-bit processors available at the time.

Keyboard

Main article: Keyboard (computing)

A keyboard is an arrangement of buttons that each corre-

A "Model M" IBM computer keyboard from the early 1980s. Commonly called the "Clicky Keyboard" due to its buckling spring key spring design, which gives the keyboard its iconic 'Click' sound with each keystroke.

spond to a function, letter, or number. They are the primary devices used for inputting text. In most cases, they contain an array of keys specifically organized with the corresponding letters, numbers, and functions printed or engraved on the button. They are generally designed around an operators language, and many different versions for different languages exist.

In English, the most common layout is the QWERTY layout, which was originally used in typewriters. They have evolved over time, and have been modified for use in computers with the addition of function keys, number keys, arrow keys, and keys specific to an operating system. Often, specific functions can be achieved by pressing multiple keys at once or in succession, such as inputting characters with accents or opening a task manager. Programs use keyboard shortcuts very differently and all use different keyboard shortcuts for different program specific operations, such as refreshing a web page in a web browser or selecting all text in a word processor.

Mouse

Main article: Mouse (computing)

A computer mouse is a small handheld device that users

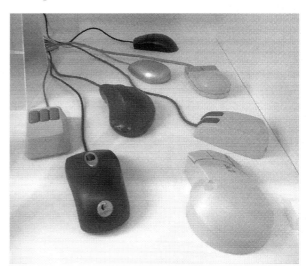

A selection of computer mice built between 1986 and 2007

hold and slide across a flat surface, pointing at various elements of a graphical user interface with an on-screen cursor, and selecting and moving objects using the mouse buttons. Almost all modern personal computers include a mouse; it may be plugged into a computer's rear mouse socket, or as a USB device, or, more recently, may be connected wirelessly via an USB dongle or Bluetooth link.

In the past, mice had a single button that users could press down on the device to "click" on whatever the pointer on the screen was hovering over. Modern mice have two, three or more buttons, providing a "right click" function button on the mouse, which performs a secondary action on a selected object, and a scroll wheel, which users can rotate using their fingers to "scroll" up or down. The scroll wheel can also be pressed down, and therefore be used as a third button. Some mouse wheels may be tilted from side to side to allow sideways scrolling. Different programs make use of these functions differently, and may scroll horizontally by default with the scroll wheel, open different menus with different buttons, etc. These functions may be also user-defined through software utilities.

Mice traditionally detected movement and communicated with the computer with an internal "mouse ball", and used optical encoders to detect rotation of the ball and tell the computer where the mouse has moved. However, these systems were subject to low durability, accuracy and required internal cleaning. Modern mice use optical technology to directly trace movement of the surface under the mouse and are much more accurate, durable and almost maintenance free. They work on a wider variety of surfaces and can even operate on walls, ceilings or other non-horizontal surfaces.

Other components

All computers require either fixed or removable storage for their operating system, programs and user-generated material. Early home computers used compact audio cassettes for file storage; these were at the time a very low cost storage solution, but were displaced by floppy disk drives when manufacturing costs dropped, by the mid-1980s.

Initially, the 5.25-inch and 3.5-inch floppy drives were the principal forms of removable storage for backup of user files and distribution of software. As memory sizes increased, the capacity of the floppy did not keep pace; the Zip drive and other higher-capacity removable media were introduced but never became as prevalent as the floppy drive.

By the late 1990s, the optical drive, in CD and later DVD and Blu-ray Disc forms, became the main method for software distribution, and writeable media provided means for data backup and file interchange. As a result, floppy drives became uncommon in desktop personal computers since about 2000, and were dropped from many laptop systems even earlier.[note 1]

A second generation of tape recorders was provided when videocassette recorders were pressed into service as backup media for larger disk drives. All these systems were less reliable and slower than purpose-built magnetic tape drives. Such tape drives were uncommon in consumer-type personal computers but were a necessity in business or industrial use.

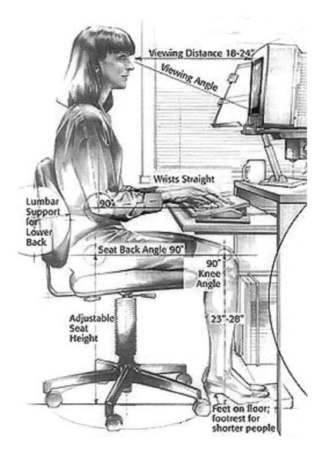

A proper ergonomic design of a personal computer workplace is necessary to prevent repetitive strain injuries, which can develop over time and can lead to long-term disability.[66]

Interchange of data such as photographs from digital cameras is greatly expedited by installation of a card reader, which is often compatible with several forms of flash memory devices. It is usually faster and more convenient to move large amounts of data by removing the card from the mobile device, instead of communicating with the mobile device through a USB interface.

A USB flash drive performs much of the data transfer and backup functions formerly done with floppy drives, Zip disks and other devices. Mainstream operating systems for personal computers provide built-in support for USB flash drives, allowing interchange even between computers with different processors and operating systems. The compact size and lack of moving parts or dirt-sensitive media, combined with low cost and high capacity, have made USB flash drives a popular and useful accessory for any personal computer user.

The operating system can be located on any storage, but is typically installed on a hard disk or solid-state drive. A Live CD represents the concept of running an operating system directly from a CD. While this is slow compared to storing the operating system on a hard disk drive, it is typically used for installation of operating systems, demonstrations, system recovery, or other special purposes. Large flash memory is currently more expensive than hard disk drives of similar size (as of mid-2014) but are starting to appear in laptop computers because of their low weight, small size and low power requirements.

Computer communications involve internal modem cards, modems, network adapter cards, and routers. Common peripherals and adapter cards include headsets, joysticks, microphones, printers, scanners, sound adapter cards (as a separate card rather than located on the motherboard), speakers and webcams.

1.18.5 Software

Main article: Computer software
  Computer software is any kind of computer program,

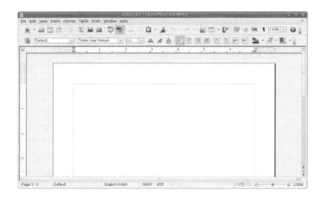

A screenshot of the OpenOffice.org Writer software

procedure, or documentation that performs some task on a computer system.[67] The term includes application software such as word processors that perform productive tasks for users, system software such as operating systems that interface with computer hardware to provide the necessary services for application software, and middleware that controls and co-ordinates distributed systems.

Software applications are common for word processing, Internet browsing, Internet faxing, e-mail and other digital messaging, multimedia playback, playing of computer game, and computer programming. The user of a modern personal computer may have significant knowledge of the operating environment and application programs, but is not necessarily interested in programming nor even able to write programs for the computer. Therefore, most software written primarily for personal computers tends to be designed with simplicity of use, or "user-friendliness" in mind. However, the software industry continuously provide a wide

range of new products for use in personal computers, targeted at both the expert and the non-expert user.

Operating system

Main article: Operating system
See also: Usage share of operating systems

An operating system (OS) manages computer resources and provides programmers with an interface used to access those resources. An operating system processes system data and user input, and responds by allocating and managing tasks and internal system resources as a service to users and programs of the system. An operating system performs basic tasks such as controlling and allocating memory, prioritizing system requests, controlling input and output devices, facilitating computer networking, and managing files.

Common contemporary desktop operating systems are Microsoft Windows, OS X, Linux, Solaris and FreeBSD. Windows, OS X, and Linux all have server and personal variants. With the exception of Microsoft Windows, the designs of each of the them were inspired by or directly inherited from the Unix operating system, which was developed at Bell Labs beginning in the late 1960s and spawned the development of numerous free and proprietary operating systems.

Microsoft Windows   Main article: Microsoft Windows

Microsoft Windows is the collective brand name of several operating systems made by Microsoft. Microsoft first introduced an operating environment named Windows in November 1985,[68] as an add-on to MS-DOS and in response to the growing interest in graphical user interfaces (GUIs)[69][70] generated by Apple's 1984 introduction of the Macintosh.[71] As of August 2015, the most recent client and server version of Windows are Windows 10 and Windows Server 2012 R2, respectively.

OS X   Main article: OS X

OS X (formerly Mac OS X) is a line of operating systems developed, marketed and sold by Apple Inc.. OS X is the successor to the original Mac OS, which had been Apple's primary operating system since 1984. OS X is a Unix-based graphical operating system, and Snow Leopard, Leopard, Lion, Mountain Lion, Mavericks and Yosemite are its version codenames. The most recent version of OS X is codenamed El Capitan.

On iPhone, iPad and iPod, versions of iOS (which is an OS

X derivative) are available from iOS 1.0 to the recent iOS 9. The iOS devices, however, are not considered PCs.

Linux   Main article: Linux
Linux is a family of Unix-like computer operating systems.

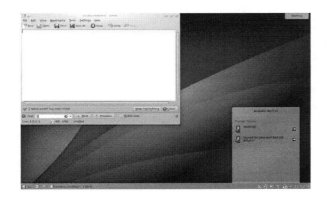

A Linux distribution running KDE Plasma Desktop.

Linux is one of the most prominent examples of free software and open source development: typically all underlying source code can be freely modified, used, and redistributed by anyone.[72] The name "Linux" refers to the Linux kernel, started in 1991 by Linus Torvalds. The system's utilities and libraries usually come from the GNU operating system, announced in 1983 by Richard Stallman. The GNU contribution is the basis for the alternative name GNU/Linux.[73]

Known for its use in servers, with the LAMP application stack as one of prominent examples, Linux is supported by corporations such as Dell, Hewlett-Packard, IBM, Novell, Oracle Corporation, Red Hat, Canonical Ltd. and Sun Microsystems. It is used as an operating system for a wide variety of computer hardware, including desktop computers, netbooks, supercomputers,[74] video game systems such as the Steam Machine or PlayStation 3 (until this option was removed remotely by Sony in 2010[75]), several arcade games, and embedded devices such as mobile phones, portable media players, routers, and stage lighting systems.

Applications

Main article: Application software
Generally, a computer user uses application software to carry out a specific task. System software supports applications and provides common services such as memory management, network connectivity and device drivers, all of which may be used by applications but are not directly of interest to the end user. A simplified analogy in the world of hardware would be the relationship of an electric light bulb (an application) to an electric power generation plant

A screenshot of GIMP, which is a raster graphics editor

(a system): the power plant merely generates electricity, not itself of any real use until harnessed to an application like the electric light that performs a service that benefits the user.

Typical examples of software applications are word processors, spreadsheets, and media players. Multiple applications bundled together as a package are sometimes referred to as an *application suite*. Microsoft Office and OpenOffice.org, which bundle together a word processor, a spreadsheet, and several other discrete applications, are typical examples. The separate applications in a suite usually have a user interface that has some commonality making it easier for the user to learn and use each application. Often, they may have some capability to interact with each other in ways beneficial to the user; for example, a spreadsheet might be able to be embedded in a word processor document even though it had been created in the separate spreadsheet application.

End-user development tailors systems to meet the user's specific needs. User-written software include spreadsheet templates, word processor macros, scientific simulations, graphics and animation scripts; even email filters are a kind of user software. Users create this software themselves and often overlook how important it is.

Gaming

PC gaming is popular among the high-end PC market. According to an April 2014 market analysis, Gaming platforms like Steam (software), Uplay, Origin, and GOG.com (as well as competitive e-sports titles like League of Legends) are largely responsible for PC systems overtaking console revenue in 2013.[76]

1.18.6 Toxicity

Toxic chemicals found in some computer hardware include lead, mercury, cadmium, chromium, plastic (PVC), and barium. Overall, a computer is about 17% lead, copper, zinc, mercury, and cadmium; 23% is plastic, 14% is aluminum, and 20% is iron.

Lead is found in a cathode ray tube (CRT) display, and on all of the printed circuit boards and most expansion cards. Mercury is located in the screen's fluorescent lamp, in the laser light generators in the optical disk drive, and in the round, silver-looking batteries on the motherboard. Plastic is found mostly in the housing of the computation and display circuitry.

While daily end-users are not exposed to these toxic elements, the danger arises during the computer recycling process, which involves manually breaking down hardware and leads to the exposure of a measurable amount of lead or mercury. A measurable amount of lead or mercury can easily cause serious brain damage or ruin drinking water supplies. Computer recycling is best handled by the electronic waste (e-waste) industry, and kept segregated from the general community dump.

Electronic waste regulation

Main article: Computer recycling

Personal computers have become a large contributor to the 50 million tons of discarded electronic waste that is being generated annually, according to the United Nations Environment Programme. To address the electronic waste issue affecting developing countries and the environment, extended producer responsibility (EPR) acts have been implemented in various countries and states.[77]

Organizations, such as the Silicon Valley Toxics Coalition, Basel Action Network, Toxics Link India, SCOPE, and Greenpeace have contributed to these efforts. In the absence of comprehensive national legislation or regulation on the export and import of electronic waste, the Silicon Valley Toxics Coalition and BAN (Basel Action Network) teamed up with 32 electronic recyclers in the US and Canada to create an e-steward program for the orderly disposal of manufacturers and customers electronic waste. The Silicon Valley Toxics Coalition founded the Electronics Take-Back Coalition, a coalition that advocates for the production of environmentally friendly products. The TakeBack Coalition works with policy makers, recyclers, and smart businesses to get manufacturers to take full responsibility of their products.

There are organizations opposing EPR regulation, such as

the Reason Foundation. They see flaws in two principal tenants of EPR: First EPR relies on the idea that if the manufacturers have to pay for environmental harm, they will adapt their practices. Second EPR assumes the current design practices are environmentally inefficient. The Reason Foundation claims that manufacturers naturally move toward reduced material and energy use.

1.18.7 See also

- Computer case
- Computer virus
- Desktop computer
- Desktop replacement computer
- e-waste
- IBM 5100
- Information and communication technologies for development
- Laptop
- List of computer system manufacturers
- Market share of personal computer vendors
- Personal Computer Museum
- Portable computer
- Public computer
- Quiet PC
- PC game

1.18.8 Notes

[1] The NeXT computer introduced in 1988 did not include a floppy drive, which at the time was unusual.

1.18.9 References

[1] Conlon, Tom (January 29, 2010), *The iPad's Closed System: Sometimes I Hate Being Right*, Popular Science, retrieved 2010-10-14, The iPad is not a personal computer in the sense that we currently understand.

[2] "Steve Jobs Offers World 'Freedom From Porn'", *Gawker*, May 15, 2010, retrieved 2010-10-14

[3] "The incredible story of the first PC, from 1965". Pingdom. Retrieved August 28, 2012.

[4] Pospelov, Dmitry. ЭВМ серии МИР - первые персональные ЭВМ[MIR series of computers. The first personal computers]. *Glushkov Foundation* (in Russian). Institute of Applied Informatics. Retrieved November 19, 2012.

[5] IBM Archives

[6] *PC Magazine*, Vol. 2, No. 6, November 1983, "SCAMP: The Missing Link in the PC's Past?"

[7] Jim Battle (August 9, 2008). "The Wang 2200". *Wang2200.org*. Jim Battle. Retrieved November 13, 2013.

[8] What's New (February 1978), "Commodore Ships First PET Computers", *BYTE* (Byte Publications) **3** (2): 190 Commodore press release. "The PET computer made its debut recently as the first 100 units were shipped to waiting customers in mid-October 1977."

[9] "Apple II History". Apple II History. Retrieved May 8, 2014.

[10] "Sinclair Research website". Retrieved 2014-08-06.

[11] Reimer, Jeremy (November 2, 2009). "Personal Computer Market Share: 1975–2004". Retrieved 2009-07-17.

[12] Reimer, Jeremy (December 2, 2012). "Personal Computer Market Share: 1975–2004". Retrieved 2013-02-09.

[13] "Computing Japan". *Computing Japan* (LINC Japan). 54-59: 18. 1999. Retrieved February 6, 2012. ...its venerable PC 9800 series, which has sold more than 18 million units over the years, and is the reason why NEC has been the number one PC vendor in Japan for as long as anyone can remember.

[14] Polsson, Ken. "Chronology of Amiga Computers". Retrieved May 9, 2014.

[15] Angler, Martin. "Obituary: The PC is Dead". JACKED IN. Retrieved February 12, 2014.

[16] Kanellos, Michael. "PCs: More than 1 billion served". CNET News. Retrieved August 9, 2001.

[17] Kanellos, Michael (June 30, 2002). "personal computers: More than 1 billion served". CNET News. Retrieved 2010-10-14.

[18] "Computers reach one billion mark". BBC News. July 1, 2002. Retrieved 2010-10-14.

[19] Global PC shipments grew 13.8 percent in 2010 – Gartner study, Jan 13, 2011, retrieved at September 12, 2011

[20] Laptop Sales Soaring Amid Wider PC Growth: Gartner, May 27, 2010, Andy Patrizio, earthweb.com, retrieved at September 12, 2011

[21] Worldwide PC Shipments in 2008, March 16, 2009, ZDNet, retrieved at September 12, 2011

[22] PC Sales Up for 2008, but Barely, January 14, 2009, Andy Patrizio, internetnews.com, retrieved at September 12, 2011

[23] *ISuppli Raises 2007 Computer Sales Forecast*, pcworld.com, retrieved January 13, 2009

[24] *iSuppli raises 2007 computer sales forecast*, Macworld UK, retrieved January 13, 2009

[25] *Global PC Sales Leveling Off*, newsfactor.com, retrieved January 13, 2009

[26] *HP back on top of PC market*, retrieved January 13, 2009

[27] Yates, Nona (January 24, 2000). "Dell Passes Compaq as Top PC Seller in U.S". Los Angeles Times. Retrieved January 13, 2009.

[28] *Economic recovery bumps AP 1999 PC shipments to record high*, zdnetasia.com, retrieved January 13, 2009

[29] "Worldwide PC use to reach 1 billion by 2008: report". CBC News. Retrieved June 12, 2007.

[30] "Gartner Says More than 1 Billion PCs In Use Worldwide and Headed to 2 Billion Units by 2014" (Press release). Gartner. June 23, 2008. Retrieved 2010-10-14.

[31] Tarmo Virki (June 23, 2008). "Computers in use pass 1 billion mark: Gartner". Reuters. Retrieved 2010-10-14.

[32] "China hits tech milestone: PC shipments pass US". August 23, 2011.

[33] "4P Computing - Negroponte's 14 Million Laptop Impact". OLPC News. December 11, 2008. Retrieved 2010-10-14.

[34] Conrad H. Blickenstorfer. "Rugged PC leaders". Ruggedpcreview.com. Retrieved 2010-10-14.

[35] "PC Rebound in Mature Regions Stabilizes Market, But Falls Short of Overall Growth in the Second Quarter of 2014". International Data Corporation.

[36] "After Two Years of Decline, Worldwide PC Shipments Experienced Flat Growth in Second Quarter of 2014". Gartner.

[37] Tablets, smartphones to outsell PCs http://news.yahoo.com/s/afp/20110210/tc_afp/itinternettelecomequipmentmobileconsumerproduct

[38] "Gartner Says Declining Worldwide PC Shipments in Fourth Quarter of 2012 Signal Structural Shift of PC Market". *Gartner.Com* (Press release). January 14, 2013. Retrieved January 18, 2013.

[39] "Feeble PC industry stumbles to steep sales drop during 1st quarter as Windows makeover flops". *Washington Times*. Associated Press. April 10, 2013. Retrieved April 11, 2013.

[40] Nick Wingfield (April 10, 2013). "PC Sales Still in a Slump, Despite New Offerings". *New York Times*. Retrieved April 11, 2013.

[41] "Steve Ballmer's retirement leaves Microsoft in a replacement crisis". August 24, 2013.

[42] "The Apple Vs. Samsung Title Fight for Mobile Supremacy". *The Financialist.* Credit Suisse. August 8, 2013. Retrieved August 13, 2013.

[43] John Fingas (March 4, 2014). "PC shipments faced their steepest-ever drop in 2013".

[44] Marvin B. Sussman *Personal Computers and the Family* Routledge, 1985 ISBN 0-86656-361-X, page 90

[45] Kateri M. Drexler *Icons of business: an encyclopedia of mavericks, movers, and shakers, Volume 1*, Greenwood Publishing Group, 2007 ISBN 0-313-33863-9 page 102

[46] Nancy Weil, *Average PC Price drops below $1000*, PC World December 1998, Retrieved November 17, 2010

[47] Joe Wilcox (April 16, 2009). "Netbooks Are Destroying the Laptop Market and Microsoft Needs to Act Now". eWeek. Retrieved 2010-10-14.

[48] Shane O'Neill (December 2, 2009). "Falling PC Prices Pit Microsoft Against PC Makers". Retrieved 2010-10-14.

[49] "Mac* vs. PC Debate". *intel.com.* Intel. Retrieved 5 October 2014.

[50] Finnie, Scot (8 June 2007). "Mac vs. PC cost analysis: How does it all add up?". *Computerworld.* Computerworld, Inc. Retrieved 5 October 2014.

[51] Ackerman, Dan (22 August 2013). "Don't buy a new PC or Mac before you read this". *CNET.* CBS Interactive. Retrieved 5 October 2014.

[52] Haslam, Karen (11 December 2013). "Mac or PC? Ten reasons why Macs are better than PCs". *Macworld.* IDG. Retrieved 5 October 2014.

[53] Hoffman, Chris. "Macs Are PCs! Can We Stop Pretending They Aren't?". *How-To Geek.* Retrieved 15 October 2015.

[54] Ralston, Anthony; Reilly, Edwin (1993). "Workstation". *Encyclopedia of Computer Science* (Third ed.). New York: Van Nostrand Reinhold. ISBN 0-442-27679-6.

[55] Houghton, Andy. "Evolution of Custom Gaming PCs: What Really Made the Difference". *digitalstorm.com.* Retrieved 28 September 2015.

[56] Desktop notebooks stake their claim, accessed October 19, 2007

[57] Erica Ogg (August 20, 2009). "Time to drop the Netbook label". CNN.

[58] Walt Mossberg (August 6, 2009). "New Netbook Offers Long Battery Life and Room to Type". The Wall Street Journal Online, Personal Technology.

[59] "Cheap PCs Weigh on Microsoft". Business Technologies, The Wall Street Journal. December 8, 2008.

[60] "UMID Netbook Only 4.8". Elitezoom.com. Retrieved 2010-10-14.

[61] "CES 2009 - MSI Unveils the X320 "MacBook Air Clone" Netbook". Futurelooks.com. 2009-01-07. Retrieved 2010-10-14.

[62] *Netbook Trends and Solid-State Technology Forecast* (PDF). pricegrabber.com. p. 7. Retrieved 2009-01-28.

[63] *Light and Cheap, Netbooks Are Poised to Reshape PC Industry*, The New York Times, April 1, 2009, retrieved 2010-10-14, AT&T announced on Tuesday that customers in Atlanta could get a type of compact PC called a netbook for just 50 US$ if they signed up for an Internet service plan... 'The era of a perfect Internet computer for 99 US$ is coming this year,' said Jen-Hsun Huang, the chief executive of Nvidia, a maker of PC graphics chips that is trying to adapt to the new technological order.

[64] "Tablet PC Redux?". *Paul Thurrott's Supersite for Windows.* Retrieved October 6, 2013.

[65] New Windows Mobile 6 Devices :: Jun/Jul 2007

[66] Berkeley Lab. *Integrated Safety Management: Ergonomics.* Website. Retrieved July 9, 2008.

[67] "Wordreference.com: WordNet 2.0". Princeton University, Princeton, NJ. Retrieved 2007-08-19.

[68] "A history of Windows: Highlights from the first 25 years".

[69] Mary Bellis. "The Unusual History of Microsoft Windows". About.com. Retrieved 2010-10-14.

[70] "IDC: Consolidation to Windows won't happen". Linuxworld. Retrieved 2010-10-14.

[71] "Thirty Years of Mac: 1984 - Macintosh". Apple. Retrieved May 8, 2014.

[72] "Linux Online — About the Linux Operating System". Linux.org. Retrieved 2007-07-06.

[73] Weeks, Alex (2004). "1.1". *Linux System Administrator's Guide* (version 0.9 ed.). Retrieved 2007-01-18.

[74] Lyons, Daniel (March 15, 2005). "Linux rules supercomputers". *Forbes.* Retrieved 2007-02-22.

[75] Patrick Seybold (March 28, 2010). "PS3 Firmware (v3.21) Update". PlayStation.Blog. Retrieved March 29, 2010.

[76] Mark Serrels. "PC Gaming Revenue Has Now Overtaken Console Gaming". *kotaku.com.au.* Retrieved June 8, 2015.

[77] Nash, Jennifer; Bosso, Christopher (2013). "Extended Producer Responsibility in the United States: Full Speed Ahead?" (PDF). *Journal of Industrial Ecology* **17** (2 - RPP-2013-04): 175–185. doi:10.1111/j.1530-9290.2012.00572.x. Retrieved August 23, 2014.

1.18.10 Further reading

- *Accidental Empires: How the boys of Silicon Valley make their millions, battle foreign competition, and still can't get a date*, Robert X. Cringely, Addison-Wesley Publishing, (1992), ISBN 0-201-57032-7

- *PC Magazine*, Vol. 2, No. 6, November 1983, "SCAMP: The Missing Link in the PC's Past?"

1.18.11 External links

- How Stuff Works pages:
  - Dissecting a PC
  - How PCs Work
  - How to Upgrade Your Computer
  - How to Build a Computer

1.19 Sound chip

A **sound chip** is an integrated circuit (i.e. "chip") designed to produce sound (see chiptune). It might be doing this through digital, analog or mixed-mode electronics. Sound chips normally contain things like oscillators, envelope controllers, samplers, filters and amplifiers. During the late 20th century, sound chips were widely used in arcade game system boards, video game consoles, home computers, and PC sound cards.

1.19.1 Programmable sound generators (PSG)

Atari

- Atari TIA, combined sound and graphics chip, used in the Atari 2600 and Atari 7800 video game consoles.

- Atari POKEY, used in Atari 8-bit home computers, the Atari 5200 console, and certain Atari 7800 cartridges.

- Atari AMY, intended for the 65XEM, but never released.

General Instrument

- General Instrument AY-3-8910, used in arcade boards (DECO,[1] Taito Z80,[2] Konami Scramble,[3] Irem M27,[4] Konami 6809,[5] Capcom Z80[6]), computers (Colour Genie, Oric 1, Elektor TVGC, Mockingboard), and the Intellivision.

- General Instrument SP0250, LPC (linear predictive coding) speech synthesis chip used in the Sega G80 arcade system board.

- General Instrument SP0256, LPC speech synthesis chip.

Konami

- Konami RC, used in the Konami Scramble[7] and *Gyruss*[8] arcade system boards.

- Konami VRC6, used in certain Konami-produced Famicom cartridges.

MOS Technology

- MOS Technology 6560/6561 "VIC", used in the Commodore VIC-1001 and VIC-20.

- MOS Technology 6581/8580 "SID", used in the Commodore 64 and Commodore 128.

- MOS Technology 7360/8360 "TED", used in the Commodore 16 and Commodore Plus/4.

Philips

- Philips SAA1099, used in the SAM Coupé.

Ricoh

- Ricoh 2A03/2A07, used in the Nintendo Entertainment System/Famicom home console (hardware expandable) and the arcade game *Punch-Out!!*

Sega

- Sega Melody Generator, used in the Sega G80 arcade system board.[9]

- Sega PSG (SN76496), used in the Sega Z80,[10] Sega Zaxxon and System E arcade boards, and the Sega Master System and Mega Drive/Genesis consoles.[11]

Sunsoft

- Sunsoft 5B (derivative of Yamaha YM2149F), used in the Famicom cartridge *Gimmick!*

Texas Instruments

- Texas Instruments SN76477, used in the *Space Invaders* arcade system board.

- Texas Instruments SN76489 "DCSG", used in various arcade system boards, the Sega SG-1000 console, and the BBC Micro and Texas Instruments TI-99/4A computers.

- Texas Instruments SN76489A "DCSG", used in the ColecoVision, Sega Master System and Mega Drive/Genesis consoles, and the Sega Game Gear and Pico handheld game consoles.

- Texas Instruments SN76496, used in the Tandy 1000 computer.

Yamaha

- Yamaha YM2149 (based on General Instrument AY-3-8910), used in various arcade boards, and the Atari ST, MSX, Amstrad CPC and ZX Spectrum computers with 128K RAM.

1.19.2 Wavetable-lookup synthesis ("wavetable")

Note: Wavetable-lookup synthesis chips are sometimes incorrectly referred as *wavetable synthesis*.

Atari

- Jerry, used in the Atari Jaguar. Also supports FM synthesis and PCM (sample-based synthesis).

Hudson Soft/Epson

- Hudson Soft HuC6280, used in NEC's PC Engine/TurboGrafx-16 console.

Konami

- Konami SCC, used in certain arcade boards and game carts for the MSX.

Namco

- Namco WSG (Waveform Sound Generator),[12] used in several Namco arcade system boards, including Namco Pac-Man and Namco Galaga.[13]

- Namco 15xx (WSG), used in the Namco Super Pac-Man arcade system board.[13][14]

- Namco 52xx (Audio Processor), used in the Namco Galaga and Namco Pole Position arcade system boards.[15]

- Namco 54xx (Audio Generator), used in the Namco Pole Position arcade system board.[15]

- Namco CUS30, used in the Namco System 1,[13] Namco Thunder Ceptor and System 86 arcade boards.

- Namco 163, used in Namco-produced Famicom games.

1.19.3 Frequency modulation synthesis (FM synth)

Atari

- Jerry, used in the Atari Jaguar. Also supports single-cycle wavetable-lookup synthesis and PCM (sample-based synthesis).

Konami

- Konami VRC7, a modified derivative of Yamaha's YM2413, used in the Famicom cartridge *Lagrange Point*

Yamaha

- Yamaha YM2413 (a.k.a. OPLL), used in the Japanese Sega Master System, and in the MSX in MSX Music cartridges like the FM-PAC and internally in several Japanese models by Panasonic, Sony and Sanyo

- Yamaha YM2203 (a.k.a. OPN), used in some 80's arcade games and the NEC PC-88 and PC-98 computers

- Yamaha YM2151 (a.k.a. OPM), used in mid-80's to mid-90's arcade games (the most prolific FM chip used in arcades), the Sharp X68000 computer, and the Yamaha SFG-01 and SFG-05 FM Sound Synthesizer Unit cartridges for the MSX

- Yamaha YM2608 (a.k.a. OPNA), used in the NEC PC-88 and PC-98 computers

- Yamaha YM2610 (a.k.a. OPNB), used in the SNK Neo Geo console

- Yamaha YM2612 (a.k.a. OPN2), used in the Sega Mega Drive / Genesis console and FM Towns computer

- Yamaha YM3526 (a.k.a. OPL)

- Yamaha Y8950 (a.k.a. MSX-AUDIO, very similar to Yamaha YM3526), used in MSX-Audio cartridges for the MSX: Panasonic FS-CA1, Toshiba HX-MU900, and Philips NMS-1205

- Yamaha YM3812 (a.k.a. OPL2), used in AdLib and early Sound Blaster sound cards for the PC

- Yamaha YMF262 (a.k.a. OPL3), used in Sound Blaster Pro 2.0 and later cards for the PC

- Yamaha YMF278 (a.k.a. OPL4), used in the Moonsound cartridge for the MSX computer

- Yamaha YMF288 (a.k.a. OPN3), used in the NEC PC-98 computer

- Yamaha YMF7xx (Embedded audio chipset in some laptops and soundcards)

1.19.4 Pulse-code modulation (PCM, sample-based)

Atari

- Jerry, used in the Atari Jaguar. Also supports FM and single-cycle wavetable-lookup synthesis.

Drucegrove

- Digitalker MM54104, a DM (delta modulation) DPCM (differential PCM) speech synthesis chip used in the Namco Galaxian (*King & Balloon*) and *Scorpion* arcade system boards

Harris

- HC-55516, a CVSD (continuously variable slope delta modulation) ADM (adaptive delta modulation) speech coding decoder used in the *Red Alert*,[16] *Sinistar*[17] and Midway Y Unit[18] arcade system boards

MOS Technology

- MOS Technology 8364 "Paula", used in the Commodore Amiga computer

Namco

- Namco C140, used in the Namco System 21 arcade board

- Namco C352, used in the Namco System 22 arcade board

Oki

- Oki MSM5205, ADPCM chip used in various arcade system boards (Irem M-52,[19] Data East Z80,[20] Capcom 68000)[21] and NEC's PC Engine CD-ROM²/TurboGrafx-CD console

- Oki MSM6258, used in Sharp's X68000 computer

- Oki MSM6295

Ricoh

- Ricoh RF5c68, used in the Fujitsu FM Towns computer and the Sega System 18 and System 32 arcade boards

Sanyo

- VLM5030 Speech Synthesizer, a speech synthesis chip used in the arcade game *Punch-Out!!*

Sega

- SegaPCM, used in the Sega Space Harrier, Sega Out-Run, X Board and Y Board arcade system boards

- Sega MultiPCM, used in the Sega System Multi 32, Sega Model 1 and Model 2 arcade boards

Sony

- Sony SPC700, used in the Super Nintendo Entertainment System console

1.19.5 See also

- Programmable sound generator

- Sound card

1.19.6 References

[1] http://www.system16.com/hardware.php?id=913

[2] http://www.system16.com/hardware.php?id=628

[3] http://www.system16.com/hardware.php?id=554

[4] http://www.system16.com/hardware.php?id=735

[5] http://www.system16.com/hardware.php?id=556

[6] http://www.system16.com/hardware.php?id=787

[7] http://www.arcade-history.com/?n= scramble-model-gx387&page=detail&id=2328

[8] http://www.arcade-history.com/?n=gyruss-model-gx347& page=detail&id=1063

[9] https://github.com/mamedev/mame/blob/master/src/ mame/audio/segag80r.c

[10] http://system16.com/hardware.php?id=688&gid=3239

[11] https://github.com/mamedev/mame/blob/master/src/emu/ sound/sn76496.c

[12] http://webcache.googleusercontent.com/search?q=cache: FU_nncKCzgIJ:pacman.shaunew.com/redmine/projects/ pacman/repository/revisions/master/raw/doc/pie/wsg3.htm

[13] https://github.com/mamedev/mame/blob/master/src/emu/ sound/namco.c

[14] http://www.system16.com/hardware.php?id=519

[15] http://www.multigame.com/NAMCO.html

[16] https://github.com/mamedev/mame/blob/master/src/ mame/audio/redalert.c

[17] http://www.mamereviews.hubmed.org/set/sinistar

[18] http://www.system16.com/hardware.php?id=610

[19] http://www.system16.com/hardware.php?id=736

[20] http://www.system16.com/hardware.php?id=931

[21] http://www.system16.com/hardware.php?id=791

1.19.7 External links

- Sound generators of the 1980s home computers - Has a list of chips, pictures, datasheets, etc.

1.20 Synthwave

Synthwave; also called **Retrowave** or **outrun**,[1] is a musical style that emerged in the mid-2000s, influenced by 1980s soundtrack music.[1][2][3][4]

1.20.1 Style

Musically, synthwave is heavily inspired by new wave and the soundtracks of many 1980s films, videogames, cartoons and television shows.[3][5][6] Composers such as John Carpenter and Tangerine Dream are frequently cited as influences.[1][7] The style is mainly instrumental, and often contain 80s cliché elements in the sound such as electronic drums, gated reverb, analog synthesizer bass lines and leads, all to resemble tracks from that time period. However, synthwave incorporates modern production techniques such as sidechained compression and placing the bassline and kick drum prominentliy in the mix as heard in modern electronic music genres such as electro house.[7]

Aesthetically, synthwave gives a retrofuturistic perspective, emulating 1980s science fiction, action, and horror media.[5][8] In this sense, it can be considered the inverse of vaporwave; while the latter expresses disdain for 80s culture, synthwave expresses nostalgia for it[7] and attempts to capture the era's atmosphere.[9] Examples of this aesthetic may be viewed in films and video games such as *Drive*,[6] *Hotline Miami*,[10][11] the upcoming game *Power Drive 2000*,[10][12] and *Far Cry 3: Blood Dragon*.[13][14]

1.20.2 History

Background

In 2005 French Electronic Musician David Grellier began making music under the name College. In 2008 he released the EP "Teenage Color" which, because of its structure, chord progression and sound character is very characteristic for synthwave as a genre, can be looked upon as a starting point of the style as we know it today. In an interview Grellier says his music is influenced from "80's soaps and an aesthetic which I particularly like: color, images, silvery films and the sun – images of Los Angeles, Chicago and all of the other cities that [...] continue to fascinate me".[15] In 2011 he released the album "Northern Council"[16] and the same year the track "Real Hero" with Electric Youth, that was featured in the movie *Drive* which drew more attention to the music as a genre.[17][18]

During the same time period, French artists Lifelike[19] and Anoraak contributed to the synthwave sound with similar musical references: Anoraak states in a 2014 interview: "American pop culture is definitely my background as a kid. I was born in 1980, so I grew up in a world taken by American music and movies".[20]

Growth

Following the movie Drive, several artists emerged influenced by the sound and the imagery of the movie.[21][22] Swedish artist Mitch Murder [23][24] was one of the other early artists starting in 2009, and paved the way in introducing the video game music as a part of the Synthwave sound.[25][26][27]

During the same time period, several independent record labels emerged where the main focus was releasing artists in the retroesque synthwave genre, such as Telefuture Records, Rosso Corsa Records, Aphasia Records, Future City Records, Future 80s Records, and 30th Floor Records.[28][29][30][31]

Present

Apart from the early artists College and Kavinsky, a significant number of artists have emerged.[32] The darker sound from Kavinsky has been carried on by artists such as Power Glove,[33] Lazerhawk, Perturbator,[7] Lost Years, Bourgeoisie and Waveshaper,[34] and the more easy-listening heritage of the genre brought by College, Lifelike and Anoraak is continued by artists like Miami Nights 1984,[35] Futurecop!,[36] Timecop1983,[37] Le Cassette, Betamaxx,[38] Robert Parker ,[39] Highway Superstar and Phaserland.[6][40]

Com Truise also describes his music as synthwave.[41] Other synthwave artists include Magic Sword[42] and Cold Cave.[43]

Following a successful crowdfunding campaign in 2014,[44] the Youtube short *Kung Fury* further lifted Synthwave into a mainstream audience, with both its visual language from 1980s cop and sci-fi movies, combined with a soundtrack containing several artists from the synthwave scene such as Lost Years, Mitch Murder, Betamaxx, and Highway Superstar.[45][46]

Alex Westaway and Dan Haigh of the post-hardcore band Fightstar started a synthwave side project, "Gunship", with a debut album released on 24 July 2015.[47]

1.20.3 Artists commonly associated with Synthwave

- Absolute Valentine
- Perturbator
- Mitch Murder[23][24]
- Miami Nights 1984
- Cold Cave[43]

- College[15]
- Com Truise[41]
- Electric Youth[17]
- Futurecop![36]
- Kavinsky[6]
- Power Glove[33]
- Valerie collective[7]

1.20.4 See also

- Vaporwave
- Chillwave
- Cyberspace
- Retrofuturism

1.20.5 References

[1] Hunt, Jon (9 April 2014). "We Will Rock You: Welcome To The Future. This is Synthwave.". l'etoile. Retrieved 18 May 2015.

[2] "A Retrowave Primer: 9 Artists Bringing Back the '80s". MTV Iggy. Retrieved 23 June 2015.

[3] Disabato, Catie. *The Ghost Network: A Novel*. ISBN 978-1612194349. Retrieved 19 May 2015.

[4] Young, Bryan (25 March 2015). "Synthwave: If Tron and Megaman had a music baby.". Glitchslap.com. Retrieved 2015-05-19.

[5] Raymer, Miles (2013-02-27). "Kavinsky: Outrun". Pitchfork Media. Retrieved 2015-05-24.

[6] Christopher Higgins (2014-07-29). "The 7 Most Essential Synthwave Artists". Nerdglow.com. Retrieved 2015-05-18.

[7] McCasker, Toby (2014-06-22). "Riding the Cyber Doom Synthwave With Perturbator | NOISEY". Noisey.vice.com. Retrieved 2015-05-19. Electronic music has lost a lot of its musicality lately. It's all drops and bass lines looped for five minutes non-stop. Back in the '80s, you had classic themes and iconic melodies. I try to take the best of '80s music and the best of what modern electro has. The 80s were the golden age of synths too, with master composers like Vangelis and Tangerine Dream, who are huge inspirations for most of us in this genre. There's this special imagery that comes up in your mind when you think about this decade. There's a lot of '80s cliché that I find to be extremely cool, like gory practical effects or over-saturated neon colours.

[8] "Perturbator - DANGEROUS DAYS". Scene Point Blank. 2014-12-01. Retrieved 2015-05-24.

[9] Calvert, John (13 October 2011). "Xeno and Oaklander - Sets & Lights". Drowned in Sound. Retrieved 8 June 2015.

[10] Haulica, Radu (7 May 2015). "Power Drive 2000 Is an '80s Inspired Arcade Racer with a Great Soundtrack". Softpedia.

[11] Inverno, Julien (12 May 2015). "Perturbator et Hotline miami : du sang sur le beat". IGN France.

[12] Fekete, Bob. "Power Drive 2000 Mixes Mario Kart, Knight Rider, And Blade Runner". iDigitalTimes. Retrieved 30 May 2015.

[13] Roche, Antoine (19 May 2015). "Power Drive 2000 : un KickStarter pour un jeu de course bourré de nostalgie". *begeek.fr*. Retrieved 30 May 2015.

[14] "Discipline Reviews: Power Glove - Far Cry 3: Blood Dragon (2013)". *EscapistMagazine.com*. The Escapist Magazine. 7 January 2015. Retrieved 30 May 2015.

[15] "Interview with David Grellier of College and founder of the Valerie Collective 2009". Whatsonthehifi.com. Retrieved 2015-05-18.

[16] "Search Results for college northern council - Magicrpm". *magicrpm.com*.

[17] "Record Makers - Drive (OST)". *recordmakers.com*. Archived from the original on 5 August 2013.

[18] "sexy sushi : À l'Ouest du son". Alouestduson.blogs.ouest-france.fr. 2011-12-17. Retrieved 2015-05-18.

[19] "Lifelike Interview: Killahbeez Exclusive". Killahbeez.com. Retrieved 2015-05-19.

[20] "Interview with Anoraak". Whatsonthehifi.com. Retrieved 2015-05-19.

[21] Eric James Lyman (2015-01-11). "Eric James Lyman - Synthwave". Ericlyman.net. Retrieved 2015-05-19.

[22] "Spotify". *spotify.com*.

[23] "Sveriges nästa superstjärna älskar synthen 29 juli 2014 kl 17:30 - Musikguiden i P3 I Sveriges Radio". T.sr.se. 2014-07-29. Retrieved 2015-05-19.

[24] "Music I mitch murder". Mitchmurder.bandcamp.com. 2010-07-22. Retrieved 2015-05-18.

[25] "Mitch Murder Profile I Rosso Corsa". Rossocorsarecords.com. 2011-04-01. Retrieved 2015-05-18.

[26] "Smooth as Chrome – An Interview with Sweden's Mitch Murder". Synconation.com. Retrieved 2015-05-18.

[27] "TILLBAKA TILL ÅTTIOTALET MED MITCH MURDER I Upplevgbg - Livets goda, På djupet". Upplevgbg.se. Retrieved 2015-05-18.

[28] "Telefuture - Releases". Telefuturenow.com. Retrieved 2015-05-18.

[29] "Rosso Corsa I Music Cars Fashion Lifestyle". Rossocorsarecords.com. Retrieved 2015-05-18.

[30] "Future City Records". Futurecityrecords.com. Retrieved 2015-05-18.

[31] Robert Moog. "Future 80's Records I The True Sound Of The Future". Future80srecords.com. Retrieved 2015-05-18.

[32] "DREAMWAVE-MUSIK, AXELVADDAR OCH NEON I Upplevgbg - Livets goda, På djupet". Upplevgbg.se. Retrieved 2015-05-18.

[33] "Power Glove Interview: Reviving the 80s (July 2013)". Game-ost.com. 1970-01-01. Retrieved 2015-05-19.

[34] "Interview w/Waveshaper". *The French Shuffle*.

[35] "Miami Nights 1984 presents: Stallions · Stoney Roads". Stoneyroads.com. Retrieved 2015-05-19.

[36] "Disco Unchained: Saturday Sit-down with Futurecop!". Discounchained.blogspot.se. 2014-07-05. Retrieved 2015-05-19.

[37] "Interview - Timecop1983". *NewRetroWave*.

[38] "Interview: Betamaxx". *NEONVICE*.

[39] "Music - Robert Parker".

[40] Caliandro, Christian (8 March 2015). "Dreamwave, synthwave, new retro wave. Appunti sulla nostalgia sintetica". *artribune.com*. Attribune. Retrieved 30 May 2015.

[41] "Meet Com Truise: Synthwave Wunderkind". 1 September 2011. Retrieved 19 May 2015.

[42] Stuart, Keith (12 January 2015). "Hotline Miami 2 – listen to Magic Sword's contribution to the soundtrack". The Guardian. Retrieved 19 May 2015.

[43] Misir, Timothy (8 November 2013). "Appleseed Cast Gives Memorable Moscow Concert". The Moscow Times. Retrieved 19 May 2015. [...] as the gig calendar in the capital was packed with the likes of American synthwave band Cold Cave [...]

[44] Jess Denham (2013-12-27). "Wacky trailer for new action comedy Kung Fury released on Kickstarter - News - Films". Independent.co.uk. Retrieved 2015-05-18.

[45] Kooser, Amanda (2014-03-25). "David Hasselhoff rides a T. rex in 'Kung Fury' music video". CNET.com. Retrieved 2015-05-18.

[46] "Kung Fury: Beyond Awesome". Futurecityrecords.com. 2013-12-29. Retrieved 2015-05-18.

[47] Interview: Fightstar "We're going to write new material", *fortitudemagazine.co.uk*

1.21 Video game music

Video game music is the soundtrack or background music accompanying video games. Originally limited to simple melodies by early sound synthesizer technology, video game music has grown to include the same breadth and complexity associated with television and movie soundtracks. While simple synthesizer pieces are still common, game music now can include full orchestral pieces and licensed popular music. Video games can now also generate or alter their soundtrack based on the player's current actions or situation, such as indicating missed actions in rhythm games.

Beginning in the early 2000s, it became increasingly common for video game soundtracks to be commercially sold or performed in concerts that focus on video game music.[1] The early limitations on video game music also inspired the style of music known as chiptunes that use the original simple melodic styles, sometimes sampled directly from classic games, with more complex patterns or mixed with the traditional music styles.

With the expansion of the video game market, artists going between popular music, classical music, the film industry and video games has become more common. Composers and artists famous for other music—such as film composers Harry Gregson-Williams, Trent Reznor and Hans Zimmer—have worked on soundtracks for recent games, while Michael Giacchino, now normally known for his film scores, began with *Mickey Mania* and continued with the *Medal of Honor* series.[2][3][4]

1.21.1 History

Early video game technology and computer chip music

See also: Chiptune

At the time video games emerged as a popular form of entertainment in the late 1970s (the golden age of arcade video games and second-generation consoles), music was stored on physical medium in analog waveforms such as compact cassettes and phonograph records. Such components were expensive and prone to breakage under heavy use making them less than ideal for use in an arcade cabinet, though in rare cases, they were used (*Journey*). A more affordable method of having music in a video game was to use digital means, where a specific computer chip would change electrical impulses from computer code into analog sound waves on the fly for output on a speaker. Sound effects for the games were also generated in this fashion. An early example of such an approach to video game music was the opening chiptune in Tomohiro Nishikado's *Gun Fight* (1975).[5]

While this allowed for inclusion of music in early arcade video games, it was usually monophonic, looped or used sparingly between stages or at the start of a new game, such as the Namco titles *Pac-Man* (1980) composed by Toshio Kai or *Pole Position* (1982) composed by Nobuyuki Ohnogi.[6] The first game to use a continuous background soundtrack was Tomohiro Nishikado's *Space Invaders*, released by Taito in 1978. It had four simple chromatic descending bass notes repeating in a loop, though it was dynamic and interacted with the player, increasing pace as the enemies descended on the player.[7] The first video game to feature continuous, melodic background music was *Rally-X*, released by Namco in 1980, featuring a simple tune that repeats continuously during gameplay.[8] The decision to include any music into a video game meant that at some point it would have to be transcribed into computer code by a programmer, whether or not the programmer had musical experience. Some music was original, some was public domain music such as folk songs. Sound capabilities were limited; the popular Atari 2600 home system, for example, was capable of generating only two tones, or "notes", at a time.

As advances were made in silicon technology and costs fell, a definitively new generation of arcade machines and home consoles allowed for great changes in accompanying music. In arcades, machines based on the Motorola 68000 CPU and accompanying various Yamaha YM programmable sound generator sound chips allowed for several more tones or "channels" of sound, sometimes eight or more. The earliest known example of this was Sega's 1980 arcade game *Carnival*, which used an AY-3-8910 chip to create an electronic rendition of the classical 1889 composition "Over The Waves" by Juventino Rosas.[9]

Konami's 1981 arcade game *Frogger* introduced a dynamic approach to video game music, using at least eleven different gameplay tracks, in addition to level-starting and game over themes, which change according to the player's actions. This was further improved upon by Namco's 1982 arcade game *Dig Dug*, where the music stopped when the player stopped moving.[10] *Dig Dug* was composed by Yuriko Keino, who also composed the music for other Namco games such as *Xevious* (1982) and *Phozon* (1983).[6] Sega's 1982 arcade game *Super Locomotive* featured a chiptune rendition of Yellow Magic Orchestra's "Rydeen" (1979);[11] several later computer games also covered the song, such as *Trooper Truck* (1983) by Rabbit Software as well as *Daley Thompson's Decathlon* (1984) and *Stryker's Run* (1986) composed by Martin Galway.[12]

Home console systems also had a comparable upgrade in sound ability beginning with the ColecoVision in 1982 capable of four channels. However, more notable was the Japanese release of the Famicom in 1983 which was later released in the US as the Nintendo Entertainment System in 1985. It was capable of five channels, one being capable of simple PCM sampled sound. The home computer Commodore 64 released in 1982 was capable of early forms of filtering effects, different types of waveforms and eventually the ability to play 4-bit samples on a fourth sound channel. Its comparatively low cost made it a popular alternative to other home computers, as well as its ability to use a TV for an affordable display monitor.

Approach to game music development in this time period usually involved using simple tone generation and/or frequency modulation synthesis to simulate instruments for melodies, and use of a "noise channel" for simulating percussive noises. Early use of PCM samples in this era was limited to short sound bites(*Monopoly*), or as an alternate for percussion sounds (*Super Mario Bros 3*). The music on home consoles often had to share the available channels with other sound effects. For example, if a laser beam was fired by a spaceship, and the laser used a 1400 Hz tone, then whichever channel was in use by music would stop playing music and start playing the sound effect.

The mid-to-late 1980s software releases for these platforms had music developed by more people with greater musical experience than before. Quality of composition improved noticeably, and evidence of the popularity of music of this time period remains even today. Composers who made a name for themselves with their software include Koichi Sugiyama (*Dragon Quest*),[13] Nobuo Uematsu (*Final Fantasy*), Rob Hubbard (*Monty On the Run, International Karate*), Koji Kondo (*Super Mario Bros., The Legend of Zelda*), Miki Higashino (*Gradius, Yie-Ar Kung Fu, Teenage Mutant Ninja Turtles*), Hiroshi Kawaguchi (*Space Harrier, Hang-On, Out Run*), Hirokazu Tanaka (*Metroid, Kid Icarus, EarthBound*), Martin Galway (*Daley Thompson's Decathlon, Stryker's Run, Times of Lore*), Yuzo Koshiro (*Dragon Slayer, Ys, Shinobi, ActRaiser, Streets of Rage*), Mieko Ishikawa (*Dragon Slayer, Ys*), and Ryu Umemoto (visual novels, shoot 'em ups). By the late 1980s, video game music was being sold as cassette tape soundtracks in Japan, inspiring American companies such as Sierra, Cinemaware and Interplay to give more serious attention to video game music by 1988.[14] The Golden Joystick Awards introduced a category for *Best Soundtrack of the Year* in 1986, won by Sanxion.

Near the end of the life-cycle of the Famicom, some game producers at their own expense custom manufactured their cartridges with an additional tone generating chip. These chips added to the existing sound chip in the Famicom, but also sported extra features to modulate the additional channels.

Early digital synthesis and sampling

See also: Chiptune

From around 1980, some arcade games began taking steps toward digitized, or sampled, sounds. Namco's 1980 arcade game *Rally-X* was the first known game to use a digital-to-analog converter (DAC) to produce sampled tones instead of a tone generator.[9] That same year, the first known video game to feature speech synthesis was also released: Sunsoft's shoot 'em up game *Stratovox*.[8] Around the same time,[15] the introduction of frequency modulation synthesis (FM synthesis), first commercially released by Yamaha for their digital synthesizers and FM sound chips, allowed the tones to be manipulated to have different sound characteristics, where before the tone generated by the chip was limited to the design of the chip itself. Konami's 1983 arcade game *Gyruss* utilized five synthesis sound chips along with a DAC, which were partly used to create an electronic rendition of J. S. Bach's *Toccata and Fugue in D minor*.[16]

Beyond arcade games, significant improvements to personal computer game music were made possible with the introduction of digital FM synth boards, which Yamaha released for Japanese computers such as the NEC PC-8801 and PC-9801 in the early 1980s, and by the mid-1980s, the PC-8801 and FM-7 had built-in FM sound. This allowed computer game music to have greater complexity than the simplistic beeps from internal speakers. These FM synth boards produced a "warm and pleasant sound" that musicians such as Yuzo Koshiro and Takeshi Abo utilized to produce music that is still highly regarded within the chiptune community.[17] The widespread adoption of FM synthesis by consoles would later be one of the major advances of the 16-bit era, by which time 16-bit arcade machines were using multiple FM synthesis chips.[15]

One of the earliest home computers to make use of digital signal processing in the form of sampling was the Commodore Amiga in 1985. The computer's sound chip featured four independent 8-bit digital-to-analog converters. Developers could use this platform to take samples of a music performance, sometimes just a single note long, and play it back through the computer's sound chip from memory. This differed from *Rally-X* in that its hardware DAC was used to play back simple waveform samples, and a sampled sound allowed for a complexity and authenticity of a real instrument that an FM simulation could not offer. For its role in being one of the first and affordable, the Amiga would remain a staple tool of early sequenced music composing, especially in Europe.

The Amiga offered these features before other competing home computer platforms. The Amiga's main rival, the Atari ST, sourced the Yamaha YM2149 Programmable

Sound Generator (PSG). Compared to the in-house designed Amiga sound engine, the PSG could only handle 1 channel of sampled sound, and needed the computer's CPU to process the data for it. This made it impractical for game development use until 1989 with the release of the Atari STE which used DMA techniques to play back PCM samples at up to 50 kHz. The ST however remained relevant as it was equipped with a MIDI controller and external ports. It became the choice of by many professional musicians as a MIDI programming device.

IBM PC clones in 1985 would not see any significant development in multimedia abilities for a few more years, and sampling would not become popular in other video game systems for several years. Though sampling had the potential to produce much more realistic sounds, each sample required much more data in memory. This was at a time when all memory, solid state (ROM cartridge), magnetic (floppy disk) or otherwise was still very costly per kilobyte. Sequenced soundchip generated music on the other hand was generated with a few lines of comparatively simple code and took up far less precious memory.

Arcade systems pushed game music forward in 1984 with the introduction of FM (Frequency Modulation) synthesis, providing more realistic sounds than previous PSGs. The first such game, Marble Madness used the Yamaha YM2151 FM synthesis chip.[18]

As home consoles moved into the fourth generation, or 16-bit era, the hybrid approach (sampled and tone) to music composing continued to be used. In 1988 the Sega Mega Drive (Sega Genesis in the US) offered advanced graphics over the NES and improved sound synthesis features (also using a Yamaha chip, the YM2612),[19] but largely held the same approach to sound design. Ten channels in total for tone generation with one for PCM samples were available in stereo instead of the NES's five channels in mono, one for PCM. As before, it was often used for percussion samples, or "drum kits" (*Sonic the Hedgehog 3*). The 16-bit Sega referred to was the CPU and should not be confused with 16-bit sound samples. The Genesis did not support 16-bit sampled sounds. Despite the additional tone channels, writing music still posed a challenge to traditional composers and it forced much more imaginative use of the FM synthesizer to create an enjoyable listening experience. The composer Yuzo Koshiro utilized the Mega Drive/Genesis hardware effectively to produce "progressive, catchy, techno-style compositions far more advanced than what players were used to" for games such as *The Revenge of Shinobi* (1989) and the *Streets of Rage* series, setting a "new high watermark for what music in games could sound like."[20] The soundtrack for *Streets of Rage 2* (1992) in particular is considered "revolutionary" and "ahead of its time" for its blend of house music with "dirty" electro basslines and "trancey electronic textures" that "would feel as comfort-

able in a nightclub as a video game."[21] Another important FM synth composer was the late Ryu Umemoto, who composed music for many visual novels and shoot 'em ups during the 1990s.[22]

As cost of magnetic memory declined in the form of diskettes, the evolution of video game music on the Amiga, and some years later game music development in general, shifted to sampling in some form. It took some years before Amiga game designers learned to wholly use digitized sound effects in music (an early exception case was the title music of text adventure game *The Pawn*, 1986). By this time, computer and game music had already begun to form its own identity, and thus many music makers intentionally tried to produce music that sounded like that heard on the Commodore 64 and NES, which resulted in the chiptune genre.

The release of a freely-distributed Amiga program named Soundtracker by Karsten Obarski in 1987 started the era of MOD-format which made it easy for anyone to produce music based on digitized samples. Module files were made with programs called "trackers" after Obarski's Soundtracker. This MOD/tracker tradition continued with PC computers in the 1990s. Examples of Amiga games using digitized instrument samples include David Whittaker's soundtrack for *Shadow of the Beast*, Chris Hülsbeck's soundtrack for *Turrican 2* and Matt Furniss's tunes for *Laser Squad*. Richard Joseph also composed some theme songs featuring vocals and lyrics for games by Sensible Software most famous being *Cannon Fodder* (1993) with a song "War Has Never Been So Much Fun" and *Sensible World of Soccer* (1994) with a song "Goal Scoring Superstar Hero". These songs used long vocal samples.

A similar approach to sound and music developments had become common in the arcades by this time and had been used in many arcade system boards since the mid-1980s.[23] This was further popularized in the early 1990s by games like *Street Fighter II* (1991) on the CPS-1, which used voice samples extensively along with sampled sound effects and percussion. Neo Geo's MVS system also carried powerful sound development which often included surround sound.

The SNES (1990) brought digitized sound to console games.

The evolution also carried into home console video games, such as the release of the Super Famicom in 1990, and its US/EU version SNES in 1991. It sported a specialized custom Sony chip for both the sound generation and for special hardware DSP. It was capable of eight channels of sampled sounds at up to 16-bit resolution, had a wide selection of DSP effects, including a type of ADSR usually seen in high end synthesizers of the time, and full stereo sound. This allowed experimentation with applied acoustics in video games, such as musical acoustics (early games like *Super Castlevania IV*, *F-Zero*, *Final Fantasy IV*, *Gradius III*, and later games like *Chrono Trigger*), directional (*Star Fox*) and spatial acoustics (Dolby Pro-Logic was used in some games, like *King Arthur's World* and *Jurassic Park*), as well as environmental and architectural acoustics (*Zelda III*, *Secret of Evermore*). Many games also made heavy use of the high quality sample playback capabilities (*Super Star Wars*, *Tales of Phantasia*). The only real limitation to this powerful setup was the still-costly solid state memory. Other consoles of the generation could boast similar abilities yet did not have the same circulation levels as the SNES/SFC. The Neo-Geo home system was capable of the same powerful sample processing as its arcade counterpart, but was several times the cost of a SNES. The Mega-CD (Sega-CD in the US) hardware upgrade to the Mega Drive (Genesis in the US) offered multiple PCM channels, but they were often passed over instead to use its capabilities with the CD-ROM itself.

Popularity of the SNES and its software remained limited to regions where NTSC television was the broadcast standard. Partly because of the difference in frame rates of PAL broadcast equipment, many titles released were never redesigned to play appropriately and ran much slower than originally intended, or were never released. This showed a divergence in popular video game music between PAL and NTSC countries that still shows to this day. This divergence would be lessened as the fifth generation of home consoles launched globally, and as Commodore began to take a back seat to general purpose PCs and Macs for developing and gaming.

Though the Sega-CD/Mega-CD, and to a greater extent the PC Engine in Japan, would give gamers a preview of the direction video game music would take in streaming music, the use of both sampled and sequenced music continues in game consoles even today. The huge data storage benefit of optical media would be coupled with progressively more powerful audio generation hardware and higher quality samples in the Fifth Generation. In 1994, the CD-ROM equipped PlayStation supported 24 channels of 16-bit samples of up to 44.1 kHz sample rate, samples equal to CD audio in quality. It also sported a few hardware DSP effects like reverb. Many Square titles continued to use sequenced music, such as *Final Fantasy 7*, *Legend of Mana*,

and *Final Fantasy Tactics*. The Sega Saturn also with a CD drive supported 32 channels of PCM at the same resolution as the PSX. In 1996, the Nintendo 64, still using a solid state cartridge, actually supported an integrated and scalable sound system that was potentially capable of 100 channels of PCM, and an improved sample rate of 48 kHz. Games for the N64, because of the cost of the solid state memory, typically had samples of lesser quality than the other two however, and music tended to be simpler in construct.

The more dominant approach for games based on CDs, however, was shifting toward streaming audio.

MIDI on the PC

The first developers of IBM PC computers neglected audio capabilities (first IBM model, 1981).

In the same timeframe of the late 1980s to mid-1990s, the IBM PC clones using the x86 architecture became more ubiquitous, yet had a very different path in sound design than other PCs and consoles. Early PC gaming was limited to the PC speaker, and some proprietary standards such as the IBM PCjr 3-voice chip. While sampled sound could be achieved on the PC speaker using pulse width modulation, doing so required a significant proportion of the available processor power, rendering its use in games rare.

With the increase of x86 PCs in the market, there was a vacuum in sound performance in home computing that expansion cards attempted to fill. The first two recognizable standards were the Roland MT-32, followed by the AdLib sound card. Roland's solution was driven by MIDI sequencing using advanced LA synthesizers. This made it the first choice for game developers to produce upon, but its higher cost as an end-user solution made it prohibitive. The AdLib used a low-cost FM synthesis chip from Yamaha, and many boards could operate compatibly using the MIDI standard.

The AdLib card was usurped in 1989 by Creative's Sound

Blaster, which used the same Yamaha FM chip in the AdLib, for compatibility, but also added 8-bit 22.05 kHz (later 44.1 kHz) digital audio recording and playback of a single stereo channel. As an affordable end-user product, the Sound Blaster constituted the core sound technology of the early 1990s; a combination of a simple FM engine that supported midi, and a DAC engine of one or more streams. Only a minority of developers ever used Amiga-style tracker formats in commercial PC games, (*Unreal*) typically preferring to use the MT-32 or AdLib/SB-compatible devices. As general purpose PCs using x86 became more ubiquitous than the other PC platforms, developers drew their focus towards that platform.

The last major development before streaming music came in 1992: Roland Corporation released the first General MIDI card, the sample-based SCC-1, an add-in card version of the SC-55 desktop MIDI module. The comparative quality of the samples spurred similar offerings from Soundblaster, but costs for both products were still high. Both companies offered 'daughterboards' with sample-based synthesizers that could be later added to a less expensive soundcard (which only had a DAC and a MIDI controller) to give it the features of a fully integrated card.

Unlike the standards of Amiga or Atari, a PC using x86 even then could be using a broad mix of hardware. Developers increasingly used MIDI sequences: instead of writing soundtrack data for each type of soundcard, they generally wrote a fully featured data set for the Roland application that would be compatible with lesser featured equipment so long as it had a MIDI controller to run the sequence. However, different products used different sounds attached to their MIDI controllers. Some tied into the Yamaha FM chip to simulate instruments, some daughterboards of samples had very different sound qualities; meaning that no single sequence performance would be accurate to every other General Midi device.

All of these considerations in the products reflected the high cost of memory storage which rapidly declined with the optical CD format.

Pre-recorded and streaming music

Main article: Streaming audio in video games

Taking entirely pre-recorded music had many advantages over sequencing for sound quality. Music could be produced freely with any kind and number of instruments, allowing developers to simply record one track to be played back during the game. Quality was only limited by the effort put into mastering the track itself. Memory space costs that was previously a concern was somewhat addressed with optical media becoming the dominant media for software

games. CD quality audio allowed for music and voice that had the potential to be truly indistinguishable from any other source or genre of music.

In fourth generation home video games and PCs this was limited to playing a Mixed Mode CD audio track from a CD while the game was in play (such as *Sonic CD*). The earliest examples of Mixed Mode CD audio in video games include the TurboGrafx-CD RPG franchises *Tengai Makyō*, composed by Ryuichi Sakamoto from 1989,[24] and the *Ys* series, composed by Yuzo Koshiro and Mieko Ishikawa and arranged by Ryo Yonemitsu in 1989. The *Ys* soundtracks, particularly *Ys I & II* (1989), are still regarded as some of the most influential video game music ever composed.[25][26][27]

However, there were several disadvantages of regular CD-audio. Optical drive technology was still limited in spindle speed, so playing an audio track from the game CD meant that the system could not access data again until it stopped the track from playing. Looping, the most common form of game music, was also problem as when the laser reached the end of a track, it had to move itself back to the beginning to start reading again causing an audible gap in playback.

To address these drawbacks, some PC game developers designed their own container formats in house, for each application in some cases, to stream compressed audio. This would cut back on memory used for music on the CD, allowed for much lower latency and seek time when finding and starting to play music, and also allowed for much smoother looping due to being able to buffer the data. A minor drawback was that use of compressed audio meant it had to be decompressed which put load on the CPU of a system. As computing power increased, this load became minimal, and in some cases dedicated chips in a computer (such as a sound card) would actually handle all the decompressing.

Fifth generation home console systems also developed specialised streaming formats and containers for compressed audio playback. Games would take full advantage of this ability, sometimes with highly praised results (*Castlevania: Symphony of the Night*). Games ported from arcade machines, which continued to use FM synthesis, often saw superior pre-recorded music streams on their home console counterparts (*Street Fighter Alpha 2*). Even though the game systems were capable of "CD quality" sound, these compressed audio tracks were not true "CD quality." Many of them had lower sampling rates, but not so significant that most consumers would notice. Using a compressed stream allowed game designers to play back streamed music and still be able to access other data on the disc without interruption of the music, at the cost of CPU power used to render the audio stream. Manipulating the stream any further would require a far more significant level of CPU power available in the 5th generation.

Some games, such as the *Wipeout* series, continued to use full Mixed Mode CD audio for their soundtracks.

This overall freedom offered to music composers gave video game music the equal footing with other popular music it had lacked. A musician could now, with no need to learn about programming or the game architecture itself, independently produce the music to their satisfaction. This flexibility would be exercised as popular mainstream musicians would be using their talents for video games specifically. An early example is *Way of the Warrior* on the 3DO, with music by White Zombie. A more well-known example is Trent Reznor's score for *Quake*.

An alternate approach, as with the *TMNT* arcade, was to take pre-existing music not written exclusively for the game and use it in the game. The game *Star Wars: X-Wing vs. TIE Fighter* and subsequent *Star Wars* games took music composed by John Williams for the *Star Wars* films of the 1970s and 1980s and used it for the game soundtracks.

Both using new music streams made specifically for the game, and using previously released/recorded music streams are common approaches for developing sound tracks to this day. It is common for X-games sports-based video games to come with some popular artists recent releases (*SSX*, *Tony Hawk*, *Initial D*), as well as any game with heavy cultural demographic theme that has tie-in to music (*Need For Speed: Underground*, *Gran Turismo*, and *Grand Theft Auto*). Sometimes a hybrid of the two are used, such as in *Dance Dance Revolution*.

Sequencing samples continue to be used in modern gaming for many uses, mostly RPGs. Sometimes a cross between sequencing samples, and streaming music is used. Games such as *Republic: The Revolution* (music composed by James Hannigan[28]) and *Command & Conquer: Generals* (music composed by Bill Brown) have utilised sophisticated systems governing the flow of incidental music by stringing together short phrases based on the action on screen and the player's most recent choices (see dynamic music). Other games dynamically mixed the sound on the game based on cues of the game environment.

As processing power increased dramatically in the 6th generation of home consoles, it became possible to apply special effects in realtime to streamed audio. In *SSX*, a recent video game series, if a snowboarder takes to the air after jumping from a ramp, the music softens or muffles a bit, and the ambient noise of wind and air blowing becomes louder to emphasize being airborne. When the snowboarder lands, the music resumes regular playback until its next "cue". The LucasArts company pioneered this interactive music technique with their iMUSE system, used in their early adventure games and the *Star Wars* flight simulators *Star Wars: X-Wing* and *Star Wars: TIE Fighter*. Action games such as these will change dynamically to match the amount of danger. Stealth-based games will sometimes rely on such music, either by handling streams differently, or dynamically changing the composition of a sequenced soundtrack.

Personalized soundtracks

Being able to play one's own music during a game in the past usually meant turning down the game audio and using an alternative music player. Some early exceptions were possible on PC/Windows gaming in which it was possible to independently adjust game audio while playing music with a separate program running in the background. Some PC games, such as *Quake*, play music from the CD while retrieving game data exclusively from the hard disk, thereby allowing the game CD to be swapped for any music CD. The first PC game to introduce in-game support for custom soundtracks was Lionhead Studio's Black and White. The 2001 game included an in-game interface for Winamp that enabled the players to play audio tracks from their own playlists. In addition, this would sometimes trigger various reactions from the player's Creature, like dancing or laughing.

Some PlayStation games supported this by swapping the game CD with a music CD, although when the game needed data, players had to swap the CDs again. One of the earliest games, *Ridge Racer*, was loaded entirely into RAM, letting the player insert a music CD to provide a soundtrack throughout the entirety of the gameplay. In *Vib Ribbon*, this became a gameplay feature, with the game generating levels based entirely on the music on whatever CD the player inserted.

Microsoft's Xbox, a competitor in the sixth generation of home consoles opened new possibilities. Its ability to copy music from a CD onto its internal hard drive allowed gamers to use their own music more seamlessly with gameplay than ever before. The feature, called Custom Soundtrack, had to be enabled by the game developer. The feature carried over into the seventh generation with the Xbox 360 except it is now supported by the system software and enabled at any point.

The Wii is also able to play custom soundtracks if it is enabled by the game (*Excite Truck*,[29] *Endless Ocean*[30]).

The PlayStation Portable can, in games like *Need for Speed Carbon: Own the City* and *FIFA 08*, play music from a Memory Stick.

The PlayStation 3 has the ability to utilize custom soundtracks in games using music saved on the hard drive, however few game developers have used this function so far.

MLB 08: The Show, released in North America on March 4, 2008, has a My MLB sound track feature which allows the user to play music tracks of their choice saved on the hard drive of their PS3, rather than the preprogrammed tracks incorporated into the game by the developer. An update to *Wipeout HD*, released on the PlayStation Network, was made to also incorporate this feature.

In *Audiosurf*, custom soundtracks are the main aspect of the game. Users have to pick a music file to be analyzed. The game will generate a race track based on tempo, pitch and complexity of the sound. The user will then race on this track, synchronized with the music.

Developments in the 2000s

The Xbox 360 supports Dolby Digital software, sampling and playback rate of 16-bit @ 48 kHz (internal; with 24-bit hardware D/A converters), hardware codec streaming, and potential of 256 audio simultaneous channels. While powerful and flexible, none of these features represent any major change in how game music is made from the last generation of console systems. PCs continue to rely on third-party devices for in-game sound reproduction, and SoundBlaster is largely the only major player in the entertainment audio expansion card business.

The PlayStation 3 handles multiple types of surround sound technology, including Dolby TrueHD and DTS-HD, with up to 7.1 channels, and with sampling rates of up to 192 kHz.

Nintendo's Wii console shares many audio components with the Nintendo GameCube from the previous generation, including Dolby Pro Logic II. These features are extensions of technology already currently in use.

The game developer of today has many choices on how to develop music. More likely, changes in video game music creation will have very little to do with technology and more to do with other factors of game development as a business whole. Video game music has diversified much to the point where scores for games can be presented with a full orchestra or simple 8/16-bit chiptunes. This degree of freedom has made the creative possibilities of video game music limitless to developers. As sales of video game music diverged from the game itself in the West (compared to Japan where game music CDs had been selling for years), business elements also wield a new level of influence. Music from outside the game developer's immediate employment, such as music composers and pop artists, have been contracted to produce game music just as they would for a theatrical movie. Many other factors have growing influence, such as editing for content, politics on some level of the development, and executive input.

1.21.2 Game music as a genre

See also: Chiptune

Many games for the Nintendo Entertainment System and other early game consoles feature a similar style of musical composition that is sometimes described as the "video game genre." Some aspects of this style continue to influence certain music today, though gamers do not associate many modern game soundtracks with the older style. The genre's compositional elements largely developed due to technological restraints, while also being influenced by electronic music bands, particularly Yellow Magic Orchestra (YMO), who were popular during the late 1970s to 1980s.[31] YMO sampled sounds from several classic arcade games in their early albums, most notably *Space Invaders* in the 1978 hit song "Computer Game".[32] In turn, the band would have a major influence on much of the video game music produced during the 8-bit and 16-bit eras.[31]

Features of the video game music genre include:

- Pieces designed to repeat indefinitely, rather than having an arranged ending or fading out.

- Pieces lacking lyrics and playing over gameplay sounds.

- Limited polyphony. Only three notes can be played simultaneously on the Nintendo Entertainment System. A great deal of effort was put into composition to create the illusion of more notes playing at once.

Although the tones featured in NES music can be thought of as emulating a traditional four-piece rock band (triangle wave used as a bass, two pulse waves analogous to two guitars, and a white noise channel used for drums), composers would often go out of their way to compose complex and rapid sequences of notes, in part due to the restrictions mentioned above. This is similar to music composition during the Baroque period, when composers, particularly when creating solo pieces, focused on musical embellishments to compensate for instruments such as the harpsichord that do not allow for expressive dynamics. For the same reason, many early compositions also feature a distinct jazz influence. These would overlap with later influences from heavy metal and j-pop music, resulting in an equally distinct compositional style in the 16-bit era.

In an unrelated but parallel course in the European and North American developer scene, similar limitations were driving the musical style of home computer games. Module file format music, particularly MOD, used similar techniques but was more heavily influenced from the electronic music scene as it developed, and resulted in another very distinct subgenre. Demos and the developing demoscene played a big part in the early years, and still influence video game music today.

As technological limitations gradually lifted, composers were given more freedom and with the advent of CD-ROM pre-recorded soundtracks came to dominate, resulting in a noticeable shift in composition and voicing style.[33] Popular early CD-ROM titles were released with high-resolution graphics and recorded music. Since the audio was not reliant on a sound-card's synthesis, CD-ROM technology ensured that composers and sound designers could know what audio would sound like on most consumer configurations and could also record sound effects, live instruments, vocals, and in-game dialogue.[34]

As the divisions between movies and video games has blurred, so have divisions between film scores and video game scores. Adventure and fantasy movies have similar needs to adventure and fantasy games, i.e. fanfare, traveling, hero's theme and so on. Some composers have written scores in both genres. One noted example is U.S. composer Michael Giacchino who composed the soundtrack for the game Medal of Honor and later composed for the television series *Lost* and wrote scores for movies such as *The Incredibles* (2004) and *Star Trek* (2009).

1.21.3 Video game music outside video games

See also: Chiptune

Appreciation for video game music, particularly music from the third and fourth generations of home video game console and sometimes newer generations, continues today in very strong representation in both fans and composers alike, even out of the context of a video game. Melodies and themes from 20 years ago continue to be re-used in newer generations of video games. Themes from the original *Metroid* by Hirokazu Tanaka can still be heard in *Metroid* games from today as arranged by Kenji Yamamoto.

Video game music soundtracks were sold separately on CD in Japan well before the practice spread to other countries. Interpretive albums, remixes and live performances were also common variations to original soundtracks (OSTs). Koichi Sugiyama was an early figure in this practice subgenres, and following the release of the first *Dragon Quest* game in 1986, a live performance CD of his compositions was released and performed by the London Philharmonic Orchestra (then later by other groups including the Tokyo Philharmonic Orchestra, and NHK Symphony). Yuzo Koshiro, another early figure, released a live performance of the *Actraiser* soundtrack. Both Koshiro's and fellow Falcom composer Mieko Ishikawa's contributions to Ys music would have such long lasting impact that there were more albums released of Ys music than of almost all other game-type music.

Like anime soundtracks, these soundtracks and even sheet music books were usually marketed exclusively in Japan. Therefore, interested non-Japanese gamers have to import the soundtracks and/or sheet music books through on or offline firms specifically dedicated to video game soundtrack imports. This has been somewhat less of an issue more recently as domestic publishers of anime and video games have been producing western equivalent versions of the OSTs for sale in UK and US, but only for the most popular titles in most cases.

Other original composers of the lasting themes from this time have gone on to manage symphonic concert performances to the public exhibiting their work in the games. Koichi Sugiyama was once again the first in this practice in 1987 with his "Family Classic Concert" and has continued concert performances almost annually. In 1991, he also formed a series called Orchestral Game Concerts, notable for featuring other talented game composers such as Yoko Kanno (*Nobunaga's Ambition*, *Romance of the Three Kingdoms*, *Uncharted Waters*), Nobuo Uematsu (*Final Fantasy*), Keiichi Suzuki (*Mother/Earthbound*), and Kentaro Haneda (*Wizardry*).

Following suit, compositions by Nobuo Uematsu on *Final Fantasy IV* were arranged into *Final Fantasy IV: Celtic Moon*, a live performance by string musicians with strong Celtic influence recorded in Ireland. The Love Theme from the same game has been used as an instructional piece of music in Japanese schools.

Global popularity of video game music would begin to surge with Square's 1990s successes, particularly with *Final Fantasy VI*, *Final Fantasy VII* and *Final Fantasy VIII* by Nobuo Uematsu and with *Chrono Trigger*, *Xenogears* and *Chrono Cross* by Yasunori Mitsuda. On August 20, 2003, for the first time outside Japan, music written for video games such as *Final Fantasy* and *The Legend of Zelda* was performed by a live orchestra, the Czech National Symphony Orchestra in a Symphonic Game Music Concert in Leipzig, Germany at the Gewandhaus concert hall. This event was held as the official opening ceremony of Europe's biggest trading fair for video games, the GC Games Convention and repeated in 2004, 2005, 2006 and 2007. On November 17, 2003, Square Enix launched the *Final Fantasy Radio* on America Online. The radio station has initially featured complete tracks from *Final Fantasy XI* and *Final Fantasy XI: Rise of Zilart* and samplings from *Final Fantasy VII* through *Final Fantasy X*. The first officially sanctioned Final Fantasy concert in the United States was performed by the Los Angeles Philharmonic Orchestra at Walt Disney Concert Hall in Los

Angeles, California, on May 10, 2004. All seats at the concert were sold out in a single day. "Dear Friends: Music from Final Fantasy" followed and was performed at various cities across the United States. Nobuo Uematsu has also performed a variety of Final Fantasy compositions live with his rock band, The Black Mages.[35]

On July 6, 2005, the Los Angeles Philharmonic Orchestra also held a Video Games Live concert, which was founded by video game music composers Tommy Tallarico and Jack Wall at the Hollywood Bowl. This concert featured a variety of video game music, ranging from *Pong* to *Halo 2*. It also incorporated real-time video feeds that were in sync with the music, as well as laser and light special effects. Media outside the video game industry, such as NPR and the *The New York Times*, have covered their subsequent world tours.[36][37] On August 20, 2006, the Malmö Symphonic Orchestra with host Orvar Säfström performed the outdoor game music concert Joystick in Malmö, Sweden before an audience of 17,000, currently the attendance record for a game music concert.[38] Säfström has since continued to produce game music concerts around Europe under the names Joystick and Score.[39] From April 20–27, 2007, Eminence Symphony Orchestra, an orchestra dedicated to video game and anime music, performed the first part of their annual tour, the "A Night in Fantasia" concert series in Australia. Whilst Eminence had performed video game music as part of their concerts since their inception, the 2007 concert marked the first time ever that the entire setlist was pieces from video games. Up to seven of the world's most famous game composers were also in attendance as special guests.

On March 16, 2012 the Smithsonian American Art Museum's "The Art of Video Games" exhibit opened featuring a chipmusic soundtrack at the entrance by artists 8 Bit Weapon & ComputeHer.8 Bit Weapon also created a track called "The art of Video Games Anthem" for the exhibit as well.[40]

Popular music

See also: Chiptune and Bitpop

In the popular music industry, video game music and sounds have appeared in songs by various popular artists,[41] with arcade game sounds having had a particularly strong influence on the hip hop,[42] pop music (particularly synthpop)[43] and electro music[44] genres during the golden age of arcade video games in the early 1980s. Arcade game sounds had an influence on synthpop pioneers Yellow Magic Orchestra,[45] who sampled *Space Invaders* sounds in their influential 1978 debut album, particularly the hit song "Computer Game".[32] In turn, the band would have a ma-

jor influence on much of the video game music produced during the 8-bit and 16-bit eras.[31]

Other pop songs based on *Space Invaders* soon followed, including "Disco Space Invaders" (1979) by Funny Stuff,[46] "Space Invaders" (1980) by Playback,[47] and the hit songs "Space Invader" (1980) by The Pretenders[46] and "Space Invaders" (1980) by Uncle Vic.[48] Buckner & Garcia produced a successful album dedicated to video game music in 1982, *Pac-Man Fever*.[49] Former YMO member Haruomi Hosono also released a 1984 album produced entirely from Namco arcade game samples entitled *Video Game Music*, an early example of a chiptune record[50] and the first video game music album.[51] Warp's record "Testone" (1990) by Sweet Exorcist sampled video game sounds from YMO's "Computer Game" and defined Sheffield's bleep techno scene in the early 1990s.[52]

In more recent times, "video game beats" have appeared in popular songs such as Kesha's "Tik Tok",[41] the best-selling single of 2010,[53] as well as "U Should Know Better" by Robyn featuring Snoop Dogg,[41] and "Hellbound" by Eminem. The influence of video game music can also be seen in contemporary electronica music by artists such as Dizzee Rascal and Kieran Hebden.[45] Grime music in particular samples sawtooth wave sounds from video games which were popular in East London.[54] English power metal band DragonForce is also known for their "retro video game influenced" sound.

1.21.4 Video game music education

Video game music has become part of the curriculum of traditional schools and universities.[55] Berklee College of Music, Yale University, New York University and the New England Conservatory all feature or are adding game music to their curricula. Game sound & music design has also been part of the curriculum since 2003 at the Utrecht School of the Arts (Faculty of Art, Media and Technology). Training seminars such as GameSoundCon also feature classes in how to compose video game music.[56]

Extracurricular organizations devoted to the performance of video game music are being established in tandem to these additions to the curriculum. The Gamer Symphony Orchestra at the University of Maryland performs self-arranged video game music and the Video Game Orchestra is a semiprofessional outgrowth of students from the Berklee College of Music and other Boston-area schools. The establishment of these groups is also occurring at the secondary level.[57]

1.21.5   Video game music jobs

During the arcade and early console era (1983 to the mid 90's), most game music was composed by full-time employees of the particular game company producing the game. This was largely due to the very specialized nature of video game music, where each system had its own technology and tool sets. It was not uncommon for a game company like Capcom or Konami to have a room full of composers, each at their own workstation with headphones writing music.

Once the CD-era hit and studio recorded music became more ubiquitous in games, it became increasingly common for game music to be composed by independent contractors, hired by the game developer on a per-project basis.[58][59] Most bigger budget games such as Call of Duty, Mass Effect, Ghost Recon, or Lost Planet hire composers in this fashion. Notable exceptions include composer Koji Kondo, who remains an employee at Nintendo and Martin O'Donnell, who worked at Bungie until early 2014.

The growth of casual, mobile and social games has greatly increased opportunities for game music composers, with job growth in the US market increasing more than 150% over five years.[60] Independently developed games are a frequent place where beginning game composers gain experience composing for video games.[59]

1.21.6   Awards

Since 2010, the Ivor Novello Awards has included a category for *best original video game score*. The 2010 award winner was Killzone 2 (Composed by Joris de Man), and in 2011, Napoleon: Total War (Composers: Richard Beddow, Richard Birdsall, Ian Livingstone)

Spike Video Game Awards includes awards for Best Soundtrack, Best Song in a Game, and Best Original Score.

From 2012, the Grammy Awards began including "video game music" as part of its "Visual Media (Motion, Television, Video Game Music, or Other Visual Media)" awards. The four *Visual Media* awards are: Best Music for Visual Media, Best Compilation Soundtrack for Visual Media, Best Score Soundtrack for Visual Media, Best Song Written for Visual Media.

In 2011, *Baba Yetu*, a song from Civilization IV, won the 53rd annual music awards' Best Instrumental Arrangement Accompanying Vocalists, the first video game music to be nominated for (or to win) a Grammy.

The International Film Music Critics Association (IFMCA) has a Best Original Score for Interactive Media award.

Hollywood Music In Media Awards includes a Best Original Video Game Score award.

Machinima.com's Inside Gaming Awards include Best Original Score and Best Sound Design.

The MTV Video Music Award for Best Video Game Soundtrack ran from 2004 to 2006. Additionally an award for Best Video Game Score was awarded only in 2006.

1.21.7   Fan culture

In addition to these professional deviations, a large network of English speaking fans has sprung up with the increase of emulators and the Internet beginning in the early 2000s.

Numerous fan sites such as OverClocked Remix and Rainwave have appeared that are "dedicated to the appreciation and promotion of video game music".[61]

1.21.8   See also

- Circuit bending
- Game rip (audio)
- IEZA Framework
- List of video game musicians
- List of video game soundtracks considered the best
- List of video game soundtracks released on vinyl
- MAGFest
- Music video game
- OverClocked ReMix
- Rainwave
- VGMusic.com
- Video Games Live

1.21.9   References

[1] "Distant World: International Final Fantasy Concert Series". Ffdistantworlds.com. Archived from the original on 2010-09-23. Retrieved 2011-05-25.

[2] "The Evolution of Video Game Music". NPR. 12 April 2008. Retrieved 15 October 2012.

[3] Weir, William (10 February 2011). "From the Arcade to the Grammys: The Evolution of Video Game Music". The Atlantic. Retrieved 15 October 2012.

[4] McDonald, Glenn. "A History of Video Game Music". GameSpot. Retrieved 15 October 2012.

[5] Gun Fight on YouTube

[6] "Video Game Music". *VGMdb*. Retrieved 6 September 2011.

[7] Karen Collins (2008), *From Pac-Man to pop music: interactive audio in games and new media*, Ashgate, p. 2, ISBN 0-7546-6200-4

[8] Gaming's Most Important Evolutions, GamesRadar

[9] Collins, Karen (2008). *Game sound: an introduction to the history, theory, and practice of video game music and sound design*. MIT Press. p. 12. ISBN 0-262-03378-X. Retrieved 12 June 2011.

[10] Collins, Karen (2008). *Game sound: an introduction to the history, theory, and practice of video game music and sound design*. MIT Press. pp. 19–20. ISBN 0-262-03378-X. Retrieved 12 June 2011.

[11] *Super Locomotive* at the Killer List of Videogames

[12] "Covers of Yellow Magic Orchestra songs". WhoSampled. Retrieved 21 July 2011.

[13] "Koichi Sugiyama Home Page". Sugimania.com. Retrieved 2011-05-25.

[14] "The Sound of Music", *Computer Gaming World* (49), July 1988: 8

[15] Collins, Karen (2008). *Game sound: an introduction to the history, theory, and practice of video game music and sound design*. MIT Press. pp. 10–1. ISBN 0-262-03378-X. Retrieved 12 June 2011.

[16] Collins, Karen (2008). *Game sound: an introduction to the history, theory, and practice of video game music and sound design*. MIT Press. p. 19. ISBN 0-262-03378-X. Retrieved 12 June 2011.

[17] John Szczepaniak. "Retro Japanese Computers: Gaming's Final Frontier Retro Japanese Computers". Hardcore Gaming 101. Retrieved 2011-03-29. Reprinted from *Retro Gamer (67), 2009*

[18] Grannell, Craig (August 2008). "The Making of Marble Madness". Retro Gamer (Imagine Publishing) (53): 82–87.

[19] Collins, Karen (2008). *Game sound: an introduction to the history, theory, and practice of video game music and sound design*. MIT Press. p. 40. ISBN 0-262-03378-X. Retrieved 12 June 2011.

[20] Santos, Wayne (December 2006). "Songs & Sounds In The 21st Century". *GameAxis Unwired* (SPH Magazines) (40): 39. ISSN 0219-872X.

[21] McNeilly, Joe (April 19, 2010). "Game music of the day: Streets of Rage 2". GamesRadar. Retrieved 28 July 2012.

[22] Audun Sorlie. "A Dragon's Journey: Ryu Umemoto in Europe". Hardcore Gaming 101. Retrieved 2011-08-23.

[23] Collins, Karen (2008). *Game sound: an introduction to the history, theory, and practice of video game music and sound design*. MIT Press. p. 39. ISBN 0-262-03378-X. Retrieved 12 June 2011.

[24] Kalata, Kurt. "Tengai Makyou: Ziria". *Hardcore Gaming 101*. Retrieved 7 September 2011.

[25] Kalata, Kurt (February 2014). "Ys". *Hardcore Gaming 101*. Retrieved 23 June 2015.

[26] Ryan Mattich. "Falcom Classics II". *RPGFan*. Retrieved 3 September 2011.

[27] Chris Greening & Don Kotowski (February 2011). "Interview with Yuzo Koshiro". Square Enix Music Online. Retrieved 2011-06-20.

[28] "The official website of composer James Hannigan". Jameshannigan.co.uk. Retrieved 2011-05-25.

[29] "Nintendo Wii: Review". Wiiportal.nintendo-europe.com. Retrieved 2011-05-25.

[30] "Games - Endless Ocean". Nintendo. 2010-12-07. Retrieved 2011-05-25.

[31] Daniel Robson (February 29, 2008). "YMCK takes 'chiptune' revolution major". *The Japan Times*. Retrieved 2011-06-11.

[32] David Toop (March 1996), "A-Z Of Electro", *The Wire* (145), retrieved 2011-05-29

[33] "Game Music :: Interview with Yoko Shimomura (September 2009)". Squareenixmusic.com. Retrieved 2011-05-25.

[34] Collins, Karen (2008). *Game Sound: An Introduction to the History, Theory, and Practice of Video Game Music and Sound Design*. Cambridge: The MIT Press. p. 63. ISBN 9780262033787.

[35] "From Consoles to Concert Halls". Wired. 2005-05-18. Retrieved 2012-10-12.

[36] "At the Concert Hall, a Symphony for Space Invaders". NPR. 2007-08-05. Retrieved 2012-10-12.

[37] Schiesel, Seth (2009-10-26). "Video Games (No Controller Needed)". nyt.com. Retrieved 2012-10-12.

[38] http://www.mcvuk.com/press-releases/read/jason-graves-to-conduct-at-joystick-5-0-symphony-concerts-in-sweden/0115108

[39] http://www.safeconcerts.com/news/2014/may/9561-retro-and-contemporary-gaming-titles-to-be-performed-by-the-philhar asp

[40] http://americanart.si.edu/pr/library/2012/taovg/taovg_release.pdf

[41] "Robyn: Body Talk, Pt. 2". Puls Music. 10 September 2010. Retrieved 2011-05-02. (Translation)

[42] David Toop (2000). *Rap attack 3: African rap to global hip hop, Issue 3* (3rd ed.). Serpent's Tail. p. 129. ISBN 1-85242-627-6. Retrieved 2011-06-06.

[43] Stout, Andrew (June 24, 2011). "Yellow Magic Orchestra on Kraftwerk and How to Write a Melody During a Cultural Revolution". *SF Weekly*. Retrieved 30 June 2011.

[44] "Electro". Allmusic. Archived from the original on 2010-12-09. Retrieved 2011-05-25.

[45] Lewis, John (4 July 2008). "Back to the future: Yellow Magic Orchestra helped usher in electronica - and they may just have invented hip-hop, too". *The Guardian*. Retrieved 25 May 2011.

[46] "The Wire, Issues 221-226", *The Wire*, 2002: 44, retrieved 2011-05-25

[47] *Playback – Space Invaders* at Discogs

[48] Lovelace, Craven (August 27, 2010). "Take a waka-waka-waka on the wild side". *Grand Junction Free Press*. Retrieved 15 July 2011.

[49] "Pac-Man Fever". Time Magazine. April 5, 1982. Retrieved October 15, 2009. Columbia/CBS Records' Pac-Man Fever...was No. 9 on the Billboard Hot 100 last week.

[50] *Haruomi Hosono – Video Game Music* at Discogs (list of releases)

[51] Carlo Savorelli. "Xevious". Hardcore Gaming 101. p. 2. Retrieved 2011-06-11.

[52] Dan Sicko & Bill Brewster (2010), *Techno Rebels* (2nd ed.), Wayne State University Press, p. 76, ISBN 0-8143-3438-5, retrieved 2011-05-28

[53] "IFPI publishes Digital Music Report 2011".

[54] Alex de Jong, Marc Schuilenburg (2006). *Mediapolis: popular culture and the city*. 010 Publishers. p. 106. ISBN 90-6450-628-0. Retrieved 30 July 2011.

[55] Kahn, Joseph P. (January 19, 2010). "Why Berklee is teaching its students to compose scores for video games". *The Boston Globe*.

[56] "SoundCon Launches Game Audio Conference for Audio Professionals". Mixonline.com. 2009-06-05. Retrieved 2011-05-25.

[57] Midgette, Anne (2010-07-28). "Video-game concerts, a movement that's more than a blip on orchestral landscape". *The Washington Post*. ISSN 0740-5421. Retrieved 2010-07-28.

[58] A Video Game Odyssey - a brief history of video game music

[59] http://twvideo01.ubm-us.net/o1/vault/GD_Mag_Archives/GDM_April_2013.pdf

[60] Study: Video games causing spike in music composer employment - GeekWire

[61] http://ocremix.org/info/About_Us

1.21.10   External links

- VGMdb Video Game Music and Anime Soundtrack Database | VGMdb

- GamesSound.com Academic articles on video game sound and music

- Early Video Game Soundtracks 2001 article on video game music, orig. published in *In Magazine*

- High Score: The New Era of Video Game Music at Tracksounds

- "The Evolution of Video Game Music", *All Things Considered*, April 12, 2008

- List of games with non-original music at uvlist.net

- Pretty Ugly Gamesound Study Website studying pretty and ugly game music and sound.

- CaptivatingSound.com Resources for design of game sound and music.

- Audio and Immersion PhD thesis about game audio and immersion.

- Diggin' in the Carts: A Documentary Series About Japanese Video Game Music, Red Bull Music Academy.

Chapter 2

Text and image sources, contributors, and licenses

2.1 Text

- **Chiptune** *Source:* https://en.wikipedia.org/wiki/Chiptune?oldid=685287593 *Contributors:* Damian Yerrick, Zundark, Lumpbucket, Lexor, DopefishJustin, Nixdorf, Liftarn, Ahoerstemeier, ZoeB, Smack, Schneelocke, Adam Conover, Malcohol, Furrykef, Wernher, Bloodshedder, Francs2000, Fuelbottle, Neckro, Xanzzibar, DocWatson42, Everdred, ShaneCavanaugh, AmishThrasher, Ds13, Eequor, Kaminari, Gdr, Roachgod, Sonjaaa, LucasVB, Antandrus, DragonflySixtyseven, Mike Rosoft, Alkivar, Sysy, Rich Farmbrough, Florian Blaschke, MeltBanana, R.123, Indrian, ESkog, Pedant, Tooto, Jlin, Devil Master, Bobo192, Steltek, Colin Douglas Howell, HasharBot~enwiki, Batjohan, Alansohn, Coma28, Bc429, Tek022, Rd232, Strok~enwiki, Magetoo, NTK, Radical Mallard, Here, ReyBrujo, Drbreznjev, Chiprunner, Alvis, Woohookitty, Ae-a, Easyas12c, Zilog Jones, Geedubber, Vossanova, Graham87, JIP, Rjwilmsi, Wahoofive, DeadlyAssassin, Joel D. Reid, The wub, X1987x, Far-QPwnsME, Ryanfantastic, Czar, Jonny2x4, Viznut, Liontamer, Chobot, Erif~enwiki, Kjlewis, Timeheater, Jeffthejiff, Phantomsteve, RussBot, Me and, Jengelh, CambridgeBayWeather, Pelago, Msikma, Dogcow, Irishguy, Mikeblas, Tony1, Jbrendan, Mysid, Zzuuzz, Joyrex, JLaTondre, NiTenIchiRyu, Schizobullet, SmackBot, John Lunney, Madfiddler, Elonka, McGeddon, Jagged 85, Brossow, Lainagier, Mcld, Gilliam, Ohnoitsjamie, Oscarthecat, Improbcat, Shaggorama, Keiron22, Thumperward, Martinpi, Colonies Chris, Yanksox, Hagbard Celine, Tamfang, Nixeagle, Cybercobra, CrnkMnky, Monotonehell, Godwithgun, Parrot of Doom, SashatoBot, Nishkid64, Axem Titanium, KLLvr283, AmiDaniel, Jinnai, BurnDownBabylon, Eleveneleven, IronGargoyle, Neotericz, Kflasch, TJ Spyke, Kenirwin, Kencf0618, Scsnippets, ChadyWady, The Prince of Darkness, Offensiveandconfusing, Big in albania, BuZz, DefenceForce, Lighthead, URORIN, Cydebot, Ntsimp, Crossmr, Gogo Dodo, Blue Falcon, Dancter, SamWhite, Mshick, UberScienceNerd, Thijs!bot, Mbell, Bllix, Saimhe, Shawnphase, Ste4k, LibLord, Dougher, Kaini, Caper13, Andrzejbanas, Realistik, Vanished user s4irtj34tivkj12erhskj46thgdg, Doctorhawkes, Y2kcrazyjoker4, Magioladitis, Bongwarrior, Sebras, Appraiser, JMyrleFuller, JaGa, R3z, Oicumayberight, Bleepbloopbeep, Goldenrod111, Pikolas, P music, Gwern, Ilikemusic, Anaxial, Trusilver, Qnx~enwiki, Dispenser, AdamBMorgan, RenniePet, Brianmetro, STBotD, Atama, Nikthestunned, PeaceNT, VolkovBot, Ijfinster, Msxfan, Shne, Rei-bot, Truetillbrew, Jplaney, Spinningspark, Ultimate Chuck, Red, Unused000702, Work permit, Malcolmxl5, Erier2003, Dilemmachine, GlassCobra, Jerryobject, Theaveng, Gunmetal Angel, Martarius, ClueBot, Shape84, PipepBot, The Thing That Should Not Be, Matsuiny2004, HenrikErlandsson, Auntof6, Svenzzon, Anonymous101, ResidueOfDesign, Falcojet, Cloudo90, Mlaffs, Edbles, Eik Corell, XLinkBot, JWhitt433, Roxy the dog, Ost316, Cmr08, Rudmpm, Rayghost, Trvth, Addbot, Paper Luigi, Grayfell, Non-dropframe, Bharrod0815, Critthreat, Redheylin, Qweebo, SasiSasi, Roxanarox, Luckas-bot, Robinn07, Yobot, Themfromspace, Grochim, Pcap, Bloodkurst, 1oddbins1, Valueyou, ItsAlwaysLupus, Piano non troppo, Yaneleksklus, Hexacorde, Durdos, Xqbot, Jikooworld, Belasted, Rebelj12a, Ludx, Goto80~enwiki, Doctorx0079, Abolibibelot, Sabrebd, FrescoBot, Jimcu881ns, 4bpp, Pinkvoid, JamesSNIPER, Trawen, Soundmastersam, Gamecartforaheart, Tinton5, Oxvylu, Paroxysm8bit, Theschmugest, Nacho one, Tomjoyjoy, Freemium Man, Bynight, Ondertitel, Damnsell, Dsavage87, RjwilmsiBot, ButOnMethItls, Ripchip Bot, Lopifalko, Tinman44, EmausBot, John of Reading, Jackson McArthur, Tuankiet65, RFFL, Benichan, Katherine, Alfons van Vorden, TMNTOM, Jwebst08, Chipjunk, Access Denied, Chocolatejoe, Lexusuns, Abortifacient, Sassospicco, Crimsonstitches, Joeystyle, Bazillion974, Harbngr, Evan-Amos, JohnnyLurg, ClueBot NG, Untoldpromise, Dadomusic, Agenpub, Illucifixion, Dakhart, Helpful Pixie Bot, Veyneru, Jeik Hardy, Urbanuntillllllll, SomedayCameSuddenly, Ellobo1231, The Great Cloudwatcher, The1337gamer, EricEnfermero, BattyBot, Hericlesa5, Cyberbot II, None but shining hours, Myxomatosis57, Imperial Road, Khazar2, Girandolavas, Dissident93, GlitterDream, Makecat-bot, ABunnell, Piotrusp98, Zyma, ToFeignClef, Otávio Augusto Silva, IronCurtaiNYC, Pdecalculus, Pseudonymous Rex, Rsw278, Synthwave.94, DrDevilFX, Harmonium22, Fredderico18, Uss tardis, Monkbot, SpyroFan123, SkaterLife, ClassicOnAStick, Hakken, TheCoffeeAddict, Some Gadget Geek, Destinyschilde, Farlords, DavidCarterAccount and Anonymous: 598

- **Atari Punk Console** *Source:* https://en.wikipedia.org/wiki/Atari_Punk_Console?oldid=633260696 *Contributors:* Bearcat, The stuart, Ptdecker, Joel7687, Elkman, Groyolo, Squintz, SmackBot, Gregreyj, Autarch, Elagatis, Lpgeffen, Thijs!bot, CosineKitty, Propaniac, Elugelab, Dnny, HamadaFanFFSM, CultureDrone, SoxBot, XLinkBot, Addbot, Redheylin, Luckas-bot, Yobot, Fraggle81, Prari, Clusternote, Hericlesa5, Edefines, Howicus, Sisisisol and Anonymous: 17

- **Bitpop** *Source:* https://en.wikipedia.org/wiki/Bitpop?oldid=682647057 *Contributors:* Lexor, Liftarn, Heidimo, Dysprosia, Omegatron, Secretlondon, Francs2000, Dimadick, Tlogmer, Psi36, Matt Gies, Gwalla, Zinnmann, AaronW, Tothebarricades.tk, Nicke Lilltroll~enwiki, Jason One, Magetoo, Juhtolv, Westifer, Mightyzantar, Havermayer, Jclemens, Koavf, Bruce1ee, Ianthegecko, SchuminWeb, Fresheneesz, Viznut,

105

The Rambling Man, YurikBot, Sparxster, Asmadeus, MetalSnake, SmackBot, Jagged 85, JAStewart, Pmkpmk, Zephyris, B.Wind, Mr Beige, Thumperward, Sarnath~enwiki, Hagbard Celine, Frap, Re mo, Neotericz, Filelakeshoe, Geldgeschenk, ShelfSkewed, Gary Williams, GorillazRDaBest, Blackmetalbaz, XcepticZP, Kaini, Dancingcyberman, Vanished user s4irtj34tivkj12erhskj46thgdg, AdamBMorgan, Vanished User 4517, Brianmetro, One Night In Hackney, Ijfinster, Mercurywoodrose, TheoEngell, Seraphim, January2007, Trepain, JonnyJD, Superpowerless, Malcolmxl5, Cafeganesha, Microtroy, Tec-goblin, CorenSearchBot, Johny8, Kmijj, Cavagin, PixelBot, MelonBot, XLinkBot, Ost316, Addbot, Noeln94, MuZemike, Jarble, Yobot, Madcalabrian, AnomieBOT, Piano non troppo, Yaneleksklus, Materialscientist, HFredriksen, Woad85, Cxs, Sabrebd, Erik9bot, FrescoBot, Blackguard SF, Bakartkung, Raulitoyeah, JamesSNIPER, Rodrigo Nepomuceno, Tim1357, Mir09, GriffReborn, VernoWhitney, Panthablack, Mystery train, Samumarisuro, ZéroBot, The1337gamer, BattyBot, GlitterDream and Anonymous: 126

- **Circuit bending** *Source:* https://en.wikipedia.org/wiki/Circuit_bending?oldid=678504857 *Contributors:* Tregoweth, Sugarfish, Bogdangiusca, Hyacinth, Omegatron, Carnildo, Alan Liefting, Esk, Gzornenplatz, Bobblewik, Beland, MakeRocketGoNow, Zondor, Freakofnurture, Antaeus Feldspar, Cmdrjameson, Screeble, Ardric47, Pearle, CyberSkull, Andrewpmk, ReyBrujo, HenkvD, Feezo, Jeffrey O. Gustafson, K-flow, Tabletop, Graham87, Rjwilmsi, Yamamoto Ichiro, FlaBot, Ianthegecko, RexNL, Intgr, YurikBot, CambridgeBayWeather, Msikma, Dialectric, Grafen, Misza13, Phaedrus86, Jesusjonez, TheMadBaron, GraemeL, Searchforthenewland, Garion96, Bentmonkeycage, McGeddon, Ssbohio, Chris the speller, Mr Beige, Bluebot, Snori, Robth, Krallja, Gohst, Wickethewok, Alpha Omicron, Re mo, Mets501, Hu12, OnBeyondZebrax, Eastlaw, Cyrusc, Ekans, Clackbeetle, Xdugef, Alaibot, Thijs!bot, Bllix, T-1, Ego138, Tiny.ian, Guy Macon, Holotone, Kaini, Sophie means wisdom, JamesBWatson, Potar, Wayn3w, Maurice Carbonaro, Elugelab, SmithBlue, TheBendersPad, NegativeChild, RJASE1, Tsom, Broadbot, Delfy~enwiki, DrRek, Lucironic, Joseph Banks, ClueBot, Arakunem, Circuitben, Alexbot, Semitransgenic, JB8256, Mchaddock, Thebetatesters, XLinkBot, Ugh3n, Addbot, Leszek Jańczuk, Luter80, Kick52, Lightbot, AnomieBOT, Duktepemahn, Gartist, DarrenGuitarGuy, InformationGuardian, DSP-user, Intellec7, ClueBot NG, Catlemur, HMSSolent, YokoBeatdown, Hericlesa5, Madnessfan34537, Pdecalculus, Xeletron, Wikigeek244, Andrewdubber and Anonymous: 189

- **Computer music** *Source:* https://en.wikipedia.org/wiki/Computer_music?oldid=678289218 *Contributors:* Zundark, 0, Merphant, Heron, Oystein, Ronz, Furrykef, Hyacinth, Omegatron, HarryHenryGebel, Twang, Robbot, Chris 73, Magic Window, Giftlite, Gewang, Rev3rend, Micru, Karol Langner, Marc Mongenet, Discospinster, Rich Farmbrough, Xezbeth, R.123, Tgies, Quinobi, WCityMike, Polluks, Physicistjedi, M7, Versageek, Woohookitty, Tabletop, Rjwilmsi, Quiddity, Matterson52, Sdbeck, Viznut, RobotE, CambridgeBayWeather, Tfine80, Vivenot, Ninly, Closedmouth, Droidus, Zvika, SmackBot, Jagged 85, Pkirlin, Jwolf, Mcld, Chris the speller, Davigoli, Bluebot, Neonarcade, Nixeagle, Undertoad, "alyosha", Sigma 7, Savetz, Atoll, Optimale, Toineheuvelmans, MarylandArtLover, CmdrObot, Requestion, Gilbertevich, RichardVeryard, Escarbot, Sluzzelin, Rob Kam, Appraiser, Jerome Kohl, Yaxu, Jim.lindstrom, Milkmandelivery, Geldryk, Nikthestunned, Thumbuki, Dsalks, Rmkeller, Belbernard, Digego, TedColes, Parsifal, Oscillon, Logan, TJRC, Mungo Kitsch, Midicontest, MinorContributor, CharlesGillingham, Martarius, ClueBot, Userafw, Boing! said Zebedee, Trivialist, Socrates2008, Stefanos Leon, Pierre cummings, SoxBot III, Nebula2357, Joswig, Semitransgenic, Djulio~enwiki, Bijanzelli, Dan56, Skyezx, Download, AnnaFrance, Angelus1753, Guitarmasterclass, Tide rolls, Lightbot, Jarble, Legobot, Yobot, Ptbotgourou, Amirobot, Khalfani khaldun, Valueyou, Citation bot, Wrelwser43, Quebec99, Capricorn42, Jbartman, RibotBOT, Shadowjams, LucienBOT, Sphinxyminxy, HRoestBot, Meiticheol, Canuckian89, Gopalkoduri, RjwilmsiBot, Davidqwerty, EmausBot, DD Oiseau, John of Reading, Stryn, Luisrobles, ZéroBot, Fred Gandt, Knotrice, Musictechnologist, ClueBot NG, Jank1235, Thejmc, Eneko-Gotzon, Snotbot, Unmusicologist, Jk2q3jrklse, Helpful Pixie Bot, Usernamedoesntmatter, Tianzhao470, Lucyinthesky45, Laberkiste, Dexbot, TheBeardofLenin, Pdecalculus, Monkbot, Wikigeek244, Hakken, Dylandog1979 and Anonymous: 130

- **Demoscene** *Source:* https://en.wikipedia.org/wiki/Demoscene?oldid=676069146 *Contributors:* Eloquence, Bryan Derksen, Ap, AlexWasFirst, Shd~enwiki, Arj, Camembert, MrH, Tzartzam, Spiff~enwiki, Pit~enwiki, Two halves, Lexor, Nixdorf, Liftarn, Graue, Alfio, Hybrid-2k~enwiki, Docu, Ootachi, Slovakia, Nikai, Cimon Avaro, Conti, Doradus, Wernher, Bloodshedder, Raul654, Rossumcapek, Northgrove, Twang, Robbot, Tlogmer, Kaol, Greudin, Meelar, Wikibot, Fuelbottle, Bbx, Tobias Bergemann, Philwelch, Twilek, Noone~enwiki, Everyking, Eequor, Flix~enwiki, Elmindreda, Pne, Wmahan, Alexf, Sam Hocevar, Avatar, Imre Toth, Solitude, Pak21, Sesse, Hydrox, Bneely, Caesar, Pie4all88, Ardonik, Izwalito~enwiki, MajorB, R.123, Antaeus Feldspar, Bender235, Ht1848, Project2501a, CanisRufus, *drew, Kv9, RoyBoy, Chriscf, Cje~enwiki, Enric Naval, Trevj, Themindset, Gerardmajax, Gargaj, GRider, Halsteadk, Inky, Dipswitch~enwiki, Clubmarx, Lokedhs, Juhtolv, NicholasJones, Recury, Woohookitty, Jannex, Trixx, Vossanova, Jtsiomb, Graham87, Teknic, Qwertyus, Rjwilmsi, Graibeard, FlaBot, SchuminWeb, Nsae Comp, Ewlyahoocom, Czar, Mattlach, Intgr, Viznut, WouterBot, Gdrbot, DustWolf, YurikBot, Huw Powell, Pseudomonas, Grafen, Voidxor, Tony1, Zwobot, Bota47, Black Falcon, Zer0render, SMcCandlish, Rurik, Profero, SkerHawx, TheDeathCard, SmackBot, Hux, Rtc, LocalH, Gnangarra, Jagged 85, Rmeht, Coplan, Nmrd, Oscarthecat, Winterheart, The former 134.250.72.176, FakeHarajukuKid, Fintler, Bluebot, TimBentley, 32X, Bugloaf, Mdwh, Nbarth, Can't sleep, clown will eat me, 🈯🈯🈯, NW~enwiki, Z-d, Scientizzle, Disavian, Jodamn, Menacespb, Karmus, CarlosCoppola, Aboeing, Hu12, Aeternus, CmdrObot, Crossmr, Rhe br, Hilgerdenaar, Thijs!bot, Davidhorman, Jean seb, Ssr, Mrmoocow, Vendettax, Poga, Pipedreamergrey, MER-C, Andreas Toth, Soulbot, Tranqulizer, Scoutski, CommonsDelinker, Shanethewolf, Reonox~enwiki, Chiccodoro, Useight, Cjh57, Jcea, Jalwikip, Daff555, Austriacus, Vegetable4, Theaveng, TuxyQ, Fratrep, ImageRemovalBot, Martarius, Dakinijones, HenrikErlandsson, Aalolzore, Chrono256~enwiki, Simon Strandgaard, Ib doom~enwiki, Kazayta, Ubardak, DumZiBoT, InternetMeme, XLinkBot, Ost316, Netrat, ErkinBatu, Addbot, SpBot, Fireaxe888, Soppakanuuna, Lightbot, Jarble, C64 sucks, Aalolzore9000, Themfromspace, Mopkrayz, KamikazeBot, AnomieBOT, Piano non troppo, Neurolysis, Xqbot, Nasa-verve, Jjules, Pinethicket, Trapzor, Ondertitel, Wingman4l7, ChuispastonBot, Shaddim, Helpful Pixie Bot, BG19bot, PartTimeGnome, Dexbot, CsDix, SJ Defender, Monkbot, Hakken, Rm1911 and Anonymous: 255

- **Drum machine** *Source:* https://en.wikipedia.org/wiki/Drum_machine?oldid=682198124 *Contributors:* AxelBoldt, Zundark, Sjc, Mjb, Hephaestos, ChrispyH, AdSR, Vlongocomcast.net, Lexor, Liftarn, Zanimum, Delirium, CatherineMunro, Sugarfish, Smack, Viajero, Hyacinth, Chris 73, Lupin, VampWillow, Two Bananas, Trevor MacInnis, Arcataroger, Discospinster, Samboy, Bender235, MPS, Viames, Unused0022, Emhoo~enwiki, Samadam, Slipperyweasel, Macho, CBC~enwiki, Batmanand, Feline1, Deltabeignet, BD2412, Ajnewbold, Miq, Icey, Lockley, Teklund, EvanSeeds, Eubot, Richdiesal, RexNL, GreyCat, ApolloBoy, JonathanFreed, YurikBot, RobotE, Alma Pater, Peter G Werner, Sneak, Gustavb, MistaTee, Grafen, Patrick Neylan, Anetode, BOT-Superzerocool, GraemeL, DigitalDrummer, Zvika, TorKEB, SmackBot, DCGeist, Jagged 85, Gilliam, Chris the speller, SuMadre, Bluebot, Unint, MisterHand, Nixeagle, CorbinSimpson, The tooth, Mark in wiki, NeilFraser, Spiritia, Kuru, Khazar, Fairlight cmi, AmiDaniel, BurnDownBabylon, Spiff666, Wwagner, OnBeyondZebrax, Gveret Tered, CmdrObot, Amindfv, Pr0t0type, CuriousEric, Devanatha, Barticus88, Ultimus, T-1, Mat the w, 17Drew, Jhsounds, Myanw, Ghmyrtle, JAnDbot, MER-C, Nmcclana, MegX, Magioladitis, Bongwarrior, Rbatts2000, Kz1000ps, Untchbl, Technolust, Bricology, Steel1943, TXiKiBoT, A4bot, Slysplace, Habaneroman, Dolla10gs2, Houtlijm~enwiki, PlayStation 69, SieBot, MuzikJunky, Topher385, Svick, StaticGull, Mumble45, ClueBot, Binksternet, Nsk92, Tanglewood4, Czarkoff, Vivio Testarossa, Estirabot, Sun Creator, Shotguncharlie, Yun-Yuuzhan (lost password), CP-

GACoast, Semitransgenic, XLinkBot, David Delony, Dubmill, Carefree Highway, Addbot, Sard112, TutterMouse, MrOllie, Kevin.r.marshall, Mrose77, Lightbot, Zorrobot, Greyhood, LuK3, Legobot, Luckas-bot, Yobot, AnomieBOT, Connectedtoyou, RandomAct, B137, Materialscientist, ArthurBot, Acuares, BebyB, ACDCrox123, FrescoBot, Surv1v4l1st, Martin IIIa, Tbhotch, HISTA, Occam's Shaver, John of Reading, Clusternote, Cyborg2010, Thecheesykid, Romeofahl, ClueBot NG, Castncoot, Kasirbot, Helpful Pixie Bot, HMSSolent, AlterBerg, BG19bot, Bmusician, 1jfarry23, Spidey665, Bonebones, Angus.cross, Hyperborée, Guylarosh, Arcandam, Khazar2, MadGuy7023, Kevin12xd, Pabloosena, Jptvgrey, Gill run H20, Paul Badillo, Kaschimmel, Knowledgelibrary, Doctor rhythm and Anonymous: 157

- **Electro house** *Source:* https://en.wikipedia.org/wiki/Electro_house?oldid=685562313 *Contributors:* ViperSnake151, Jagged 85, Sct72, SQGibbon, Aeternus, Filelakeshoe, Lighthead, ShelfSkewed, Jac16888, HitroMilanese, SGGH, Andrzejbanas, JAnDbot, IdentityCrisis, Sarahj2107, Ftiercel, Tgeairn, DjScrawl, BeŽet, KylieTastic, Bonadea, VolkovBot, 1337pino, Therumbler, Sphilbrick, Denisarona, Mwhit42, Binksternet, Aria1561, Semitransgenic, Addbot, Legobot, AnomieBOT, Citation bot, Sabrebd, Eractnodi, FrescoBot, Goldask2, Serols, Tbhotch, RjwilmsiBot, Chrisbkoolio, ImprovingWiki, John of Reading, Ajraddatz, STATicVapor, K6ka, Swocks, Donner60, ClueBot NG, Loginnigol, O.Koslowski, Tyroneissel, Koui², Gata dels canals, Jlmaha5, BG19bot, MusikAnimal, Frze, Picaxe01, (CA)Giacobbe, Ian Streeter, Rmdl2006, Ongepotchket, Kavy32, M3D31R0S, Mogism, GlitterDream, Diskonnection, Anirekhj, Cerabot~enwiki, ItsLuke, DJStarrfish, Thedude242u2, Spaceinvadersaresmokinggrass, MidnightRequestLine, Epicgenius, Npgust, Treisis13, Myconix, Rajko92, BBBeaverboys, Etheldavis, Vassikin94, Acortes1776, Lmr97, TheComBen, Julianciccocelli, Tigercompanion25, Andrewbf, Riata123, Pulum34, Thewatertribe, PotatoNinja, Charonder1, Dylanjulian, No.1WikiXpert, Abderrahim oussi, Thomas Dirven, Roamingeditor222226, Akirainoues, AnonymousMusician, Iamswjr, Geatx, BrandonWLam, Realh345 and Anonymous: 200

- **Electroclash** *Source:* https://en.wikipedia.org/wiki/Electroclash?oldid=685979448 *Contributors:* KF, Lexor, Jahsonic, Paul A, Tregoweth, TUF-KAT, Nikai, Ehn, Ashley Y, Janexx, Henrygb, David Edgar, Anthony, Neckro, Gandalfe, MilkMiruku, Rdash, Dissident, CyborgTosser, Alanl, Wmahan, CryptoDerk, Pacian, Jessesamuel, Milk, Blorg, Alkivar, Dbach, R.123, Disasterpiece, Jaberwocky6669, JoeSmack, MBisanz, Hurricane111, Tronker, Red Winged Duck, Reubot, Max rspct, Keepsleeping, ShampooCell, Kusma, Dennis Bratland, Mahanga, Bjones, Brhaspati, RomeW, Phlebas, Allen3, LimoWreck, Kesla, Yurik, Koavf, FlaBot, Ryanfantastic, GreyCat, Gdrbot, Petiatil, Ericorbit, Splette, Asmadeus, Gaius Cornelius, Megastar, Bloodofox, Sylvain1972, Awiseman, Kyle Barbour, Eshe, Meegs, That Guy, From That Show!, Luk, Sardanaphalus, SmackBot, Debuskjt, Zazaban, Lifebaka, Jagged 85, Doc Strange, PeterSymonds, Gilliam, Nickhac, Dolanclass, Keiron22, OrangeDog, ThirdPlateauDreamer, Mikesullivan, Chlewbot, Raynethackery, Radagast83, Fgh12, ZetaReveal, Moodybrutha, Deepred6502, SevenEightTwo, Urbs-In-Horto, Monsantoman, Robovski, Scottd, Cielomobile, Davemcarlson, Beetstra, Neotericz, Zepheus, CatZilla, Anton Max Hart, Dlohcierekim, Filelakeshoe, CmdrObot, Zarex, Shandris, (chubbstar), Cydebot, Thugitlikethis, Travelbird, Donnachadelong, PhillipPaxman, Barticus88, GordonRoss, AntiVandalBot, Gioto, 17Drew, Hoponpop69, Qwerty Binary, Davis2k, Dereckson, PlazzTT, Memphisto, Gingerlib~enwiki, Magioladitis, Cinnamongirl276, Jvhertum, SnapSnap, James3k, Shadiac, Cavale, Ftiercel, Lynnarmstrong, Qabbalah, Lifebonzza, Boston, Captain panda, Pharaoh of the Wizards, Wandering Ghost, P4k, LozaB, DjScrawl, BeŽet, Brianmetro, Nevergrowold, ShimShem, JTOToole, Ascii art, Nerdynick, Personline, Jotsko, LeaveSleaves, Room429, SabreWolfy, Sebisthlm, Newheadrecords, Someoneelser, Nite-Sirk, Systempluss, Maddmike64, ClueBot, Binksternet, Arentath8, Nnnudibranch, Trivialist, PixelBot, DumZiBoT, Semitransgenic, Ceekayone, Tim010987, Magda europa, Addbot, Monk79, Binary TSO, Kwanesum, Leszek Jańczuk, Aryder779, BecauseWhy?, The Shadow-Fighter, Lightbot, Zorrobot, Taargus taargus 1, Yobot, Daondo, Guy1890, Larrytee2001, User529, Yaneleksklus, Citation bot, Tarsierfish, Promosonica, GrouchoBot, Sabrebd, Macaronlover, Chrisbkoolio, MJf97, Hiddenstranger, Orphan Wiki, RB88public, Maashatra11, Werieth, Burnberrytree, Unreal7, SporkBot, Lexusuns, Bracelett, Dwinterwerp, EdgarFabiano, Wbm1058, Deepblue1, AvocatoBot, Ongepotchket, Vvven, BattyBot, Kavy32, Myxomatosis57, Genrallex, Acidtrash82, Tonyall87, GlitterDream, Bubbalou97, Myconix, Synthwave.94, AEIOUandsometimesYYY, Dutchcourages, Hoshirisu, Tigercompanion25, Andrewbf and Anonymous: 284

- **Electronic dance music** *Source:* https://en.wikipedia.org/wiki/Electronic_dance_music?oldid=685874507 *Contributors:* Ant, Mjb, Ixfd64, Graue, Mcarling, Darkwind, Scott, Agtx, Hyacinth, Topbanana, Dimadick, Goethean, Altenmann, Gidonb, Tobias Bergemann, DocWatson42, Aembleton, Wmahan, Gadfium, Ary29, M1ss1ontomars2k4, Mike Rosoft, Monkeyman, Discospinster, Rich Farmbrough, Vsmith, Kiand, Smalljim, Guiltyspark, Colonel Cow, Gary, Jeltz, Hu, Wtmitchell, Versageek, Dan100, Stemonitis, Woohookitty, LOL, Arru, BrenDJ, LimoWreck, BD2412, Bill37212, Bruce1ee, Vegaswikian, Krash, The wub, MapsMan, Windchaser, Paul foord, TeaDrinker, Bgwhite, Wavelength, Rapido, Mahahahaneapneap, C777, Anomalocaris, Deskana, Joel7687, Robert Moore, Irishguy, Syrthiss, Gadget850, Wknight94, Likwidshoe, Theda, Joyrex, Rotten Bastard~enwiki, ViperSnake151, TLSuda, WesleyDodds, Themacro, SmackBot, Trance88, Hydrogen Iodide, Wcquidditch, Thorseth, Jagged 85, Gilliam, Evilandi, Schmiteye, Amatulic, Chris the speller, Unint, Jstplace, DHN-bot~enwiki, Tsca.bot, Jmejia, Onorem, Nixeagle, BarryNorton, GBobly, "alyosha", Marcus Brute, Phinn, True Blue Falcon, Kuru, Minna Sora no Shita, Wickethewok, MTN~enwiki, Beetstra, Meco, Justin McConnell, OnBeyondZebrax, Aeternus, Tawkerbot2, Filelakeshoe, Heqs, Lighthead, R9tgokunks, Sky-surfer, ShelfSkewed, Bungalowbill, Gogo Dodo, Maxker, DumbBOT, Roger Roger, Zalgo, Barticus88, Sry85, Brian G. Wilson, JustAGal, Dawnseeker2000, Majorly, Nutshack1, Maryishimotomorris, Seaphoto, Jhsounds, Oblivionboy, Kaini, JAnDbot, MegX, Y2kcrazyjoker4, Bongwarrior, Jerome Kohl, Twsx, Gnu andrew, Eldumpo, Winter.Raven, Ftiercel, Qabbalah, Cybersonik, MartinBot, Jotamide, Keith D, CommonsDelinker, Lifebonzza, J.delanoy, Tikiwont, Acalamari, Rosenknospe, Swon~enwiki, Jamesontai, Fclass, Alexub, Wetdogmeat, Zenbeats, ACSE, Thykka~enwiki, Enoksrd, TheMexican2007, Draglikepull, Slysplace, Willit63, ThisIsNotReal22, Soul Train, McCoyConway, Frees, Frankmueller, Parsifal, Edkollin, Dawn Bard, Ilovewales, Seckle, Bentogoa, Happysailor, Flyer22, StateAardvark, Yerpo, Redmarkviolinist, Jdaloner, Raphy23, Fratrep, Reorgart~enwiki, Explicit, Susume-eat, ClueBot, NickCT, Binksternet, Wossit, The Thing That Should Not Be, Alecsdaniel, Aria1561, Excirial, Jusdafax, Tikilounge, Erebus Morgaine, AbsoluteZero280, Arjayeh, Tonyfey, Mlaffs, DumZiBoT, Semitransgenic, XLinkBot, Qfl247, WikiRedactor, Netrat, SilvonenBot, Raprockstail, Eborg9, Addbot, Grayfell, Sard112, Alexleroy, Percivl, Dan56, DougsTech, Ukcd, RedRose333, Moosehadley, KitchM, Fluffernutter, Aryder779, Electro - music, Cesar2, Redheylin, Charlesdickends, Tassedethe, HandThatFeeds, Lightbot, Ben Ben, Luckas-bot, Bech86, Yobot, Sekisama, Mchapel, AnomieBOT, Stormedelf, Sotoma665, ItsAlwaysLupus, Law, Radicalthinker, Bluerasberry, Materialscientist, Half past, CingSounds, ArthurBot, LilHelpa, Xqbot, CEGTalent, Daftpunker88, Sabrebd, FrescoBot, Haeinous, Macaronlover, Tetraedycal, Rznislam, Darrenpoil, I dream of horses, LadyBlacktronika, Dainiusblynas, MastiBot, Σ, Omertarecords, Sndrag7, Sebizzar, Cmcne41, Burnin Gypsy Kneeger, Jarmihi, Amyjen, Hunty1130, Theologiae, SMmoto, Onel5969, Mean as custard, RjwilmsiBot, Hiddenstranger, EmausBot, John of Reading, WikitanvirBot, ThomasWF, Dewritech, Racerx11, GoingBatty, Solarra, Clusternote, K6ka, Spamdingel, Unreal7, SporkBot, Demonkoryu, Erianna, Staszek Lem, Alexia777nasice, Carmichael, ChuispastonBot, Dottie danger, Petrb, ClueBot NG, Gareth Griffith-Jones, MelbourneStar, This lousy T-shirt, Gulfimpossible, JasonRawlins, Thejmc, Rathersilly, Loginnigol, Navops47, Frietjes, Widr, Larshei, Danceking5, Petiapee, YK163, Helpful Pixie Bot, Excitium, Titodutta, RodriM3deir0z, BG19bot, Roberticus, Chess, TCN7JM, CityOfSilver, Jord.sheehy, Atomician, Sylien, Wikiz876, Rogueleaderr, BattyBot,

Darylgolden, RichardMills65, Heyya88, Camkayymusic, ChrisGualtieri, Tehloy, Khazar2, Soulparadox, Silkysystems, JYBot, Earflaps, Jeff-Baxter, Codename Lisa, Mogism, Jlesnick, Viewmont Viking, Radiodef, Lugia2453, Electronicmusic911, Got2pedia, Ccyyrree, Frosty, Ian-brine, Juliandawikkid, King jakob c, Alakazander, Lancemcawesome, Faizan, Camyoung54, Mentordisciple, Melonkelon, Eyesnore, Sanny-bear, Kyle.smith99, Mainstream EDM, Tentinator, MV360, Taikoguide, Wuzh, BryonStout, Zerabat, ItsCrazyKevin887, WhiteOutCorrector, Mlevine2013, Hmsimha, DavidLeighEllis, Redrenae, Gregoryandres3, Prokaryotes, GrivvyWivvy, Synthwave.94, Raggib, Deleonnataly, Evan-notkelley, Belazed, DuhhJohn, Choose Happy, Wikiplaya93, Djsilviuz, Rlcrist, Sarajane135, Fl0nko 359, P-123, Trisha Agarwala, BethNaught, Leadham, Scarlettail, Madisonmcneill, Pullara93, Amortias, TerryAlex, Mcmanuster, Reasonseason, Johnsose22, Lakerlandb, Krystinaamber, Saisai.msi, GoGatorMeds, Hampred, Edmtitan69, Algebra2honors, Malmsimp, Hakken, Dcris08, Ktessler9, Fourclass, Zsteigerwald, Wowo-fundy16, Jaamess, ManMega5551, Vorpzn, Gadwal ashwaryaa, Allegory80622, Uofark92, Jaydoubleyou1, Verside, Joe12.12Moore, CromRt, RetroGameFan, Fv9208pm, Ancar562, Mike123for, Pazkaz, Apinczo, Pauladima91, Erikshoell, Aniket J3, Pwright08, Bstout101, Siqm8, Yas-mine12345, Mel123451998, Anarkive, JaredSpang, Joester4, Krstnalee, Sams891, Leonard Finley, Wobbes, Jminzer, Jmb9421, Graceaudio, Justinequinteros, Mhoard44 and Anonymous: 632

- **Game Boy music** *Source:* https://en.wikipedia.org/wiki/Game_Boy_music?oldid=684647037 *Contributors:* Damian Yerrick, Andrewman327, Furrykef, Rich Farmbrough, ESkog, Nonpareility, Gary, Woohookitty, Rjwilmsi, TheRingess, Eubot, Tedder, Melodia, Timeheater, Pelago, Sar-danaphalus, SmackBot, Quadratic, Thumperward, MichaelBillington, Golfman, Patzak~enwiki, Esposimi, Phantasy Phanatik, Alaibot, Chub-bles, SteelersFan UK06, Aka042, Lelandrb, Weakmassive, Dispenser, Barkermarker, Davehi1, AtomicCEO, Dlae, Vcfool, Winchelsea, Polysic-sarebest, CultureDrone, Rabato, The Thing That Should Not Be, The Gruber, Calbeebooth, Auntof6, Tnxman307, Account9000, Carriearch-dale, Boleyn, XLinkBot, Ost316, Ninjaspew, Anticipation of a New Lover's Arrival, The, JBsupreme, FlutieFlushed, Okamikoori, Tothwolf, Tomtheeditor, Lightbot, Kasfear, Yobot, ABaptiste, Gongshow, KristyGrl, Yaneleksklus, Kyle Robinson, Gurochu, Ralpwiki, Durdos, Streetl-ogo, Empty1012, Sabrebd, PM800, Elviomusic, Danimop, DrilBot, JamesSNIPER, Paroxysm8bit, Battlelava, John of Reading, RA0808, Nesf-reak101, Anir1uph, Benjaminoakes, Elvio66, Harbngr, ClueBot NG, Megasis105, Ilveon, Dobie80, Girandolavas, Kelzarian, Klingex, Rusty595, Theduckofdeath, Monkbot, IagoQnsi, Trystmark, Elischwat, Ruddybulbs and Anonymous: 219

- **Glitch (music)** *Source:* https://en.wikipedia.org/wiki/Glitch_(music)?oldid=685574423 *Contributors:* Kurt Jansson, Lexor, CatherineMunro, Angela, Sugarfish, Pema~enwiki, Denis Barthel, Hyacinth, Omegatron, Owen, Twang, Altenmann, MilkMiruku, Magic Window, Alerante, DocWatson42, St3vo, Lvr, Beland, Mike Rosoft, Discospinster, Rich Farmbrough, STGM, Chadparker, Shanes, Barcex, Giraffedata, Drag-onGuyver, Ardric47, Gargaj, Keenan Pepper, Snowolf, Ringbang, Awk~enwiki, Ketiltrout, Quiddity, Intgr, RussBot, Chaser, Asmadeus, Aeusoes1, Mikeblas, LodeRunner, Zwobot, Slicing, Esprit15d, WesleyDodds, Sardanaphalus, SmackBot, Krovisser, Robotonic, Jagged 85, Matveims, Evanreyes, Gilliam, Fuzzform, Darktremor, Tsca.bot, T sCale, Mwtoews, Vickei, Ian Spackman, Gatesofawesome!, IronGargoyle, Makyen, Csmills, Dreftymac, Aeternus, Nina phunsta, Matthew Meta, Tawkerbot2, Filelakeshoe, Dto, Phantasy Phanatik, Jack's Revenge, Doceddi, J Milburn, Jozef Ahmed, Cyrus XIII, BFD1, Lighthead, Epistemophiliac, Peinwod, AndrewHowse, Gogo Dodo, Omicronpersei8, Treachjuris, Electroclass, T-1, Featheredserpent, Zeroday, Alphasixzero, Aboyle, Doktor Who, Jhsounds, WWB, Kaini, Andrzejbanas, JAnD-bot, Hemingrubbish, Matthew Fennell, Freshacconci, JamesBWatson, Jackdark, Sambenito, JoyZipper, MartinBot, Origin29, P4k, Foetusized, Kemonoid, Fclass, Overcow, Countrymike, Erodecay, A4bot, Djcampblood, Ridernyc, Von9, Personline, Eight Suns, Rachmiel, MostAwe-someDude, Jotsko, Room429, Llcch, Parsifal, Gozombie, Newfarout, Ramsilver, That-boy-joe, Chphe, Peasantswithfeathers, I ate jelly, Panser-bjorne51, Lars Ingebrigtsen, Foxj, Sefranklin11, Mild Bill Hiccup, N8sound, Doughouse, Rhododendrites, Bluefoz, ChrisHodgesUK, Mi-ami33139, Happypoems, Semitransgenic, Pzqk, XLinkBot, Placesense, RichLow, Awfulcopter, Addbot, Sard112, Percivl, CanadianLinuxUser, Aryder779, Tassedethe, Prop A Gandah, Lightbot, Jarble, Luckas-bot, Yobot, TaBOT-zerem, Feteti, Gongshow, Silenceisgoldie, Sponge69, AnomieBOT, Valueyou, Hairhorn, JackieBot, Piano non troppo, RayvnEQ, Materialscientist, Nitarbell, ArthurBot, Sscochaa, Mix-sit, Measles, Karlzt, J04n, Sabrebd, 安可, Black Gold, FrescoBot, Sock, Beep21, Gartist, Pinethicket, Jonesey95, ViB, Tim1357, Kokoshky, Thisispain, Nrku, ThePhantasos, Hiddenstranger, RA0808, Aldarrof, ZéroBot, Andrew H. Goldberg, Fixblor, Lacon432, Dimitaru, SporkBot, Choco-latejoe, Marcusgabler, Dustzone, Conkern65, Therewillbehotcake, ClueBot NG, Shifted28, CactusBot, Spoken Bird, Frietjes, Ruriko inoyuki, Djstoneyj, Konekta, Wbm1058, BG19bot, Ettepuop, Heinzinsky, Pasicles, Vvven, MenkinAlRire, BattyBot, Miszatomic, Karshkarsh92, Myxo-matosis57, EuroCarGT, Tuccio9719, Laiyxs, Angstost, GlitterDream, Pinecone23777, LuaIsEpic, Kingfelixmusic, Murderer & Victim, Wywin, Ede3724, Xanatos451, Myconix, Lilxxxwill, EDM4life, Padrino 007, Vandvl, Dpandaking, Fixuture, Autumn harvest thrives, Geraldkrasner, Kaystay, EdmDistrict, Xavier917, Mcmaddo, Glennderp, Thewatertribe, Chiptronica, Mrsexyfiedman, Nerologicalstatic, ManMega5551, Grass-man0, Kroponzipir, Underblue, RetroMaya, Villanueva100, Crazedragon, Dprent and Anonymous: 437

- **HardSID** *Source:* https://en.wikipedia.org/wiki/HardSID?oldid=665147979 *Contributors:* Wwwwolf, Ds13, Edcolins, Mamizou, Guy Harris, CyberSkull, Mirror Vax, Reedy, Avanze, DabMachine, Cydebot, Krator, Shape84, Prof Wrong, Addbot, Lightbot, Pcap, J04n, Spiralofhope, Sta064 and Anonymous: 14

- **List of audio programming languages** *Source:* https://en.wikipedia.org/wiki/List_of_audio_programming_languages?oldid=683237651 *Con-tributors:* Michael Hardy, Omegatron, Plutor, Andreas Kaufmann, Smimram, Tgies, Danakil, Polluks, Quiddity, GangofOne, SmackBot, Jagged 85, Chris the speller, Frap, NNemec, Sytelus, Maslin, Seth Laphage, Digego, Peu, Biasoli, Jerryobject, Wolfcm, Rhododendrites, Snowwecocke, Boomur, Jarble, Kbarkati, AllenZh, Shmageggy, Pdecalculus, Suhaild, Communal t and Anonymous: 32

- **Module file** *Source:* https://en.wikipedia.org/wiki/Module_file?oldid=679674459 *Contributors:* Shd~enwiki, David Latapie, Furrykef, Scott McNay, Shlomif, Spoon!, JoshuaRodman, AmosWolfe, Fadookie, Corporal, Ahruman, UltraSkuzzi, Jef-Infojef, Marasmusine, Woohookitty, Tabletop, Havarhen, Vossanova, Mirror Vax, RevRaven, GreyCat, Phantomsteve, RussBot, Asmadeus, Bovineone, Tms.~enwiki, Zwobot, Open2universe, Devin A., SmackBot, Eaglizard, Eskimbot, Wormbo, Pragmat, Thumperward, TechPurism, Aeternus, Bohan, BuZz, Dogma00, DannyKitty, Texcarson, LtData, Ssr, Mentifisto, TimVickers, Fayenatic london, HyperDrive, The Fifth Horseman, Robina Fox, DirtY iCE, Frotz, STBot, Bradgib, Speck-Made, CommonsDelinker, VolkovBot, Milnivlek, Jogar2, Daff555, Xerces8, Serprex, Mastersrp, Roxor128, Dfwlms, Niceguyedc, Gürkan Sengün, Miami33139, InternetMeme, Addbot, MrOllie, KaiKemmann, Lightbot, Yobot, Pcap, AnomieBOT, Sonixten, FrescoBot, RonsonDk, Christoph hausner, Freedrull, EmausBot, Sirciny, Shaddim, Helpful Pixie Bot, WNYY98, DmitryKos, Mogism, CsDix, Hakken, Djsqueekz and Anonymous: 121

- **MOS Technology SID** *Source:* https://en.wikipedia.org/wiki/MOS_Technology_SID?oldid=683998187 *Contributors:* Robert Merkel, Taw, Christian List, D, Lezek, Lexor, DopefishJustin, Mahjongg, Nixdorf, Liftarn, Wwwwolf, ZoeB, Notheruser, Tedius Zanarukando, Malcohol, Themaxx, Slark, WhisperToMe, Furrykef, Wernher, Jeeves, Twang, Robbot, RedWolf, Dehumanizer, Kevin Saff, Honta, Ds13, Spm, Edcolins,

Chowbok, LucasVB, Mamizou, Qdr, Perey, Sysy, Pixel8, Roo72, Ylee, RoyBoy, Dgpop, JRM, Polluks, Trevj, PJ, Ashley Pomeroy, Wtshymanski, Cburnett, Derbeth, Reaverdrop, Voxadam, Forderud, Jef-Infojef, Ae-a, Al E., Bluemoose, D14BL0, Graham87, Rjwilmsi, Captain Disdain, Mirror Vax, SchuminWeb, Ysangkok, Viznut, Liontamer, Flashmorbid, Bgwhite, NSR, YurikBot, Crotalus horridus, RmM, Zafiroblue05, FromWithin, CapitalLetterBeginning, NotInventedHere, Vampyrium, 2fort5r, KnightRider~enwiki, SmackBot, Eskimbot, Fuzzform, Frap, Paulie68000, Deepred6502, PXE-M0F, JMax555, Danmoore, Wickethewok, Anescient, Tawkerbot2, ChrisCork, Ronaldvd, ShelfSkewed, WeggeBot, Mccalli, Cydebot, Silvertouch57, Lord Nightmare, Al Lemos, Electron9, X201, AntiVandalBot, Darkuni, Infindebula, Damian1983, Kaini, Daibot~enwiki, Stolsvik, Conquerist, Scoutski, Vanessaezekowitz, Rettetast, Verdatum, Wikip rhyre, Dispenser, Gigantic Killerdong, DeeKay64, BOTones, JJGD, Jcea, Leopold B. Stotch, Jalwikip, Billinghurst, Spinningspark, Nunucello, Rlendog, Lightmouse, Peepo uk, Martarius, EoGuy, Niceguyedc, Suenarmy, Rhododendrites, Pinkevin, Theinvisibleworm, InternetMeme, XLinkBot, Duncan, Imanjl, Addbot, Yobot, Pcap, Chordian, AnomieBOT, MauritsBot, Xqbot, Cybjit, C64glen, SimonInns, RedBot, Jopinder, Johnnylocust, RjwilmsiBot, EmausBot, Alfons van Vorden, ZéroBot, Plm-pro, A930913, Kent Sullivan, ClueBot NG, DieSwartzPunkt, Cntras, Park Flier, Molotovsystem, Yoyofr, AndroSID, BattyBot, Thomas.hori, Scott Samwell, BaseCochise, Monkbot and Anonymous: 207

- **Music tracker** *Source:* https://en.wikipedia.org/wiki/Music_tracker?oldid=685101539 *Contributors:* Damian Yerrick, Tarquin, Rbrwr, EddEdmondson, Booyabazooka, Kwertii, Nixdorf, Liftarn, Tannin, Graue, Dori, Emmanuel Mayorga, Minesweeper, Alfio, Guaka, Dysprosia, Furrykef, Kwantus, Bloodshedder, Rholton, Cholling, Pengo, Sloyment, Twilek, Ds13, Quinone, Ijon-Tichy, Sdfisher, Kaminari, Stevietheman, Zzo38, LucasVB, Bigpeteb, Mamizou, Bumm13, Kevyn, MakeRocketGoNow, DmitryKo, Xezbeth, R.123, Stesmo, AmosWolfe, Revolutionary, Enric Naval, Shlomital, Alphax, Jason One, Gargaj, Cpcallen, Fadookie, Halsteadk, Deadworm222, Marasmusine, Woohookitty, Skypher, Tabletop, Al E., Ariamaki, Vossanova, Joe Roe, Sjakkalle, Rjwilmsi, Moskvax, Mirror Vax, Hyphz, Pathoschild, Viznut, YurikBot, Phantomsteve, Ventolin, Peter S., Splash, Snis0r, Gaius Cornelius, Msikma, Robertvan1, Albertique, Moppet65535, BirgitteSB, TERdON, Mikeblas, Zwobot, Nlu, Donald Albury, SmackBot, Widgetphreak, E-Magination, Darklock, Lonejack, KyrilRevels, Thumperward, Mdwh, Jerome Charles Potts, Fluggo~enwiki, Firetrap9254, Jacob Poon, Killerkid, Pesalomo, Slate~enwiki, Slate2, NeoVampTrunks, Tjo~enwiki, Aleator, Kigabo, Ladybluex, JoeBot, Aeternus, Amakuru, Winston Spencer, Bohan, Nakkikorva, MichaelPloujnikov, Cydebot, Texcarson, D rand, Thijs!bot, Epbr123, BeRo, Escarbot, Ssr, Daniel Villalobos, JAnDbot, MER-C, Andreas Toth, Bongwarrior, Marko75, Ecksemmess, Rich257, DasKreestof, Ahecht, Karawapo, Conquerist, CommonsDelinker, Mike.lifeguard, Beatfox, Kyle the bot, WarddrBOT, NightRadio, Chase-san, Rumpelstilzchen, SieBot, AlphaPyro, Jdaloner, ImageRemovalBot, Mild Bill Hiccup, Gürkan Sengün, InternetMeme, Delt01, XLinkBot, SilvonenBot, Willgad, Addbot, EjsBot, Lightbot, OlEnglish, Zorrobot, Yobot, Pcap, Geraeusch, AnomieBOT, Pankaj.apiit, Rtyq2, Xqbot, Jikooworld, Wormygermy, FrescoBot, Marcus256, RjwilmsiBot, EmausBot, WikitanvirBot, GoingBatty, Clusternote, Shaddim, Widr, Be..anyone, Helpful Pixie Bot, Hza a 9, Silvrous, CitationCleanerBot, BattyBot, Arcandam, Mogism, Thisisnotadrill, CsDix, Pdecalculus, Gixce93, 178tint, ScotXW, Spacedrone808, Monkbot, Hakken, ChamithN, CoolGamer23 and Anonymous: 226

- **Nintendocore** *Source:* https://en.wikipedia.org/wiki/Nintendocore?oldid=678890625 *Contributors:* Aleron235, LGagnon, HaeB, Mu, OverlordQ, Halo, Abdull, Florian Blaschke, Lachatdelarue, MBisanz, Bobo192, Fourthords, Chirpy, Falcolombardi87, Kamezuki, Woohookitty, Uncle G, Benbest, Karam.Anthony.K, TheSock, KaisaL, Island, Jdcooper, AshTM, Bruce1ee, Voretus, Zpatterson, A Man In Black, Alphachimp, Liontamer, Hatch68, Bornhj, YurikBot, Seegoon, Avt tor, Bl4d3, Haemo, ViperSnake151, Sardanaphalus, SmackBot, C.Fred, Jagged 85, Karpsmom, Lainagier, Wieners, Rrburke, TenPoundHammer, SevenEightTwo, JzG, Guroadrunner, Disavian, Shchmue, HisSpaceResearch, Ktwx, Aeternus, Eastlaw, The Haunted Angel, FatalError, Tifego, Nosawa, Pekinpekin, URORIN, The Enslaver, Jon138, Blackmetalbaz, Njmcfreak, Inhumer, Megazodiac, Thijs!bot, Sam 323, Nirvanacr1231, JNighthawk, Dayn, John254, Vincent the ghetto asian, L33TGuy, Escarbot, AntiVandalBot, Chubbles, Mkerley, Voyaging, Just Chilling, Hoponpop69, Astavats, AndThree, V-train, Random89, Skomorokh, Graveenib, Vanished user s4irtj34tivkj12erhskj46thgdg, Clementduval, Ambrosia-, Kuyabribri, Victoreea, Torchiest, Leon Sword, Juansidious, Woffiecow, Neon white, Wandering Ghost, AdamBMorgan, Dexter prog, Tsuite, Smitty, Slpunk99, Ekaidus, Granto2004uk, TXiKiBoT, Reibot, Z.E.R.O., Anonymous Dissident, Adamrulez182, Slysplace, JJJ999, Sludgegrinder, IL7Soulhunter, Alsamisath, Cocaine white, SieBot, Skellyscribbles, Vegetable4, Nite-Sirk, Gunmetal Angel, Navnløs, Jovemkurt rockstar~enwiki, Maxschmelling, Andre1989, Fezmar9, Faithlessthewonderboy, ClueBot, General Epitaph, JamesWilson2007, SuperHamster, Alexbot, Vivio Testarossa, Wiki libs, Vromeri Stafida, Clickonchase, XLinkBot, SleepyReaper, Ost316, Solino, Netrat, ZooFari, Addbot, Tide rolls, Arbitrarily0, BloodRedFox, DEWadict, Luckas-bot, Yobot, Bi0Shokker, Gareth fritz, Epinpephrine, Tamasjake, Yaneleksklus, A7xTheRev, RavAngell, Xqbot, 3family6, Wolven531, Calzum, Sabrebd, 81&CK &18!N0 80N3$, Richard BB, Dan6hell66, FrescoBot, Ramicus, Priestofglass, SpaceFlight89, Ticklewickleukulele, Jonjonjohny, Aoidh, Ctk986, Chrisbkoolio, Mashaunix, Ol Red33, Demonwesker, The Dual Dragons, ClueBot NG, Trendcoremessiah, Bestestmanhawk, Polyversemusic, BG19bot, SomedayCameSuddenly, Der Naturfreund, The1337gamer, BattyBot, Myxomatosis57, DiendJap, TheEndOfLiberty, Hairobics, Guydude2, Synthwave.94, SJ Defender, Second Skin, Monkbot, Sadisticaddict, Thecheeseispoisoned, FRSCFan1 and Anonymous: 288

- **Personal computer** *Source:* https://en.wikipedia.org/wiki/Personal_computer?oldid=685914814 *Contributors:* AxelBoldt, Magnus Manske, Mav, The Anome, Tarquin, Stephen Gilbert, Taw, Andre Engels, Christian List, Aldie, Ortolan88, William Avery, Ben-Zin~enwiki, David spector, Fonzy, Volker, Edward, Patrick, Kchishol1970, Michael Hardy, Fred Bauder, Lexor, Norm, Blueshade, Mahjongg, Pnm, Liftarn, Tannin, Cyde, TakuyaMurata, Arpingstone, Gaz~enwiki, KAMiKAZOW, Haakon, Nanshu, Julesd, Lupinoid, Cyan, Nikai, Cimon Avaro, Mxn, Crusadeonilliteracy, Revolver, Andrevan, RickK, Dmsar, Ww, Vancouverguy, Furrykef, Ed g2s, Wernher, Mang kiko, Morn, Bloodshedder, Rohan Jayasekera, Riddley, Robbot, Moriori, Fredrik, Boffy b, RedWolf, Donreed, Nurg, Modulatum, Pingveno, Rursus, Bkell, Hadal, Iain.mcclatchie, Tobias Bergemann, Ancheta Wis, Giftlite, Graeme Bartlett, DocWatson42, Andries, DavidCary, Kim Bruning, Philwelch, Inter, Kenny sh, Obli, Peruvianllama, Curps, Mboverload, Siroxo, Marcusvox, Jaan513, Edcolins, Chowbok, Bact, Nova77, Knutux, LiDaobing, Antandrus, Beland, MisfitToys, Wikimol, Cb6, DragonflySixtyseven, PFHLai, Necrothesp, Icairns, Ktvoelker, JulieADriver, Neutrality, Hellisp, Cab88, Trevor MacInnis, Millisits, Mike Rosoft, Discospinster, Rich Farmbrough, Rhobite, Pak21, Pie4all88, Chad okere, Chowells, LindsayH, Mani1, Deelkar, Martpol, Paul August, Stereotek, Dyl, Kbh3rd, Kaisershatner, Plugwash, MaxPower, PPGMD, Hayabusa future, Shanes, Grue, Vanished user sdfkjertiwoi1212u5mcake, Func, BrokenSegue, Brim, Matt Britt, Mkapor, Davelane, Giraffedata, Juzeris, SpeedyGonsales, Kjkolb, Nk, Woodsjay, Martinultima, PochWiki, Notnoisy, Maximusnukeage, Mdd, Espoo, Stephen G. Brown, Poweroid, Alansohn, Guy Harris, Arthena, Diego Moya, Andrewpmk, MarkGallagher, Lightdarkness, Jaw959, Denniss, Hu, Snowolf, Wtmitchell, Melaen, Velella, VanillaDeath, KingTT, Rebroad, Wtshymanski, Max Naylor, RainbowOfLight, Mikeo, NicholasJones, Versageek, Mattbrundage, Stinger~enwiki, Kirev, Dtobias, Firsfron, Mel Etitis, Woohookitty, TigerShark, Rocastelo, Ae-a, TomTheHand, WPPWAH, MattGiuca, JeremyA, MONGO, Gengiskanhg, Wikiklrsc, Hotshot977, Bbatsell, Mangojuice, Frungi, Sega381, SDC, Waldir, Toussaint, Karam.Anthony.K, Mkleine, Emerson7, Mandarax, Gettingtoit, LimoWreck, Graham87, Cuvtixo, Magister Mathematicae, Keeves, BD2412, Melesse, Reisio, Vanderdecken, Sjakkalle, Rjwilmsi, Mayumashu,

Wikibofh, Vary, Loudenvier, Hiberniantears, JoshuacUK, Tangotango, Brucelee, Dcsutherland, Gudeldar, ElKevbo, SeanMack, DirkvdM, JanSuchy, Harda, FlaBot, CAPS LOCK, RobertG, The.valiant.paladin, Master Thief Garrett, Ysangkok, Who, Nivix, SuperDude115, RexNL, Ewlyahoocom, Swtpc6800, TeaDrinker, Diza, Hibana, Vchapman, King of Hearts, Chobot, Fourdee, DVdm, Random user 39849958, Bgwhite, Hahnchen, Simesa, Mr.Do!, Roboto de Ajvol, The Rambling Man, Wavelength, Eraserhead1, Sceptre, OtherPerson, Retodon8, DMahalko, Amckern, Fabartus, The Storm Surfer, Pigman, Yuhong, Hydrargyrum, Stephenb, David Woodward, Gaius Cornelius, CambridgeBayWeather, Alvinrune, Rsrikanth05, Neilbeach, SamJohnston, Thane, Gustavb, Ricree101, NawlinWiki, ENeville, Wiki alf, Msikma, Aeusoes1, Grafen, Welsh, Oberst, DarthVader, Cholmes75, PhilipO, Allynnc, Tony1, Ospalh, Mysid, Wangi, Brat32, PS2pcGAMER, Jeh, Oliverdl, Groink, Ll-lll, Robertbyrne, Searchme, Rwxrwxrwx, LarryLACa, EAderhold, J S Ayer, Zzuuzz, I kant spel, StuRat, Ageekgal, Covington, Arthur Rubin, KGasso, Eric Jack Nash, DynaBlast, JuJube, Pablo2garcia~enwiki, Petri Krohn, GraemeL, Mike1024, Kevin, HereToHelp, Anclation~enwiki, JLaTondre, ArielGold, ViperSnake151, Katieh5584, Kungfuadam, Junglecat, Captain Proton, Paul Erik, Rwwww, MansonP, Roger wilco, Nippoo, DVD R W, Kimdino, Veinor, AndersL, A bit iffy, SmackBot, Kellen, Thomas Ash, Classicfilms, Schyler, Benjaminb, Anarchist42, Aflm, KnowledgeOfSelf, VigilancePrime, Hydrogen Iodide, McGeddon, Pgk, C.Fred, Blue520, Bomac, Jagged 85, RenOfHeavens, Video99, KVDP, Delldot, Darklock, CapitalSasha, Onebravemonkey, Edgar181, Lakhim, Gilliam, Ohnoitsjamie, Hmains, Oscarthecat, Skizzik, Mushroom King, Slo-mo, Chris the speller, Master Jay, Jethero, Thom2002, Ian13, MK8, Thumperward, Miquonranger03, Nobloodyname, Mdwh, EdgeOfEpsilon, DHN-bot~enwiki, Cassivs, Colonies Chris, Para, Hallenrm, Darth Panda, Janipewter, Gsp8181, Stanthejeep, Can't sleep, clown will eat me, Shalom Yechiel, Flibbert, Boomeringue, OrphanBot, Azio, Cyber rigger, SundarBot, Flyguy649, Theonlyedge, Cybercobra, Nakon, T-borg, Valenciano, The Pondermatic, SpacemanAfrica, Warren, Weregerbil, DenisRS, Andrew c, A gx7, Acdx, Sigma 7, Luigi.a.cruz, LeoNomis, ISeeYou, Candorwien, Xufem, Clicketyclack, Chickenofbristol, Kkailas, Ed@islandnet.com, Lambiam, Gailim, Lester, Harryboyles, Rklawton, KLLvr283, Oskilian, Pkalaher, Statsone, Danorux, JH-man, Sir Nicholas de Mimsy-Porpington, Leksey, Shadowlynk, Minna Sora no Shita, IronGargoyle, Ckatz, Slakr, Werdan7, Tasc, Beetstra, Noah Salzman, Optimale, Kondspi, Xiaphias, Optakeover, Waggers, TastyPoutine, Kvng, ShakingSpirit, Hans Bauer, DabMachine, SimonD, Typelighter, Smoothtofu, Iridescent, BrainMagMo, Kaarel, JoeBot, TimTIm, Aeons, Audiosmurf, Radiant chains, FairuseBot, Tawkerbot2, Daniel5127, Pithecanthropus, ChrisCork, TheHorseCollector, Ryt, Andrés Djordjalian, Eastlaw, Coolman435, Ale jrb, Raysonho, W guice, KyraVixen, Page Up, Baiji, Lmcelhiney, Pasten, Green caterpillar, Bungalowbill, Blackbox77, Karenjc, 0xF, AndrewHowse, Jac16888, Cydebot, Atomaton, Reywas92, Meno25, Gogo Dodo, ST47, Pascal.Tesson, Roketjack, Clovis Sangrail, Gvil, Christian75, Mallanox, Quadrius, Kozuch, Editor at Large, DalekClock, Omicronpersei8, Eb42, JodyB, Landroo, Gimmetrow, Satori Son, FrancoGG, Mattisse, Thijs!bot, Epbr123, Kubanczyk, ChunkySoup, O, Mojo Hand, Oliver202, Headbomb, James uk, Marek69, A3RO, Kathovo, X201, Tellyaddict, Not Diablo, Avitaltr, OrenBochman, Cooljuno411, CTZMSC3, M Nabil, Mentifisto, AntiVandalBot, Mr-Marmite, Majorly, Luna Santin, Widefox, Seaphoto, Prolog, Jj137, Sooriyank, Kristoferb, LibLord, Spencer, Jwisser, Jenny Wong, Wahwahpedal, Stokelake, Leuqarte, JAnDbot, Leuko, Jimothytrotter, Stanleyozoemena, TigerK 69, NapoliRoma, Thomleno, Arch dude, Blakwyte, Db099221, Plm209, Peachey88, Andonic, Greensburger, Bookinvestor, Kerotan, Robert Buzink, LittleOldMe, Geniac, DataMatrix, Magioladitis, Waterchan, Bongwarrior, VoABot II, Harryjohnston, JamesBWatson, Soulbot, Tobogganoggin, Ecksemmess, Pixel ;-), Nikevich, BilCat, A3nm, Frotz, FrederikVds, Glen, DerHexer, GermanX, Pappa11~enwiki, Alwolff55, Gwern, FisherQueen, AVRS, Rustyfence, MartinBot, Bboyskidz, Akbeancounter, Vanessaezekowitz, D thadd, Paracel63, Rettetast, Mike6271, R'n'B, CommonsDelinker, AlexiusHoratius, Snozzer, Technolust, The Anonymous One, Tgeairn, J.delanoy, Svetovid, AstroHurricane001, WarthogDemon, Cpiral, Davidm617617, WikiBone, Katalaveno, McSly, Gurchzilla, Jon83m, 97198, M-le-mot-dit, Alecperkins, Slashs-tophat, NewEnglandYankee, DadaNeem, Cobi, KCinDC, Matman00, Redskins99, Cmichael, KylieTastic, Cometstyles, Equazcion, WarFox, Gtg204y, Bonadea, Commander-64, Diggory Hardy, HighKing, Useight, Avitohol, Xiahou, Squids and Chips, Mokgen, ThePointblank, Idioma-bot, Thedec, Dezignr, Gambacort, Wikieditor06, Vranak, Jrugordon, Wilko12, Hammersoft, VolkovBot, Morenooso, Jeff G., BlueFalconLoyd, Katydidit, Coolest-tech, Zeno333, Philip Trueman, Fran Rogers, Quackdave, Erik the Red 2, BuickCenturyDriver, TheDude231, Darkrevenger, Planetary Chaos, Walor, Vyx, ElinorD, Crohnie, Qxz, Rootbeer22, Westbrom123, 1 20 O9, Raymondwinn, Jorophose, Biffthemonkey, Natg 19, Aliasxerog, K Watson1984, Ngch89, PlayStation 69, Botard1, Andy Dingley, Madman2468, Haseo9999, Synthebot, Enviroboy, MF88389DTU, Entegy, Entirelybs, Chaplin62, Julian dahl, Lyinginbedmon, S8333631, Deconstructhis, Hokie92, Red, GM matthew, FrederikHertzum, SieBot, Octmed, MuzikJunky, Sonicology, Tiddly Tom, Yo man bob, Freaky4jesus32, Bachcell, Dawn Bard, Caltas, Scorpus57, Lahs08, Roquai, Paulapie, Kartoffelsalad, Keilana, Interchange88, Android Mouse, Flyer22, Radon210, Theaveng, Nopetro, Duplico, Oxymoron83, Lightmouse, RW Marloe, Seuraza, Gamingnews, Alex.muller, Cebra, IdreamofJeanie, Nancy, JohnSawyer, Force316, P.Marlow, Cyfal, Alatari, Veldin963, Wiknerd, Ken123BOT, Pinkadelica, Denisarona, Xplogic, Wudy1, Stormycarlos, Troy 07, ClueBot, NickCT, Avenged Eightfold, Binksternet, Fyyer, The Thing That Should Not Be, Voxpuppet, IceUnshattered, Rilak, AbstractEpiphany, R000t, Saddhiyama, Drmies, Frmorrison, Mild Bill Hiccup, Tylerpimpin, Mcglone14, SuperHamster, Monica vicelli98, Niceguyedc, Homayonifar, Turnmeoncomputers, Neverquick, ChandlerMapBot, Puchiko, Pointillist, Ahelon, Flipja, DragonBot, Excirial, Eeekster, Vanisheduser12345, Lartoven, Technobadger, Cenarium, Kit Berg, Jotterbot, Dekisugi, Newyorxico, Ark25, Tjlarson90, ChrisHodgesUK, Guitarhero1992, Thingg, SteveJobs8436492, Ranjithsutari, Jnw222, 12345ear, -keeleykins-, -alexdream-, MuckFizzou, Vybr8, Johnuniq, SF007, DumZiBoT, Bones000sw, Fwn122, XLinkBot, Xxray03, Emmette Hernandez Coleman, Gwandoya, PseudoOne, Rror, Nepenthes, AnnSavage~enwiki, Mitch Ames, Bestkeeps34, IngerAlHaosului, Alexius08, Noctibus, Zodon, Dsimic, Matty4123, Dekonegawa, Addbot, Xp54321, Military-ucon, Tcncv, Cherry Red Toenails, Non-dropframe, Friginator, Xoloki, Metagraph, Ronhjones, Fieldday-sunday, Roiba803~enwiki, Scientus, MrOllie, Cpall, Luxinalibaba, PROTOTYPE10, Glane23, Wot2the, Favonian, LinkFA-Bot, Abo-Bakr, Tassedethe, Tide rolls, BraedenP, D10Krumped, Krano, Aarsalankhalid, Greepnik, Luckas-bot, Yobot, JSimmonz, Senator Palpatine, TaBOT-zerem, II MusLiM HyBRiD II, I Love SVG, Unknown Subject, Mmxx, QueenCake, Jerebin, Dylpickleh8, OregonD00d, Synchronism, AnomieBOT, DemocraticLuntz, ThaddeusB, Jim1138, Galoubet, Piano non troppo, Solidsandie, HELLO11152111, DEFCON 3, RandomAct, Materialscientist, Danno uk, Mysteryfm, GB fan, LilHelpa, Smith00783, Xqbot, Belasted, Begkurp, Madkid981, Iadrian yu, CoolingGibbon, Topilsky, Laguna CA, J04n, BohaiZhuangyong, Morten Isaksen, Shirik, Holypoopmobs, Mark Schierbecker, SassoBot, Mpgenius, 78.26, SCARECROW, Yoganate79, Doulos Christos, The Wiki Octopus, Cyfraw, Dell1010, E0steven, SchnitzelMannGreek, PM800, Haploidavey, A.amitkumar, Yoshidude22, Timer9918, FrescoBot, NKristensen, Klyppi123, MISTYFAN4EVER8887, Sandgem Addict, Tobby72, Pepper, GEBStgo, Comm12group, Lonaowna, Recognizance, Wifione, Urasmart1, Orion 8, Edgar8207, DigbyDalton, Simple Bob, Pinethicket, Recipe For Hate, LittleWink, Jonesey95, Calmer Waters, Jschnur, Jaguar, SpaceFlight89, Rltcheer12, Full-date unlinking bot, Horst-schlaemma, FoxBot, Rh cool, Tgv8925, AmpicoJSteinway, Ravenperch, Orb85750, Callanecc, Vrenator, Sarina132, DragonofFire, Radar scanner, EggNogInTheMorning, Diannaa, Balben, Engande, Jesse V., What? Wham!, Genetixs, 11james22, Cryptichaos, Shannonarmstrong, DARTH SIDIOUS 2, Onel5969, The Utahraptor, RjwilmsiBot, TjBot, Rahul ram bhat, Larry.europe, Ripchip Bot, VernoWhitney, Bing Widder, Hajatvrc, MANGEJ KUMAR, Balph Eubank, Yojoisbob, EmausBot, John of Reading, Brian S. Elliott, MrFawwaz, Immunize, Gfoley4, JteB, Ajraddatz, Angrytoast, Senorclean1212, Dewritech, Golfandme, Shannon Bradley, Minimac's Clone, RenamedUser01302013, Vanished user zq46pw21, F1tutorials, Mo ainm, Zaixionito, K6ka, Thecheesykid, Kkm010, MithrandirAgain, Wackywace, Allforrous, Lateg, Shatsky, Nahferrari66, Netknowle, Misabharis, Mtiddens, Okboyfriend, Wayne Slam, John9278, EricWesBrown, Rcsprinter123, Rvrcopy, Rostz, Ctiner, Gsarwa, Donner60, Wipsenade, MainFrame, ChuispastonBot, Jona612, Floydvirginia, Targaryen, Milad Mosapoor, Xyzzyavatar, Buthunter, 28bot, Rocketrod1960, Georgy90, ClueBot NG, Vaio-911, JetBlast, Cbissell, MelbourneStar, This lousy T-shirt, Wikinium, Satellizer, Tyyin, Misterseal, Thvranken~enwiki, Alexander E Ross, Kellyzac, DanielDPeterson, Cyborg4, Egreenberg1232, Widr, JordoCo, Ajjuddn, Nanainthe-butt, Helpful Pixie Bot, Thomas tom99, HMSSolent, Titodutta, Wbm1058, Lowercase sigmabot, BG19bot, Ciscoh, Comm122011, Emayv, ערן117, Ricaj19, Ramunnoodles, Nikos 1993, Kristoff Clarke, Mrjoerizkallah, Mark Arsten, Dr. Whooves, Awesomemiles42, FutureTril-lionaire, Fsfoster, DLCasper, Velem~enwiki, Kelton2, Snivels1, Ultimatecomputernerd, Suren Harutyunyan, Shaun, Trevoraaron, Jackmaver-ick2, BattyBot, Pratyya Ghosh, Jimw338, The Illusive Man, Johnleo1, Naelix, TheJJJunk, Khazar2, Soulparadox, 4p5p6, Overd, MadGuy7023, Dexbot, Codename Lisa, Dominiktesla, Webclient101, Kephir, VidyaBoy, UsefulWikipedia, TwoTwoHello, Weezermanic94, Lugia2453, Isarra (HG), Frosty, UNOwenNYC, WikiTyson, Leem235, Jonhope123, Tefrd99, Edz997, Reatlas, Frickawiz, VanishedUser 2313214sad1, Mon-freres, Greengreengreenred, Spencer.mccormick, G PViB, 中文, I am One of Many, Bennybenbenbenbenny, Bennyboybenben, Petemclaren, Provacitu74, Ifidel1, Ayub407, Captain Conundrum, Syamsunders, Haephrati, Muhammadbabarzaman, Hldavis17, Nordsen, Bsbingam, Kap-itanCookie, Connor Waffles, Hn1711, Daftano, LieutenantLatvia, Zahrazohre, My name is not dave, Waiben, Ginsuloft, Kahtar, Dannyruthe, Zynerd, SouthGal62, Sharmin.h, ScotXW, JaconaFrere, Nycee79, Monkbot, Finskipojki, In Ratio Veritas, Mickung, Ninjabob25, Tman the wiki troll, Gmoney12345, Thebookman2, Shahean Cozad, Mcswaggins999, UglowT, SurealGod, Julianhopkins, Cgadis, PieCrafted, Artcrunchy, RoboticGoatse, Patrykq, CyanLights, GeorginaMat, Japones123, VortexJasper, Kingtantan, Some Gadget Geek, Junaid sipra, Dhdhdhdffx, Nils-gunnar27, Ggfdzr, Fghjbvv, Ffdddsf, Hx7, Johnathan the tortoise, Tjhill0110 subscribe2me, Cdimauro, KasparBot, Poo1138, Pootisdispencer-here, Sweepy, Snaddyvich21, IConnect POS, BD2412bot, Idahoprogrammer, CreeperSheeepertrd, Sanjays0011, Mike basic, CAPTAIN RAJU, Therealgoldace, Morfy35, Townparker, Hi 123456789dngubidfubg and Anonymous: 1292

- **Sound chip** *Source:* https://en.wikipedia.org/wiki/Sound_chip?oldid=685463303 *Contributors:* Maury Markowitz, Lexor, Nixdorf, Harvester, Smack, Malcohol, Wernher, Ashley Y, Cutler, Zigger, Mamizou, Pixel8, Polluks, Hooperbloob, Magetoo, Ae-a, Paxsimius, BD2412, RadioAc-tive~enwiki, Mirror Vax, Liontamer, Roboto de Ajvol, Generalleoff, KnightRider~enwiki, Jagged 85, Edgar181, Shalroth, Bluebot, Thumper-ward, Rainwarrior, Ronaldvd, Thijs!bot, Rob Kam, Lidnariq, Ferritecore, R'n'B, Vranak, Spinningspark, Alexbot, Addbot, AnomieBOT, Xqbot, DSisyphBot, FrescoBot, Dexter Nextnumber, EmausBot, WikitanvirBot, Alfons van Vorden, Clusternote and Anonymous: 42

- **Synthwave** *Source:* https://en.wikipedia.org/wiki/Synthwave?oldid=685500563 *Contributors:* The Anome, Intgr, Benlisquare, NickD, Nikki-maria, Tropylium, Seduisant, Derek R Bullamore, Andrzejbanas, Philg88, Yobot, AnomieBOT, TheUnbeholden, Sabrebd, BG19bot, Reddogsix, Myxomatosis57, Myconix, YiFeiBot, Fixuture, JackySpence, November49, UnknownToMost, JohanAnderssonSynthwave, DavidCarterAc-count, Uptowndogg7, Stefanwest919, Getonthemike and Anonymous: 38

- **Video game music** *Source:* https://en.wikipedia.org/wiki/Video_game_music?oldid=686084200 *Contributors:* Ed Poor, Grouse, Apollia, Mr-wojo, Edward, Mahjongg, Nixdorf, Wintran, Haakon, ZoeB, TUF-KAT, Amcaja, Charles Matthews, Andrevan, Tedius Zanarukando, Zoicon5, Maximus Rex, Furrykef, Itai, Wernher, Paranoid, Fredrik, RedWolf, Naddy, Rholton, Meelar, DeciusMagnus, Pengo, Dave6, Honta, Dben-benn, DocWatson42, Jacoplane, ShaunMacPherson, Darkhunger, Kerahna, Maroux, Gilgamesh~enwiki, Iceberg3k, Bobblewik, TerokNor, Neilc, Gadfium, Farside~enwiki, Gdr, LucasVB, Phil Sandifer, Mitaphane, Bumm13, Spottedowl, Andy Christ, OwlofDoom, Grunt, SYSS Mouse, Kaleb.G, CALR, ElTyrant, Rich Farmbrough, Vague Rant, Pixel8, Mikkel, Shadow Hog, Indrian, DcoetzeeBot~enwiki, Bobdoe, JeDi, Bobo192, ERW1980, BrokenSegue, Cmdrjameson, Giraffedata, Diceman, FredOrAlive, PiccoloNamek, Pearle, Jason One, Gargaj, Halsteadk, CyberSkull, Diego Moya, InShaneee, Seancdaug, Alexpenev, Radical Mallard, BRW, ReyBrujo, Moogy, Pauli133, KelisFan2K5, Y0u, Jef-Infojef, Smoke, Woohookitty, LOL, Boco XLVII, Commander Keane, Iisryan, Sega381, Domfeargrieve, Revolver Ocelot, Jarkka Saariluoma, Graham87, BD2412, JIP, Krymson, Rjwilmsi, Rydia, Vile Requiem, Captain Disdain, Sumpygump, Remurmur, A Man In Black, Stuart-Brady, Andrew Rodland, Master Thief Garrett, Coll7, TeaDrinker, D.brodale, Alphachimp, GreyCat, Liontamer, Chobot, Igordebraga, Eclipsed Moon, Melodia, Wavelength, Taurrandir, Retodon8, Flameviper, Phantomsteve, RussBot, DT28, Toquinha, Bhny, Travisowens@hotmail.com, NateDan, Pelago, DBPhil, Daveswagon, WulfTheSaxon, Pagrashtak, Dark Pulse, Sitearm, Mikeblas, EEMIV, Alus~enwiki, Glenn Magus Harvey, WarpstarRider, Zero1328, Pukachu, Ultravisitor, Canley, 2fort5r, Shawnc, Jimbob1630, Staxringold, Ilthanar, WormNut, Mael0010, Samuel Blanning, NiTenIchiRyu, Aresmo, Ryūkotsusei, Kicking222, Alextrevelian 006, SmackBot, Teh Pogo, Madfiddler, Mattyatty, McGed-don, Jagged 85, TheKillerAngel, Koorogi, Brossow, AKismet, JimmyBlackwing, Commander Keane bot, Gilliam, Portillo, Shalroth, Mas-ter Jay, Bluebot, Fuzzform, Desolation0, Oatmeal batman, Frap, OrphanBot, Jam packed, Phaedriel, Fuhghettaboutit, Jc215flip, Mr Pres-ident, Micromicro, Wikipedical, Cookie90, JoeTrumpet, Swatjester, Kuru, Khazar, Euchiasmus, Sjöðar, Kuhan, JHunterJ, MTN~enwiki, Beetstra, RCIWesner, TJ Spyke, DabMachine, ZombiePosessor, Woodroar, Impy4ever, Sameboat, Aeternus, IvanDíaz, Tawkerbot2, Mecca-neer, Biiaru, The Prince of Darkness, CmdrObot, BuZz, Naq, Matthew Auger, Juhachi, Dogman15, Cydebot, Jeriaska, Arrowned, Zomic13, UnDeRsCoRe, UberScienceNerd, EmmSeeMusic, Thijs!bot, Jpark3909, Sputnikpanicpuppet, X201, Zerothis, Haha169, Salavat, Mr Bun-gle, Rehnn83, RCHM, Xbox360wraith, Scepia, Jhsounds, MER-C, Janejellyroll, GurchBot, Rocktacity, Archard, Ecksemmess, Jackthes-mack, Corsarius, Torchiest, Mkdw, Ours18, Thibbs, MNegrello, JaGa, Wozzaofrare, Fethroesforia, Tranhoa, P music, Gwern, Paunaro, R'n'B, Jzli, Ssjevot, Rednote~enwiki, Acalamari, SharkD, Tarinth, STBotD, Useight, Squids and Chips, Sergey Snajney, Hammersoft, Floppydog66, TheAlmightyGuru, AeronPeryton, Kecko1, Jayzoo, VivaPB, AtaruMoroboshi, Master Bigode, Goaty69, Crasher7, Piecemealcranky, Halbm0nd, Austriacus, Unused000702, GreaterWikiholic, Dpotiris, SieBot, Mystp, Teh nubkilr, Vanished user 82345ijgeke4tg, Lightmouse, Hjaelee, Thee darcy, Jamierichie, Thechickwhopwn3dyou, Cocoapropo, Explicit, Martarius, Cake taken, ClueBot, Andrelim1, Doommaster1994, Dekisugi, Carriearchdale, Pongopigmayiss, DrDavidWright, Swindbot, DumZiBoT, InternetMeme, XLinkBot, CheShA, RkOrton, Ost316, Avoided, Erk-inBatu, Pusehit, BrucePodger, Sendermen, Addbot, LaaknorBot, Redheylin, Xoxkirrenxox, The mikergmp3s, Mps, Drpickem, TheCreator4, Yobot, Ptbotgourou, AnomieBOT, LilHelpa, Xqbot, Meewam, RibotBOT, Sabrebd, MOTOI Kenkichi, Naru-chu12, Linearity, Parvid, Canno-lis, Hellknowz, Salvidrim!, RjwilmsiBot, Pierceistruth, Chrisbkoolio, Hajatvrc, John of Reading, GoingBatty, Majed, Bluezone101, JamaUtil, Truesician, Carmichael, Tyros1972, Evan-Amos, SimpsonsMan1234, Sven Manguard, ClueBot NG, Helpful Pixie Bot, Wbm1058, BG19bot, Fabien BRANCHUT, M0rphzone, Audun sorlie, Krystoff10, MouthlessBobcat, The1337gamer, BattyBot, Shade Of Wolf, YFdyh-bot, Khazar2, JefferyTheGambler, JYBot, Dissident93, Shane Murphy Jackson, Pytor, Sanchezy161, Themopp, Monkbot, SpyroFan123, 4rr0ws99, Hakken, DangerousJXD, Maplestrip, RynhardtVanBlerk and Anonymous: 470

2.2 Images

- **File:Chiptune-Setup-Game-Boys.jpg** *Source:* https://upload.wikimedia.org/wikipedia/commons/e/eb/Chiptune-Setup-Game-Boys.jpg *License:* CC BY-SA 2.0 *Contributors:* http://www.flickr.com/photos/luciuskwok/5743942878/ *Original artist:* Lucius Kwok

- **File:Chiptune2.ogg** *Source:* https://upload.wikimedia.org/wikipedia/commons/8/82/Chiptune2.ogg *License:* CC BY-SA 3.0 *Contributors:* Written in NerdTracker II v2.1 by Mysid and rendered in Festalon v0.2.4, emulating the NES sound chip. *Original artist:* Oona Räisänen (Mysid)

- **File:Commodore_PET_Exhibit_at_American_Museum_of_Science_and_Energy_Oak_Ridge_Tennessee.jpg** *Source:* https://upload.wikimedia.org/wikipedia/commons/1/15/Commodore_PET_Exhibit_at_American_Museum_of_Science_and_Energy_Oak_Ridge_Tennessee.jpg *License:* Public domain *Contributors:* 83-841 DOE photo by Frank Hoffman *Original artist:* doe-oakridge

- **File:Commons-logo.svg** *Source:* https://upload.wikimedia.org/wikipedia/en/4/4a/Commons-logo.svg *License:* ? *Contributors:* ? *Original artist:* ?

- **File:Computer-aj_aj_ashton_01.svg** *Source:* https://upload.wikimedia.org/wikipedia/commons/d/d7/Desktop_computer_clipart_-_Yellow_theme.svg *License:* CC0 *Contributors:* https://openclipart.org/detail/105871/computeraj-aj-ashton-01 *Original artist:* AJ from openclipart.org

- **File:Computer_Workstation_Variables.jpg** *Source:* https://upload.wikimedia.org/wikipedia/commons/3/35/Computer_Workstation_Variables.jpg *License:* Public domain *Contributors:* Ergonomics, Integrated Safety Management, Berkeley Lab. *Original artist:* Berkeley Lab

- **File:DDRSDRAM400-1GB.jpg** *Source:* https://upload.wikimedia.org/wikipedia/commons/1/18/DDRSDRAM400-1GB.jpg *License:* CC BY 2.5 *Contributors:* ? *Original artist:* ?

- **File:David_Whittaker_-_Lazy_Jones.ogg** *Source:* https://upload.wikimedia.org/wikipedia/en/1/15/David_Whittaker_-_Lazy_Jones.ogg *License:* Fair use *Contributors:*

  CD

  Original artist: ?

- **File:Demo_PC_BlackMaiden_Interceptor.jpg** *Source:* https://upload.wikimedia.org/wikipedia/commons/0/00/Demo_PC_BlackMaiden_Interceptor.jpg *License:* CC-BY-SA-3.0 *Contributors:* ? *Original artist:* ?

- **File:Desktop_personal_computer.jpg** *Source:* https://upload.wikimedia.org/wikipedia/commons/b/b6/Desktop_personal_computer.jpg *License:* CC BY 2.0 *Contributors:* originally posted to **Flickr** as New Computers *Original artist:* Jeremy Banks

- **File:Drozerix_-_Computer_Adventures.wav** *Source:* https://upload.wikimedia.org/wikipedia/commons/e/e8/Drozerix_-_Computer_Adventures.wav *License:* CC0 *Contributors:* http://modarchive.org/index.php?request=view_by_moduleid&query=173937 *Original artist:* Drozerix

- **File:Drumstick.svg** *Source:* https://upload.wikimedia.org/wikipedia/commons/6/69/Drumstick.svg *License:* Public domain *Contributors:* en: Image:Drumstick anatomy.png *Original artist:* en:User:Lupin, User:Stannered

- **File:Edit-clear.svg** *Source:* https://upload.wikimedia.org/wikipedia/en/f/f2/Edit-clear.svg *License:* Public domain *Contributors:* The *Tango! Desktop Project. Original artist:*

  The people from the Tango! project. And according to the meta-data in the file, specifically: "Andreas Nilsson, and Jakub Steiner (although minimally)."

- **File:Eko_ComputeRhythm.png** *Source:* https://upload.wikimedia.org/wikipedia/commons/5/52/Eko_ComputeRhythm.png *License:* CC BY-SA 3.0 *Contributors:*

- Eko_ComputeRhythm.svg *Original artist:* Eko_ComputeRhythm.svg: Clusternote

- **File:Electric_Love_2013.jpg** *Source:* https://upload.wikimedia.org/wikipedia/commons/a/a0/Electric_Love_2013.jpg *License:* CC BY-SA 2.0 *Contributors:* IMG_5056 *Original artist:* Avarty Photos from Straubing, Deutschland

- **File:Elwood_-_Dead_Lock.ogg** *Source:* https://upload.wikimedia.org/wikipedia/commons/0/00/Elwood_-_Dead_Lock.ogg *License:* CC BY-SA 4.0 *Contributors:* Sent to me by email. *Original artist:* Jussi-Matti Salmela

- **File:FC-SR-logo.jpg** *Source:* https://upload.wikimedia.org/wikipedia/commons/a/ac/FC-SR-logo.jpg *License:* Public domain *Contributors:* https://github.com/mtuomi/SecondReality *Original artist:* Future Crew

- **File:Flag_of_Japan.svg** *Source:* https://upload.wikimedia.org/wikipedia/en/9/9e/Flag_of_Japan.svg *License:* PD *Contributors:* ? *Original artist:* ?

- **File:Folder_Hexagonal_Icon.svg** *Source:* https://upload.wikimedia.org/wikipedia/en/4/48/Folder_Hexagonal_Icon.svg *License:* Cc-by-sa-3.0 *Contributors:* ? *Original artist:* ?

- **File:Four_to_the_floor_Roland_TR-707.jpg** *Source:* https://upload.wikimedia.org/wikipedia/commons/c/c5/Four_to_the_floor_Roland_TR-707.jpg *License:* CC BY 4.0 *Contributors:* This file was derived from Four to the floor Roland TR-707.svg: <a href='//commons.wikimedia.org/wiki/File:Four_to_the_floor_Roland_TR-707.svg' class='image'><img alt='Four to the floor Roland TR-707.svg' src='https://upload.wikimedia.org/wikipedia/commons/thumb/9/93/Four_to_the_floor_Roland_TR-707.svg/50px-Four_to_the_floor_Roland_TR-707.svg.png' width='50' height='25' srcset='https://upload.wikimedia.org/wikipedia/commons/thumb/9/93/Four_to_the_floor_Roland_TR-707.svg/75px-Four_to_the_floor_Roland_TR-707.svg.png 1.5x, https://upload.wikimedia.org/wikipedia/commons/thumb/9/93/Four_to_the_floor_Roland_TR-707.svg/100px-Four_to_the_floor_Roland_TR-707.svg.png 2x' data-file-width='2276' data-file-height='1151' /></a>
  Original artist: Roland TR-707 LCD.jpg: Brandon Daniel from Sunnyvale, CA, USA

- **File:Gameboytracker.JPG** *Source:* https://upload.wikimedia.org/wikipedia/commons/9/9e/Gameboytracker.JPG *License:* CC BY-SA 4.0 *Contributors:* Own work *Original artist:* Destinyschilde

- **File:Nuvola_apps_ksim.png** *Source:* https://upload.wikimedia.org/wikipedia/commons/8/8d/Nuvola_apps_ksim.png *License:* LGPL *Contributors:* http://icon-king.com *Original artist:* David Vignoni / ICON KING

- **File:O2xda2i.jpg** *Source:* https://upload.wikimedia.org/wikipedia/commons/4/40/O2xda2i.jpg *License:* CC BY-SA 3.0 *Contributors:* ? *Original artist:* ?

- **File:Oberheim_DMX.jpg** *Source:* https://upload.wikimedia.org/wikipedia/commons/b/b7/Oberheim_DMX.jpg *License:* CC BY-SA 2.0 *Contributors:*

- Electric_musical_instrument_section_of_the_Deutsches_Museum.jpg *Original artist:* Electric_musical_instrument_section_of_the_Deutsches_Museum.jpg: Matt Mechtley

- **File:OpenOffice.org_Writer.png** *Source:* https://upload.wikimedia.org/wikipedia/commons/8/85/OpenOffice.org_Writer.png *License:* LGPL *Contributors:* http://hacktolive.org/images *Original artist:* http://hacktolive.org/

- **File:Open_Cubic_Player.png** *Source:* https://upload.wikimedia.org/wikipedia/commons/9/92/Open_Cubic_Player.png *License:* Public domain *Contributors:* Own work *Original artist:* ?

- **File:PMD_85-1.jpg** *Source:* https://upload.wikimedia.org/wikipedia/commons/6/69/PMD_85-1.jpg *License:* Public domain *Contributors:* Own work *Original artist:* Zdeněk Starý

- **File:PSU-Open1.jpg** *Source:* https://upload.wikimedia.org/wikipedia/commons/6/62/PSU-Open1.jpg *License:* Public domain *Contributors:* ? *Original artist:* ?

- **File:Personal_computer,_exploded_6.svg** *Source:* https://upload.wikimedia.org/wikipedia/commons/4/4e/Personal_computer%2C_exploded_6.svg *License:* CC BY 2.5 *Contributors:* Self-published work by User:HereToHelp and File:Personal computer, exploded 5.svg *Original artist:* User:HereToHelp

- **File:Personal_computers_(million)_ITU.png** *Source:* https://upload.wikimedia.org/wikipedia/commons/5/53/Personal_computers_%28million%29_ITU.png *License:* CC BY-SA 3.0 *Contributors:* Own work *Original artist:* Kozuch

- **File:Portal-puzzle.svg** *Source:* https://upload.wikimedia.org/wikipedia/en/f/fd/Portal-puzzle.svg *License:* Public domain *Contributors:* ? *Original artist:* ?

- **File:Porter_Robinson,_Zedd,_and_Skrillex_at_the_2012_SXSW_cropped.jpg** *Source:* https://upload.wikimedia.org/wikipedia/commons/c/c8/Porter_Robinson%2C_Zedd%2C_and_Skrillex_at_the_2012_SXSW_cropped.jpg *License:* CC BY-SA 2.0 *Contributors:* http://www.flickr.com/photos/weeklydig/6987391899 *Original artist:* **http://digboston.com/** ("weeklydig" on Flickr)

- **File:PowerColor_Radeon_X850XT_PE.jpg** *Source:* https://upload.wikimedia.org/wikipedia/commons/0/0b/PowerColor_Radeon_X850XT_PE.jpg *License:* CC BY-SA 2.5 *Contributors:* ? *Original artist:* ?

- **File:Question_book-new.svg** *Source:* https://upload.wikimedia.org/wikipedia/en/9/99/Question_book-new.svg *License:* Cc-by-sa-3.0 *Contributors:*
  Created from scratch in Adobe Illustrator. Based on Image:Question book.png created by User:Equazcion *Original artist:*
  Tkgd2007

- **File:Renoise_2.6.png** *Source:* https://upload.wikimedia.org/wikipedia/commons/d/da/Renoise_2.6.png *License:* GFDL *Contributors:* http://www.renoise.com/board/index.php?showtopic=26675&st=0&gopid=209721&#entry209721
  Original artist: conner_bw

- **File:Roland_TR-808_drum_machine.jpg** *Source:* https://upload.wikimedia.org/wikipedia/commons/b/be/Roland_TR-808_drum_machine.jpg *License:* CC-BY-SA-3.0 *Contributors:* Transferred from nl.wikipedia to Commons. *Original artist:* Eriq at Dutch Wikipedia

- **File:SCI_model_400_drumtraks.jpg** *Source:* https://upload.wikimedia.org/wikipedia/commons/4/40/SCI_model_400_drumtraks.jpg *License:* CC BY 2.0 *Contributors:* 0002-140510 *Original artist:* Gerald Moore

- **File:SID_6581R1.jpg** *Source:* https://upload.wikimedia.org/wikipedia/commons/f/fa/SID_6581R1.jpg *License:* CC BY-SA 4.0 *Contributors:* Own work *Original artist:* AndroSID

- **File:SNES-Mod1-Console-Set.jpg** *Source:* https://upload.wikimedia.org/wikipedia/commons/3/31/SNES-Mod1-Console-Set.jpg *License:* CC BY-SA 3.0 *Contributors:* Own work *Original artist:* Evan-Amos

- **File:SPARCstation_1.jpg** *Source:* https://upload.wikimedia.org/wikipedia/commons/3/32/SPARCstation_1.jpg *License:* Public domain *Contributors:* Transferred from en.wikipedia to Commons by Mu301. *Original artist:* Fourdee at English Wikipedia

- **File:Schism-beyond.gif** *Source:* https://upload.wikimedia.org/wikipedia/commons/7/7e/Schism-beyond.gif *License:* Public domain *Contributors:* Transferred from en.wikipedia to Commons. *Original artist:* Delt01 at English Wikipedia

- **File:Screamtracker_321.png** *Source:* https://upload.wikimedia.org/wikipedia/en/5/53/Screamtracker_321.png *License:* ? *Contributors:* ? *Original artist:* ?

- **File:Seeburg_Rhythm_Prince_(without_left_panel).jpg** *Source:* https://upload.wikimedia.org/wikipedia/commons/d/da/Seeburg_Rhythm_Prince_%28without_left_panel%29.jpg *License:* CC BY-SA 2.0 *Contributors:* Derived from Synths_i_cannot_afford.jpg *Original artist:* Flickr user stereogab; modified by Clusternote

- **File:Seeburg_Select-A-Rhythm.jpg** *Source:* https://upload.wikimedia.org/wikipedia/commons/0/01/Seeburg_Select-A-Rhythm.jpg *License:* CC BY-SA 2.0 *Contributors:*

- Synths_i_cannot_afford.jpg *Original artist:* Synths_i_cannot_afford.jpg: stereogab

- **File:SoundtrackerEditor.png** *Source:* https://upload.wikimedia.org/wikipedia/commons/5/5a/SoundtrackerEditor.png *License:* Public domain *Contributors:* Captured by User:Marasmusine.
  Original artist: Marasmusine at en.wikipedia

- **File:Streets_of_Rage_2_-_Expander.ogg** *Source:* https://upload.wikimedia.org/wikipedia/en/2/22/Streets_of_Rage_2_-_Expander.ogg *License:* Fair use *Contributors:* ? *Original artist:* ?
- **File:Stripped-computer-case.JPG** *Source:* https://upload.wikimedia.org/wikipedia/commons/2/2d/Stripped-computer-case.JPG *License:* Public domain *Contributors:* ? *Original artist:* ?
- **File:Super_Locomotive.ogg** *Source:* https://upload.wikimedia.org/wikipedia/en/6/6a/Super_Locomotive.ogg *License:* Fair use *Contributors:* ? *Original artist:* ?
- **File:TB-303.jpg** *Source:* https://upload.wikimedia.org/wikipedia/commons/1/1d/TB-303.jpg *License:* CC-BY-SA-3.0 *Contributors:*
  - Quelle: selbst fotografiert
  - Fotograf oder Zeichner: 口口口口

  Original artist: User 口口口口 on de.wikipedia
- **File:Text_document_with_red_question_mark.svg** *Source:* https://upload.wikimedia.org/wikipedia/commons/a/a4/Text_document_with_red_question_mark.svg *License:* Public domain *Contributors:* Created by bdesham with Inkscape; based upon Text-x-generic.svg from the Tango project. *Original artist:* Benjamin D. Esham (bdesham)
- **File:The_Adventure_Lights.ogg** *Source:* https://upload.wikimedia.org/wikipedia/commons/d/df/The_Adventure_Lights.ogg *License:* CC BY 3.0 *Contributors:* https://soundcloud.com/skipcloud/the-adventure-lights *Original artist:* Skip Cloud
- **File:The_Depreciation_Guild_In_Her_Gentle_Jaws.ogg** *Source:* https://upload.wikimedia.org/wikipedia/en/5/53/The_Depreciation_Guild_In_Her_Gentle_Jaws.ogg *License:* Fair use *Contributors:* ? *Original artist:* ?
- **File:The_Minibosses.jpg** *Source:* https://upload.wikimedia.org/wikipedia/commons/f/fa/The_Minibosses.jpg *License:* CC BY 2.0 *Contributors:* originally posted to **Flickr** as The Minibosses *Original artist:* Benjamin Hollis
- **File:UMPC_Samsung-Q1-Ultra.JPG** *Source:* https://upload.wikimedia.org/wikipedia/commons/d/d8/UMPC_Samsung-Q1-Ultra.JPG *License:* CC-BY-SA-3.0 *Contributors:* Own work *Original artist:* User:Coaster J
- **File:Unreal_music_sample.ogg** *Source:* https://upload.wikimedia.org/wikipedia/en/3/3a/Unreal_music_sample.ogg *License:* Fair use *Contributors:*

  Derived from a digital capture (photo/scan) of the soundfile (creator of this digital version is irrelevant as the copyright in all equivalent soundfile is still held by the same party). Copyright held by the publisher or the artist. Claimed as fair use regardless.
  Original artist: ?
- **File:Vg_icon.svg** *Source:* https://upload.wikimedia.org/wikipedia/commons/1/1a/Vg_icon.svg *License:* LGPL *Contributors:*
- Kasteroids.svg *Original artist:* Kasteroids.svg: David Vignoni
- **File:Wesnothmusic.ogg** *Source:* https://upload.wikimedia.org/wikipedia/commons/e/ec/Wesnothmusic.ogg *License:* GPL *Contributors:* ? *Original artist:* ?
- **File:Wiki_letter_w_cropped.svg** *Source:* https://upload.wikimedia.org/wikipedia/commons/1/1c/Wiki_letter_w_cropped.svg *License:* CC-BY-SA-3.0 *Contributors:*
- Wiki_letter_w.svg *Original artist:* Wiki_letter_w.svg: Jarkko Piiroinen
- **File:Wikiquote-logo.svg** *Source:* https://upload.wikimedia.org/wikipedia/commons/f/fa/Wikiquote-logo.svg *License:* Public domain *Contributors:* ? *Original artist:* ?
- **File:Wikiversity-logo.svg** *Source:* https://upload.wikimedia.org/wikipedia/commons/9/91/Wikiversity-logo.svg *License:* CC BY-SA 3.0 *Contributors:* Snorky (optimized and cleaned up by verdy_p) *Original artist:* Snorky (optimized and cleaned up by verdy_p)
- **File:Wiktionary-logo-en.svg** *Source:* https://upload.wikimedia.org/wikipedia/commons/f/f8/Wiktionary-logo-en.svg *License:* Public domain *Contributors:* Vector version of Image:Wiktionary-logo-en.png. *Original artist:* Vectorized by Fvasconcellos (talk · contribs), based on original logo tossed together by Brion Vibber
- **File:Wurlitzer_Sideman_drum_machine_(inside).jpg** *Source:* https://upload.wikimedia.org/wikipedia/commons/2/23/Wurlitzer_Sideman_drum_machine_%28inside%29.jpg *License:* CC BY 2.0 *Contributors:* originally posted to **Flickr** as First drum machine *Original artist:* guiltysin
- **File:Yamaha_PSR-6_circuit_bended_@_Dorkbot_Helsinki_2007.jpg** *Source:* https://upload.wikimedia.org/wikipedia/commons/a/ac/Yamaha_PSR-6_circuit_bended_%40_Dorkbot_Helsinki_2007.jpg *License:* CC BY 2.0 *Contributors:* originally posted to **Flickr** as IMG_4262.JPG *Original artist:* Aleksi Pihkanen
- **File:Yamaha_RY30_front.png** *Source:* https://upload.wikimedia.org/wikipedia/commons/d/d3/Yamaha_RY30_front.png *License:* CC-BY-SA-3.0 *Contributors:* Own work *Original artist:* Matt Perry

2.3   Content license

- Creative Commons Attribution-Share Alike 3.0

Made in United States
Orlando, FL
15 January 2022

13491900R00067